Science for All Children

Lessons for Constructing Understanding

François

Science for All Children

Lessons for Constructing Understanding

Ralph Martin
Ohio University

Colleen M. Sexton
Ohio SchoolNet

with

Jack Gerlovich
Drake University

Allyn and Bacon
Boston   London   Toronto   Sydney   Tokyo   Singapore

Vice President and Publisher, Education: Sean Wakely
Series Editor: Frances Helland
Editorial Assistant: Bridget Keane
Marketing Managers: Ellen Mann Dolberg and Brad Parkins
Cover Administrator: Jenny Hart
Composition Buyer: Linda Cox
Manufacturing Buyer: Suzanne Lareau
Editorial-Production Service: Anne Rebecca Starr
Text Designer: Glenna Collett

Portions of this book first appeared in *Teaching Science for All Children*, Second Edition, by Ralph Martin, Colleen Sexton, Kay Wagner, and Jack
Gerlovich, copyright © 1997, 1994 by Allyn and Bacon.

Library of Congress Cataloging-In-Publication Data
Martin, Ralph E.
    Science for all children : lessons for constructing understanding
/ Ralph Martin, Colleen M. Sexton with Jack Gerlovich.
        p.   cm.
    Includes index.
    ISBN 0-205-29373-5
    1. Science—Study and teaching—Methodology.   2. Science—Study
and teaching (Elementary)—Methodology.   3. Teachers—Training of.
4. Constructivism (Education)   I. Sexton, Colleen M.
II. Gerlovich, Jack A.   III. Title.
Q181.M1778   1998
372.3'5044—dc21   98-26027
                                                              CIP

Special thanks to the following companies for use of their photos on p. 13:
(top left), Courtesy of H. L. Bouton Co., Inc.; (top right), Courtesy of Boekel
Industries, Inc.; (center), Courtesy of Lab Safety Supply; (bottom left and
right), Courtesy of Sargent-Welch Company.

The material in this book is based upon work supported by the National
Science Foundation under grant number 91-47392. Any opinions, findings,
conclusions, or recommendations expressed in this publication are those of
the authors and do not necessarily reflect the views of the Foundation.

Printed in the United States of America

10   9   8   7   6   5   4   3   2   03   02   01   00

DEDICATIONS

For Donald and Marjorie—model citizens, wonderful parents, nurturing grandparents, and the best in-laws one could ever hope to have.

r. m.

To my former teachers who exemplified effective teaching and inspired me to follow in their footsteps.

c. s.

To the Elementary Science Methods students at Drake University who have been, and continue to be, inspirations for my science activity ideas, as well as enthusiastic supporters of hands-on, and often electronically delivered, quality science teaching.

j. g.

Contents

◆3 Lessons for Constructing Understanding 25

SECTION I Life Science Lessons 26

SECTION II Physical Science Lessons 90

SECTION III   Earth and Space Science Lessons   159

APPENDIXES

Preface

This book was written to accomplish two things: (1) to provide conceptually based lessons that allow children to construct their understanding of science using carefully planned experiences, and (2) to integrate the newer dimensions of science—science as inquiry, science and technology, science in personal and social perspectives, and the history and nature of science—into each lesson. Proper concept formation requires students to reflect on their experiences, and through carefully guided questioning, the concept is made concrete.

In Chapter 1, the 4-E learning cycle of *exploration, explanation, expansion,* and *evaluation* is examined. This teaching strategy is consistent with our views of how children construct their understanding through constructivist teaching practices. Chapter 2 examines the classroom management strategies that allow for safe and efficient activity-based science lessons. Tips on how to order supplies, where and how to store them, necessary safety equipment, how to use that equipment, and strategies for classroom management while carrying out engaging lessons are detailed in this chapter.

The final chapter of this book contains more than 60 complete science lessons, organized according to the disciplines identified by the National Science Education Standards (NSES): life, physical, and earth/space science. Each lesson is correlated with the grade levels and concepts recommended by the NSES framework. These lessons contain more than 150 different activities that are experienced in a very powerful way—a way that encourages the highest level of hands-on, minds-on student activity and stimulates high levels of concept formation. Our plans are consistent with the 4-E learning cycle detailed in Chapter 1. The exploration phase prepares the students for science as an inquiry process, while the explanation phase stimulates them to construct conceptual understanding. This fundamental understanding is expanded by addressing the new dimensions of the NSES content standards, such as the history and nature of science, the interrelationship of science and technology, and science in personal and social perspectives. Evaluation embeds assessment in the instruction throughout the cycle and uses performance-based techniques such as pictorial assessment, reflective questioning, and hands-on assessment. The evaluation expectations are written as performance outcomes. As you use the lessons, the outcomes listed will guide the type of assessment you create to provide your students with a variety of opportunities to demonstrate to you that they truly have grasped the concept. The lessons provided have been classroom-tested by our own undergraduate and graduate students as well as by practicing teachers.

The National Science Education Standards content standards are provided in the appendix. The spirit of the NSES content standards is reflected in the lessons found in this book. As you gain experience in using these lessons, we encourage you to choose from the NSES concepts and try your hand at creating your own 4-E learning cycle science lessons.

ACKNOWLEDGMENTS

As we grow in our professions, our career paths and colleagues change, and distance tends to separate us from peers whose talents and skills have made us all better educators. The creation of this book owes a lot to the mutual respect and friendship we three authors have for one another, our sincere belief in good science teaching, and the careful prodding and encouragement of our editor Frances Helland, as well as to the wonders of modern technology—e-mail, voicemail, and the fax machine—that have made up for the miles that distance the three of us.

Our special thanks go to the reviewers who offered substantial suggestions that helped to shape this text. They are:

Leonard Garigliano, Salisbury State University;
William Hughes, Ashland University;
Larry Kellerman, Bradley University;
Michael Leyden, Eastern Illinois University;
Robert Lonning, University of Connecticut;
J. Preston Prather, University of Virginia;
Mary Rubeck, Friends University.

We are also thankful to our families for their support and understanding as long nights in front of our computer monitors kept us from their company. Spe-cial thanks to Marilyn, Jennifer, Jessica, Jonathan, Tim, Sarah, Celeste, Pat, Jacque, and Kelly.

SPECIAL ACKNOWLEDGMENT

The author order printed on the cover of a book is often viewed as an acknowledgment of who made the largest contribution to the project. The lead author typically serves as the primary conceptualizer, organizer, writer, editor, voice, and producer for the author team. This is not true in the case of this particular book. Dr. Colleen Sexton deserves to be acknowledged as the primary author of this volume. Her skill in translating theory into practice shows in her writing of these constructivist lessons. I write this acknowledgment to credit her for writing the major part of this book, and for editing it, and for being the taskmaster for the author team. It is Colleen's voice that is heard in most of this volume, and I am grateful for her efforts.

R. M.

CHAPTER 1

Why Are the Lessons in This Book Different Than in Other Books?

An unbiased observer may conclude that we have entered an era when our schoolchildren are tested mercilessly and give us disappointing results. Indeed, major testing initiatives such as the National Assessment of Educational Progress (NAEP) and the Third International Mathematics and Science Study (TIMSS) provide reams of insightful information, but to the general public, the mass media message is that our children are not able to compete with their peers from other developed countries. The achievement scores for recalling factual science knowledge are quite high. However, the real shortcoming has consistently been what our children have been able to *do* with what they appear to know. Achievement scores that measure our children's deep conceptual understanding and their abilities to apply scientific information in problem-solving situations have been consistently disappointing.

The National Science Education Standards (NSES), among other sources, speak of the need to educate our children so they can use what they know to deepen their understanding and become scientifically literate. As educators, we are encouraged to interact with children so we can uncover and attempt to correct their common misconceptions about science, and to help children complete their preconceptions by developing their notions into scientifically correct conceptions about their universe.

More than just an education buzzword, *constructivism* is a modern mission that provides teachers and children with cooperative opportunities for authentic learning. Indeed, the constructivist teacher may learn more than the children, but all have the opportunity for meaningful, experiential, problem-based learning. These shared experiences provide the basis for inquiring, making discoveries, constructing meaning, using newly formed ideas and skills, investigating phenomena, and solving problems. This book provides these types of experiences.

This book contains more than 150 different science activities. Several activities are carefully woven into each lesson; there are more than 60 complete lessons. The fabric of each lesson contains a story: a visual and experiential message that is organized around a central concept. Therefore, each lesson is focused upon helping teachers to guide and students to discover by constructing its point (concept). These lessons come from our popular book *Teaching Science for All Children*, Second Edition, which promotes the National Science Education Standards. All of the lessons have been classroom-tested and used by scores of experienced teachers and thousands of preservice teachers. The lessons work primarily because of the method.

THE 4-E METHOD

A cycle of learning helps children to construct meaning from their experiences. It is important for children to *explore*—the first E—with teacher assistance, but not with a prescriptive recipe. From very personal insights gained by exploring, children are able to construct meaning from what they have seen, felt, smelled, heard, and (if safe) tasted. Figure 1.1 helps to illustrate the relationships among the different phases in our learning cycle.

Similarities and differences are identified and compared, teachers pose guiding questions, and children form conceptual conclusions by completing an *explanation* phase of learning, the second E. Indeed, questions are very important for guiding the students in each phase of our method. Figure 1.2 helps to give some tips about the types of questions that are most effective in each phase.

Many books tend to stop and move on to another topic once the point of a lesson has been raised, but more must be done to help children move beyond a preliminary understanding, which carries a high risk for students to form misconceptions. This moving beyond is accomplished by the third E, *expansion*. This phase of our lessons often leads to the beginning of another lesson, which starts the exploring over again.

No cycle of learning is complete without authentically determining what the children know and can do. The fourth E, *evaluation*, completes this cycle. It works best when fitted to the proper task in each of the prior phases; the evaluation does not have to wait until the end of the lesson. The naturalness and completeness of the learning cycle nurtures constructed understanding and gives us a good model to use for addressing all of the science content expectations that are described in the National Science Education Standards.

FIGURE 1.1   The 4-E Science Learning Cycle

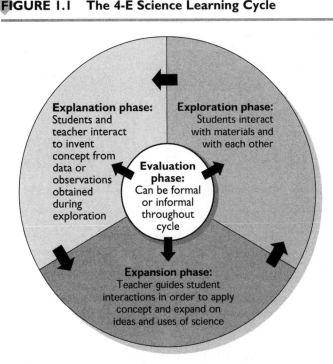

Source: Adapted from a figure by Charles Barman, "The Learning Cycle: Making It Work," *Science Scope* (February 1989): 28–31.

It is important to understand more about your various roles and functions if you are to use our lessons successfully. Let us explore each of the 4 E's a bit further.

Phase 1: Exploration

The *exploration* phase of our lessons is student-centered, stimulates learner mental disequilibrium, and fosters mental assimilation. (You might recall these concepts from Piagetian learning theory.) In this phase, you are responsible for giving students sufficient directions and materials. The materials you use must stimulate children's thinking in ways that are related to the concept. (See Appendix A for examples of concepts from the NSES.) Your directions *must not tell* students what they should learn and *must not explain* the concept. Your role is to:

- answer students' questions,
- ask questions to guide student observations and to cause students to engage in proper science processes or thinking skills, and
- give hints and cues to keep the exploration going.

◆**FIGURE 1.2   Using Questions During a Learning Cycle**

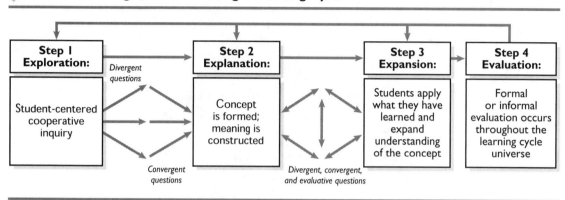

Your students will be responsible for exploring the materials and for gathering and/or recording their own information. To guide learning, you might find it helpful to rely on questioning skills like those shown in Figure 1.2.

Children must have concrete materials and experiences if they are to construct science concepts for themselves.

Phase 2: Explanation

The *explanation* phase is less student-centered and provides for learner mental accommodation. Your role in this phase is to guide student thinking so the concept of the lesson is constructed cooperatively, not merely given, told, or lectured. Encourage your students to construct the point (concept) of the lesson mentally. To accomplish this, you will need to select and set the desired class environment, perhaps by gathering the children near a poster board, chalkboard, or demonstration table to help focus their thinking. Ask your students to give the information they have collected, and then help them to process and organize the information. Constructing graphs, data tables, or simple comparative lists often helps. Once the information is organized, you can introduce the specific language needed for the concept. For example, after playing a game about the food chain, you might use the word *predator* to describe one of the roles and then ask the children to tell, in their own words, what a predator is and to give some other examples of predators.

Phase 3: Expansion

The *expansion* phase should be as student-centered as possible and structured to encourage group cooperation. The purpose of this phase is to help children to organize mentally the experiences they have acquired by finding connections to similar previous experiences and then to discover new applications for what they have learned. Constructed concepts must be linked to other related ideas or experiences to take the students' thinking beyond where it currently is. To do this, you must require children to use the language or labels of the new concept, so they add depth to their understanding. This is a proper phase for helping students apply what they have learned by expanding examples or by providing additional experiences through related activities. It is also a particularly good time to include the new content dimensions from the National Science Education Standards (more about this later). The expansion phase can automatically lead to the exploration phase of the next lesson, hence establishing a continuing cycle for teaching and learning.

Phase 4: Evaluation

The purpose of this phase is to overcome the limits of standard types of testing. Often learning must occur in small increments before larger mental leaps of insight are possible. Therefore, evaluation should be continuous, not just the typical end-of-chapter or unit approach. That is, evaluation can be included in each phase of the learning cycle, not just held for the end. Several types of measures are necessary to form an authentic and holistic evaluation of the students' learning and to encourage mental construction of concepts and science skills. In constructing these lessons, we have asked ourselves:

- What appropriate learning outcomes should teachers expect?
- What types of hands-on evaluation techniques can the students do to demonstrate the basic skills of observation, classification, communication, measurement, prediction, and inference?
- What techniques are appropriate for students to demonstrate the integrated science process skills of identifying and controlling variables, defining operationally, forming hypotheses, experimenting, interpreting data, and forming models?
- How can pictures be used to help students demonstrate how well they can think through problems that require understanding fundamental concepts and the integration of ideas?
- What types of questions can students be asked to help them reflect and to indicate how well they recall and understand what has been learned?

WHAT TYPES OF LESSONS ARE INCLUDED?

Each lesson is organized around a central concept, and the activities included are appropriate for the grade-level range indicated. The grade levels are those recommended by the National Science Education Standards (NSES). We have also used the concepts recommended by the NSES to help us match our selections with the curriculum expectations of schools. Hence, our lessons are organized into three sections—life, physical, and earth/space—the content areas recommended by the standards. In addition, the National Science Education Standards now recommend four new dimensions of content, typically not previously included in science lessons. We address this new content by integrating each new dimension in each lesson. You will find that this naturally fits in the Expansion phase. These new dimensions are very important in helping to prepare children to be scientifically literate. A brief description of what is intended by each of these new science content dimensions follows.

Science as Inquiry

Inquiry includes the use of the processes of science, scientific knowledge, and attitudes to reason and to think critically as a way to construct understanding of science ideas. As described by the standards, inquiry assists in constructing an understanding of scientific concepts, learning how to learn, becoming an independent lifelong learner, and further developing the habits of mind associated with science. Learning outcomes for the inquiry dimension require students to be able to understand about inquiry and do a variety of types of science activities in order to learn the uses and skills of inquiry and develop a greater capacity to inquire.

Inquiry is the process that students should use to learn science. They should be able to ask questions, use their questions to plan and conduct a scientific investigation, use appropriate science tools and scientific techniques, evaluate evidence and use it logically to construct several alternative explanations, and communicate (argue) their conclusions scientifically.

Science and Technology

Science and technology complements the inquiry dimension. This content dimension places emphasis on helping students develop scientific abilities and science understandings to establish connections between the natural world and the human-designed world. Decision making is an important student outcome that arises from student activity associated with the process of identifying scientific problems, determining risks and benefits, and designing solutions and evaluating.

Science in Personal and Social Perspectives

Addressing this dimension assures that learners understand that science is a part of personal and social issues. This dimension encourages teachers to help learners achieve outcomes that will help them develop decision-making skills for solving personal and community problems. It provides ideas to help expose students to matters of making personal health choices, help students understand changes in populations and the complications of resource usage, and become aware of science and society issues on local, national, and global levels.

History and Nature of Science

Science is ongoing, and the thoughts of science change over time. The history and nature of science dimension encourages teachers to provide learning experiences that use the history of science to inform the present, predict likely changes in the future, and appreciate that science is not a static or absolute discipline. This dimension of scientific literacy helps students appreciate the human role in science and how that role has helped to shape various cultures.

CHAPTER SUMMARY

Science has seen many reform efforts since the Russian satellite Sputnik was launched in 1957. Past efforts have helped to inform us as we contemplate new changes in our science programs, adjust expectations for learners, and modify teaching habits. The ways and means for change are presented in the new National Science Education Standards, which describe seven essential content areas that are necessary for systemic reform in teaching and learning. As teachers we cannot meet all of the standards by ourselves, but we can focus our efforts on the content standards that fall within our responsibility. This book can help you focus your efforts through meaningful classroom science activities. Although understanding fundamental science content concepts is important, some may misperceive that the standards are concerned only with the physical, life, and earth and space science concepts and learning activities for children. This is not true; to focus only on those topics shortchanges our students, depriving them of additional essential experiences.

The physical, life, and earth and space science content is an important context for developing scientific literacy. The standards require four new dimensions of science learning to assure that real progress is made toward helping students achieve literacy in science. These new dimensions challenge us to help students understand science as a process of inquiry, understand the interrelationships between science and technology, benefit from science personally and understand the social perspective of science, and understand and appreciate the history and nature of science. Parts of the many outcomes for these new dimensions predictably overlap and complement natural learning.

As an educator, your challenge is to find a way to link all of these dimensions of science learning and literacy to the content context. This book will help you to do so through the lessons provided. We hope that our lessons give a model that you will use as you construct your own cycles of learning. However, please exercise caution as you do. Safety and proper supervision are important tasks, and it is just as important to help children to think and choose to behave safely as it is to shield them from potential hazards. The next chapter should help you to do this more effectively.

How Can You Teach Activity-Based Science Lessons Safely and Efficiently?

A safe science classroom does not have to be a place where no exploration occurs. Conceptual understanding requires students to engage in a variety of science processes. It also requires that strict attention be given to science safety. Each lesson in this book identifies safety precautions necessary for safe explorations. Before your students participate in any science activities, it is important for you to ask yourself three questions: *What materials are necessary for the activities?*, *What is the safest and most efficient way to store and distribute materials?*, and *What classroom management strategies will I use to insure my students' safety?* How you answer these questions depends upon your philosophy of safe science teaching. You may also choose to add to this list, depending on your students' abilities. As you read through our answers to these questions, we encourage you to ask yourself what you believe is necessary for providing a safe learning environment. A variety of factors will impact your answer, learner characteristics being the most important. While you cannot control those characteristics, you can create a learning environment that will make the most of the positive ones, while downplaying the ones that impact the students' ability to learn.

This chapter provides classroom management strategies designed to promote safe, efficient, activity-based science lessons. It examines the questions raised above by:

1. identifying criteria for choosing and maintaining safety equipment,
2. examining the tasks necessary for safe and efficient storage of equipment and materials,
3. suggesting methods for distributing, maintaining, and inventorying science materials,
4. encouraging you to develop a philosophy of safe science teaching that demonstrates your understanding of your legal responsibilities,
5. providing ways to arrange the classroom and students physically for activity-based science lessons, and
6. encouraging you to perform safety assessments regularly.

WHAT MATERIALS ARE NECESSARY FOR THE ACTIVITIES?

Each lesson in this book provides a materials list. You will need to determine the availability of those items. Identify the readily available items, and determine where additional items can be obtained. A good suggestion is to divide the remaining items into categories: items to be purchased through a scientific supplier, items that can be purchased locally through a discount or hardware store, and items that can be made for little or no cost from recycled materials. Items such as test tubes, chemicals, beakers, and the like can be purchased from a scientific supplier. Consumable items such as paper cups and straws can be purchased locally, and items such as cans and pie pans may be found in the recycling bin.

A Science Activity Planner form (Figure 2.1) will facilitate your ordering needs. Fill out this sheet at least six weeks before you teach the lesson to allow time for vendor shipping and/or the steps your order must go through for approval of purchases and appropriation of funds in your school district. Figure 2.2 provides an example of how this form can be used.

When purchasing items for science activities, consider the maturity level of the students you are teaching. You can avoid some safety problems right from the start by only ordering supplies that meet federal, state, or locally established safety standards. Decision making can be difficult because of the variety and type of some of the more commonly used items. How do you know which to choose? Table 2.1 lists the basic safety equipment that should be available during science activities, and the safety criteria for selecting and maintaining the equipment.

WHAT IS THE SAFEST AND MOST EFFICIENT WAY TO STORE AND DISTRIBUTE MATERIALS?

The variables to consider when storing science materials in the classroom are space, safety, and access. When any of these three criteria are not adequate, materials should be stored in a secure central location elsewhere within the school.

◆FIGURE 2.1 Form for Science Activity Planner

Concept to be taught: _____

Safety considerations: _____

Material needs: _____

_____

Items available through school inventory: _____

_____

Items available at no cost/recycle: _____

_____

Scientific supplier (indicate vendor name, catalog number, description, number needed, cost per unit, total cost):

Local store (indicate store name and exact cost):

◆FIGURE 2.2 Science Activity Planner Example

Concept to be taught: The circular path electrons follow is called a _circuit._

Safety considerations: Wear goggles to prevent eye injury when using wires. Caution students not to attempt to short out batteries because burns could result. Pick up materials dropped on the floor immediately to prevent slips and falls.

Material needs: _For each student:_ Battery, flashlight bulb, insulated copper wire, switch, bulb socket, cardboard tube (toilet paper tube), paper clip, two brass fasteners, plastic cap from a gallon milk container or a 35mm film can.

Items available through:

School inventory	Bulbs, switches, wire
No cost/recycle	Cardboard tubes, milk caps, film canister caps
Scientific supplier	Delta Supply, Nashua, New Hampshire
	57–020–9769, Bucket of Batteries, 30, $29.95
	57–020–5644, Bulb Sockets, 30, $4.85/pkg. of 6, $24.25
Local store	John's Dollar Store on Main Street
	1 box of paper clips, 79¢
	2 boxes of brass fasteners, $1.45

TABLE 2.1   Criteria for Selecting and Maintaining Safety Equipment

Equipment	Selection Criteria	Maintenance
Goggles	Must meet the American National Standards Institute (ANSI) standard for safety. Look for a Z87 on the faceplate. Should fit face securely around the eye, with side vents to avoid chemical fume build-up.	Store in a dust-free environment, such as a box or cabinet. Clean with sterile isopropyl alcohol pads before the students wear them.
Hot plates	Should have an on-off indicator light. Use whenever possible in place of an open flame. Do not use extension cords for operation; hot plates purposely come with short cords so there is less danger of students tripping.	When not in use, be sure indicator light shows hot plate is off. Unplug it, and keep electrical outlets capped so students cannot stick items into them, causing burns or electrocution. Keep out of reach of students until it is cool to touch.
Alcohol lamp	Purchase alcohol specifically identified for use in lamps. Do not substitute inexpensive rubbing alcohol. Add a small amount of table salt to the lamp so the alcohol will burn with a bright orange flame; plain alcohol burns with a blue flame that is difficult to see.	Do not store large quantities in the classroom; transfer to smaller containers that are clearly labeled, preferably in a safety can. 100% alcohol does not have the odor associated with lesser grades. Be sure to keep away from areas where it may be mistaken for water. In case of spills during use, place lamp in a pie pan of wet sand.
Fire blanket	Should be made of fire retardant wool. Choose one that is not too large for students to use in an emergency. You can purchase storage containers; some are metal cylinders with a latch, others are vinyl or leather pouches that close with Velcro.	Place in a conspicuous location where it can be retrieved easily by both handicapped and non–handicapped students and staff. Avoid chimney effect, in which flames fly up blanket and across the face. Practice the stop, drop, and roll method with students.
Fire extinguisher	ABC triclass—dry powder—are preferred because of their ability to extinguish most fires, such as paper products, electrical, solvents.	Store in area accessible to all. Check the pressure gauge regularly. Students and teachers should practice lifting and using comfortably.
Eyewash	A fountain fixture eyewash allows a classroom faucet to be used as an eyewash station. Fairly inexpensive and easy to install. Sufficient to supply the recommended 15 minutes of aerated (60–90 degrees Fahrenheit), running water to flush the eyes of a person who has suffered a chemical splash.	Should be available for emergency use at all times. Be sure it is installed on a faucet that is accessible to all students. Do not purchase bottled water stations; they cannot deliver the fifteen minutes of aerated running water. Use only when there is no alternative, such as for field use.
First aid kit	Select a physician-approved kit. Keep in classroom and take on field trips or when using outdoor study areas such as land labs. Keep list or poster of emergency telephone numbers readily available.	Replace consumables—e.g., surgical masks, gloves, and sanitary wipes— in order to address HIV and hepatitis concerns.

Safety goggles

Alcohol lamp

Fire blanket

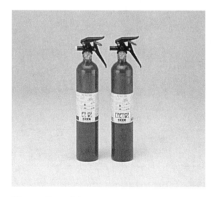

Fire extinguisher

Eyewash station

Central Storage Area

When a school building has a central storage area for science supplies and teaching materials, the following precautions are necessary. A central storage area should:

- maintain an inventory of the items stored there.
- have one person who is responsible for keeping the inventory current.
- provide a secure area with adequate ventilation for all hazardous materials.
- store flammable liquids in their original containers with the manufacturer's safety information clearly visible.
- have available a safety checklist that itemizes the hazardous ingredients of the materials stored in the area, their physical and chemical characteristics, how they react with other substances, any fire or explosion hazards, precautions for safe handling and use, and steps necessary in case of accidental ingestion.
- require that the teachers who borrow materials be responsible for their use and prompt return.
- authorize one person to request the return of borrowed materials (from other teachers) after a reasonable time period.
- require the use of a sign-out sheet (see Figure 2.3) to be completed by any staff member who uses materials.

FIGURE 2.3   Science Equipment Checkout Form

Science Equipment Checkout Form

Name: _____

Grade and/or subject area: _____

Room number: _____

Date of checkout: Expected date of return:

_____   _____

Items borrowed:

_____

_____

_____

Signature: _____

Classroom Storage

When science supplies and teaching materials are stored within the classroom, the following must occur to insure student and teacher safety.

- Hazardous materials must be stored in locked, well-ventilated cabinets. A safety checklist that itemizes the hazardous ingredients of the materials stored in the area, their physical and chemical characteristics, how they react with other substances, any fire or explosion hazards, precautions for safe handling and use, and steps necessary in case of accidental ingestion should be easily accessible. Such documents are referred to as Material Safety Data Sheets (MSDS) and are provided by the chemical manufacturer upon purchase. They are also available via Internet Web sites: http://www.sargentwelch.com or http://www.pdc.cornell.edu/ISSEARCH/MSDSrch.htm.
- Materials that students are allowed access to should be stored on shelves or in cabinets within easy reach below eye level. The students must be taught which materials they are allowed to handle and which they cannot. The students should be involved in creating a classroom safety policy.
- Plants should be stored in an area near windows to facilitate growth. Artificial light be should be available where windows do not exist.
- Plants that present potential physical or chemical harm to the students if ingested should not be used or stored in classrooms.
- Live, nonpoisonous animals should be kept in safe cages or containers. A water source should be available. Be aware of their food requirements, and have a plan for how and where their food will be stored.
- If a live animal is kept in the classroom, be aware of your responsibility to the animal, and more important, for the students' health and safety. Know the school's policy on live animals in the classroom. Find out if any of your students have allergies to certain animals. Learn what kind of insurance coverage you need should a student become injured while handling the animal. Make sure that any animal kept around children is not a carrier of infectious diseases. See Appendix B for the NSTA guidelines for responsible use of animals in classrooms.
- When students bring live animals into the classroom, the twenty-four-hour rule recommended by the American Humane Society should be followed. Students can study the animal during the day, but after a day of being in the classroom, the animal should be returned to where it was found or a similar habitat. Common sense should prevail as to the type of animal brought into the school. Do not bring wild squirrels, raccoons, and similar animals into the school. An occasional ladybug or cricket can teach valuable lessons.

Organizing and Distributing Materials

No matter where the materials are stored, you will need to decide how to organize them for safety and efficiency. Will they be arranged according to units, such as electricity, weather, and simple machines, or will the items be stored separately? Once you make this decision, you must choose how to organize the items within an area, from shelves to shoeboxes to plastic storage bins. Table 2.2 identifies the advantages and disadvantages of several storage possibilities.

Whether items are kept in a central storage area or in the classroom, you still need to think about how the students will collect them for a particular activity and how the items will be distributed. When items are stored in a central location, you may want to collect the materials at least a day ahead of time to make sure everything needed for a given activity is still available. Decide how many of what item you will need. Once the items are in the classroom, appoint students to arrange the materials for the various working groups.

In a safe, efficient, activity-based science classroom, the teacher does not need to do all of the advance work for a particular science activity. He or she can appoint responsible students to collect the science materials. A simple way to disseminate the materials is to have a materials list posted for the given activity, assign particular students to gather materials, and provide those students with buckets or plastic bins to use for collecting the materials. Each materials manager for the day would be responsible for collecting the correct number of items needed for his or her group to do the activity. He or she would also be responsible for counting the materials at the end of the lesson, collecting them in the bucket, and returning them to their proper place.

You could appoint one or two students to count the items in the buckets, making sure everything is returned after use. You can put the used materials back in their proper storage areas yourself or assign students to help. If the materials go back to a central storage area, you should make sure they are returned to their proper place as soon as possible. Other teachers may be counting on the use of those materials.

Keep safety concerns in mind when returning used materials. Were hazardous materials used during the activity? (Any material labeled toxic, ignitable, corrosive, or reactive should be considered hazardous and its use with elementary students seriously questioned.) Many common household items used at the elementary level in science activities—such as bleach or ammonia, carpet shampoos, window cleaner, paints, and glues—can be considered hazardous. Does your school have an appropriate system to handle disposal of these wastes? Which materials can be recycled? What procedures should be followed to dispose of used materials? Remember, when improperly handled, hazardous waste can pollute drinking supplies, poison humans, or contaminate soil and air. The teacher should be responsible for disposing of all used hazardous materials. If you are uncertain about disposing of a particular item, check with the local fire marshall or office of the Environmental Protection Agency. These agencies will be able to instruct you on proper disposal. Many local fire departments are equipped to handle low-level toxic waste. A local high school should already have a plan in place for handling waste from the chemistry classes. Check to see if your district

TABLE 2.2   Materials Storage

Materials Stored	Advantages	Disadvantages
As units	All material together Can present lesson at any time without rummaging through shelves for necessary materials	Question of who is responsible for replacing consumable items Scarce resources cause unit to be picked apart and used for other activities
Individually	Ideal storage in schools where resources are scarce Works well when materials are centrally stored Easier to collect	Time needed to pull several items together for each teaching unit Additional storage space necessary to store individual items in classroom
On shelves	Items can be shelved alphabetically for quick and easy retrieval Efficient method for storing glassware and large items	Difficult to determine where one letter ends and the next begins Difficult to store items in multiple quantities With multiple users, need to rearrange shelves frequently
In plastic bags	Sealable bags are ideal for small items Can be labeled with permanent markers Available in a variety of sizes to accommodate various sized materials	If seal not made, items fall out and get lost With extended use, labeling wears off Tear with frequent use
In shoeboxes or cardboard boxes	Inexpensive way to store multiple items like thermometers, magnets, and marbles Easily labeled and can be covered with an adhesive plastic for prolonged use An ideal size for storing on shelves	Since opaque, necessary to open to determine contents Even covered, eventually wear out
In plastic storage bins	Available in a variety of shapes and sizes Clear so items stored are visible Can be labeled with permanent markers Many guaranteed to last at least five years	Better-made containers are costly Lids crack on less expensive containers if heavy things are stacked on top
Using color coding	Ideal for identifying hazardous materials by using orange safety stickers Identify quickly consumed items with one color, facilitates reordering needs	Advantages lost if not all teachers understand or remember color codes If color code key not posted, difficult to locate material

has one. If not, work with local agencies to develop a safe and reliable disposal system.

WHAT CLASSROOM MANAGEMENT STRATEGIES SHOULD YOU USE TO INSURE YOUR STUDENTS' SAFETY?

Carefully planned lessons and ample supplies are not enough to conduct a successful, safe, and efficient activity-based science lesson. It is your legal responsibility to exercise *reasonable and prudent judgment* when choosing the science lessons your students will perform. If you have determined that the activity chosen is appropriate for the maturity level of your students, that all safety measures have been addressed, and that another teacher with comparable training and experience to yours would perform the same activity with their class, then you may proceed with confidence. If you believe some hazard still exists, choose a safer activity to teach the same concept. Do not use an activity if you have doubts about its safety. You must consider all hazards as you proceed. Please refer to the NSTA position statement in Appendix C concerning teacher liability for laboratories and field trips.

The students must be aware of all safety procedures. Instruct students how to restrict loose clothing and long hair when working with open flames. Long hair should be pulled back so that it does not hang down over the flame, and loose clothing such as shirts should be tucked into pants and big sleeves should be pushed up and secured with pins or elastic (non-restricting rubber) bands to keep them from falling into open flames.

Safety Contract

A safety contract can be created jointly by teacher and students. Have the students sign the contract after they have been instructed in basic safety features, such as how and when to wear safety goggles properly. Teach them the safe use of a fire extinguisher, a fire blanket, and an eyewash and shower, and have them demonstrate this use. By reporting any missing or malfunctioning safety equipment, you avoid being accused of *negligent behavior*, demonstrate *foreseeability*, and exercise *due care*. Encourage your students to identify any safety violations they become aware of as well. Teachers can demonstrate that they have a philosophy of safe science teaching when they exhibit these behaviors, provide appropriate supervision whether in the classroom or on a field trip, report any foreseeable hazards—especially overcrowded conditions that would inhibit safe supervision of classroom activities—to school administrators, and properly maintain a learning environment that addresses safety concerns.

Physical Arrangement of the Classroom

The physical arrangement of the classroom is an important consideration in maintaining a safe learning environment. Barriers such as classroom size, traffic patterns, blind spots, poles, and walls require a teacher to be creative about using the space available.

Before you begin moving furniture around, it may help to draw to scale a floorplan of your classroom. Ask yourself the following questions when deciding how to arrange the classroom:

- What is the best, yet safest, way to use the space available?
- What kinds of activities will my students be involved in?
- What kinds of materials will be used?
- What type of furniture do I have in my classroom?
- Will I need any additional furniture, or should I eliminate some of the furniture that is already there?
- What kind of flooring does the classroom have? Is it appropriate for the activities my students will be engaged in?
- Where are the entrances and exits in this classroom?
- Where are the electrical outlets?
- What kind of traffic patterns do I wish to develop?
- What are the potential hazards with the arrangement I have in mind?

The suggestions that follow are designed to help you arrange your classroom to maximize your students' science experiences, while still allowing you to maintain the flexibility needed to accommodate teaching other subject areas.

Large-Group Science Activities

Flat surfaces offer the best means of engaging in science activities when working with an entire class. If you are in a classroom with tilted desktops, you will need to be creative; flat-topped, child-sized tables are strongly recommended.

Divide the class into small working groups of three or four students each. Current recommendations are that elementary school classrooms should provide at least 40 square feet (3.6 square meters) of space for each student and should have no more than twenty-four students for labs and activities. Although elementary science classes are not laboratory-based, you will be able to provide sufficient feedback and guidance in science projects to all students if there are only twenty-four. Although the physical constraints of your classroom may not allow you this much area or your class may be larger than twenty-four students, you must allocate optimum space and maintain ideal class size whenever possible.

Whether the students are working at small tables, at several flat-topped desks pushed together to make a larger working area, or on the floor, consider the type of flooring in the classroom. A nonslip tile floor is best, but not a necessity. Carefully taping down an inexpensive vinyl floor remnant in the designated science area will save a carpet from messy spills and facilitate clean-up.

Create an area where you can collect materials for science activities before the class uses them. Science demonstrations should also occur there. Preferably, this area should be close to the science storage area if supplies are stored within the classroom. Storage space for student projects should also be planned near this area. If possible, choose an area near the sink.

The physical arrangement of the desks and tables should be dictated by the type of activity going on in the classroom on any particular day. If space and furniture availability permit, a permanent science area can be maintained within the classroom. If space is a problem, desks and tables that can be moved into configurations like those shown in Figure 2.4 will facilitate learning in an activity-based science classroom. Whenever possible, this area should be near windows to allow the use of natural light. Space should be arranged to eliminate traffic congestion and to provide a clear path to all classroom exits.

Science Learning Centers

When working with the entire class for science lessons, a teacher committed to learning cycle–constructivist approaches will find that science learning centers satisfactorily accommodate additional expansion activities for each lesson. You

FIGURE 2.4   Arranging an Activity-Based Classroom

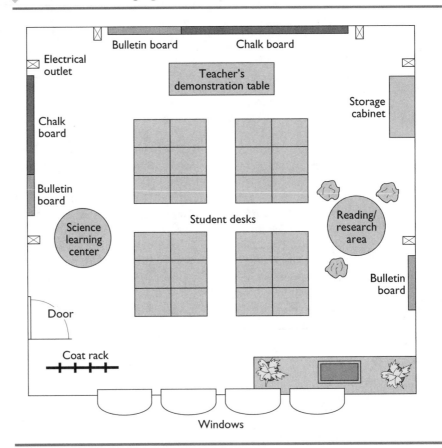

can design the learning center so that it focuses on a particular concept brought out in a class lesson and provides additional experiences for the students, who will come to a greater understanding of the concept. The center should not simply be a place where the brighter students or those who finished their assignments first get to go. All students should be encouraged to use the learning center at their convenience, to engage in activities that provide additional experiences with a particular science concept. Once all of the students have had sufficient time to use that expansion activity, change the activity at the center to address a new concept you are teaching. Be certain to address potential safety concerns for the learning center, e.g., electrical outlets, extension cords, supervision, and so forth.

Another approach to science learning centers is to design them so that students gain greater experience in the processes of science. When you present science lessons to a large group of students, it is unlikely that each student will have adequate time to make observations, predictions, measurements, and so on if a more-skilled peer blurts out the answer first. The learning center can be designed so each child has a chance to work in the area, gaining experience in solving problems, measuring, predicting, using scientific instruments, and so on. You can change the learning center weekly, with different process skills as the focus (see Figure 2.5).

A science learning center can also be designed as a *discovery area*—a place where children create inventions from a variety of materials provided. It can be considered a challenge area, where the teacher creates a problem for the week, and using the materials provided, the students work to solve the problem. Science learning centers can also be the place where students can play teacher-prepared or commercial science games.

Whatever you decide the focus of your science learning center should be, a few simple rules must be upheld to insure its success. The guidelines for a good science learning center are found in Table 2.3.

Safety Assessment

You can instill a philosophy of safe science exploration in your students by making them responsible for weekly safety assessments. Each week, student teams can do a walk-through with you to check all of the basic safety equipment—fire extinguishers, fire blankets, goggles, and the like—and any equipment unique to the upcoming lesson. You can create a standardized checklist in which you highlight the materials or the safe room arrangement necessary for a particular lesson. Along with you, the student team for the week would go down the list, inspecting the equipment to make sure it is properly functioning, or arranging the classroom so that all obstacles are removed. The same student team could be responsible for reminding—and even demonstrating for the class—proper safety behaviors expected during the upcoming activity, for example, demonstrating how to wear goggles, how to use beakers safely, how to dispose of used chemicals, and the like. Working side by side, the teacher becomes a role

◤**FIGURE 2.5   Process-Oriented Science Learning Center Lesson**

1. Obtain light bulb record books

Process Skill: Recording data

Each student will receive a light bulb record book. The outer covers are made from yellow cardboard. Several sheets of white paper for students to record their data are stapled between the covers.

2. Page 1 of record book

Process Skill: Observing

On the table is a box with a bulb sticking out of the top. A switch protrudes from one side. A card near the box states:

> Make as many observations as possible. Write the word OBSERVA-TIONS on the top of page 1 in the light bulb record book. Record your observation on that page.

3. Record Book

Process Skill: Predicting

A card that is numbered with a 3 and has a drawing of the box with the bulb will be at the center with the following directions:

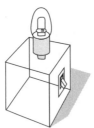

> Label the next blank page in your record book PREDICTIONS. Predict what is inside the box causing the bulb to light. List and/or draw your predictions on that page.

4. Record book, battery, bulb, wire

Process Skill: Manipulating materials

Card numbered 4 near a battery, bulb, and wire asks the students to do the following:

> Label the next blank page of your record book MANIPULAT-ING MATERIALS. Take the battery, bulb, and wire from the table. Using only those three pieces of material, get the bulb to light. Record in the record book drawings of ways you manipulated the materials—whether the bulb lit or not.

5. Record book, battery, bulb, wire, bulb holder, switch

Process Skill: Manipulating materials

At the next station the above materials will be laying near card number 5. The students will be asked to do the following:

> Label the next blank page of your record book MANIPU-LATING MATERIALS. Take the battery, bulb, wire, bulb holder, and switch from the table. Get the bulb to light as you did at station 4. This time wire it so that the switch will turn the bulb on and off. Record in the record book draw-ings of ways you manipulated the materials—whether the bulb lit or not.

6. Record book, box, battery, bulb, bulb holder, wire, switch

Process Skill: Interpreting data, inferring, formulating models

The above materials will be found at station 6. The students will be asked to do the following:

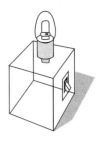

> Label the next blank page of your record book INTERPRETING DATA, INFERRING, FORMULAT-ING MODELS. Using the materi-als given and your results from activities 4 and 5, try to create a box like the one you observed at station 2 and 3. When finished go back to your prediction page in the record book. Was your prediction correct?

◆ TABLE 2.3 Science Learning Center Guidelines

1. The purpose and objectives for the activity are made clear; the students understand what they are supposed to do at each center. The activity is designed to enhance the students' understanding of a concept rather than serving to frustrate and confuse.

2. *All* students have an opportunity to work at the center before the activity is changed.

3. Activities at the center do not interfere with other lessons going on in the classroom. Activities that require darkness, loud noises, or excessive amounts of physical activity are not appropriate for a learning center. The center is in an area where the teacher can readily observe the children in action.

4. At least one 2-feet-by-4-feet table or work area of equivalent size is dedicated to this center. If the activity requires additional space, adequate floor space will be allocated. If audiovisual materials are to be used, electrical outlets are close by.

5. Consumable materials at the center are replenished frequently.

6. When water is required for an activity, the center is located close to a water source. If this is not possible, care is taken so that children running to sinks or water fountains do not interfere with students engaged in other classroom tasks. Outlets near water must be Ground Fault Circuit Interrupter (GFCI) type.

model for proper safety techniques when participating in activity-based science lessons.

SCIENCE SAFETY SOURCES AND RESOURCES

It is strongly recommended that science teachers and supervisors become aware of—and follow—applicable federal and state science safety legislation, codes, and professional standards. Several excellent resources for addressing this need are provided below.

The National Science Education Standards
National Academy Press
2101 Constitution Avenue, NW
Box 285
Washington, DC 20033
(800) 624-6242
http://www.nap.edu/readingroom/books/nses

This publication provides a vision of a scientifically literate populace, including what students need to know, understand, and be able to do at different grade levels, as well as general science safety implications.

The NSTA Handbook
National Science Teachers Association
1840 Wilson Boulevard
Arlington, VA 22201-3000
(800) 830-3232
http://www.nsta.org

This handbook provides a wealth of information concerning position papers relative to teacher duties and responsibilities. Portions of the document are also available through the Internet at the Web site indicated above.

> *The Total Science Safety System—Elementary Edition*
> JaKel, Inc.
> 585 Southfork Drive
> Waukee, IA 50263
> (515) 225-6317
> http://www/netinsnet/showcase/jakel

This is a comprehensive, interactive software program written by contributing author Jack Gerlovich and two colleagues. Currently in its fourth edition, it provides all applicable laws, codes, and professional standards. It also includes interactive science safety forms and checklists for field trips, life/earth/physical science activities, safety equipment, appropriate procedures, and assessments for chemical hazards.

CHAPTER SUMMARY

By providing thorough answers to the questions *What materials are necessary for the activities?*, *What is the safest and most efficient way to store and distribute materials?*, and *What classroom management strategies will I use to insure my students' safety?*, you can successfully create an efficient, safe environment for activity-based science lessons. Once the concepts to be taught are clearly identified and activities appropriate to the grade level are chosen, decisions about materials needed to teach those concepts, and storage and safe practices while handling those materials must be made. Generally, storage decisions depend on space restrictions in the school building and on the safety philosophy embraced by the teaching faculty.

In addition to ensuring that the environment and equipment items are properly maintained, teachers must try to foresee and address problems posed by activities; teach appropriately for the emotional, physical, and intellectual levels of their students; and provide adequate supervision for the environment and degree of hazards anticipated. Teachers who are sure that they have addressed all of these concerns can proceed with confidence. If they cannot, adjustments should be made—adding more safety features, limiting the activity to a teacher demonstration only, or eliminating the activity altogether.

The physical arrangement of the classroom directly affects the success of the activity-oriented science lesson. When physical barriers impede the completion of an activity, the students become frustrated. If materials are not readily available, a teachable moment may be lost. A flexible learning environment, carefully planned and designed to promote student exploration, will greatly facilitate science learning.

Lessons for Constructing Understanding

The next three sections contain examples of commercial and public domain supplementary materials as they are *modified* to meet the content standards for elementary and middle school science. Section I is devoted to life science lessons, Section II includes physical science lessons, and Section III contains earth and space science lessons. Our intention is to show the techniques for modification, planning, and methods of teaching. Chapter 3 is a resource for ideas and an exemplar of modification techniques.

More than 150 life, physical, and earth science activities are found within sixty lessons designed to fit the 4–E science learning cycle format suggested in the text. A clearly written *concept statement* can be found at the beginning of each lesson. Any concepts that may be important to the lesson expansion are also identified in the beginning of the lesson.

The student outcomes or objectives are included in the evaluation phase of each lesson. Those of you who expect to see objectives or *learner outcomes* listed first in an activity are encouraged to look carefully at the evaluation phase of each lesson before starting the exploration phase.

Grade levels are suggested in the beginning of each lesson. Each teacher best knows his or her students' limitations. If, upon reading the lesson, you find the activities too difficult or too easy for your students, then by all means find a lesson more suitable for your students' ability levels.

You will not find a *time limit* on the lessons. Lessons using a science learning cycle format may take one class period or several class meetings. One lesson may represent a unit or just one piece of that unit. The length of time for each lesson will depend on the ability level of your students and the amount of detail for each activity. Generally, the lessons are organized so that the *exploration* and *expansion phases* take one or two class meetings, and the *explanation phase* one class meeting. Questions designed to meet the goals of science in personal and social perspectives, science and technology, science as inquiry, and the history and the nature of science from the National Science Education Standards may be asked at any time during the lesson. Just because they are listed after the expansion phase does not mean they have to wait until after expansion to be asked. The *evaluation phase* may also be given in parts, during or after the exploration phase, as part of the explanation phase, and during or after the expansion phase.

These lessons are designed to give your students a chance to explore a science concept thoroughly. Collect materials and try each activity before you present it to your students to make sure everything works according to the plan, to make you aware of any potential problem areas, to ensure that you have foreseen all safety requirements, and to give you an opportunity to correct problems before you are with the students.

Make sure that each student is aware of any *safety precautions* before engaging in the science activity. If certain skills are required before the students can engage in an activity, then spend the time teaching those skills before starting the new activity. Advance work will ensure the success of a lesson presented in a science learning cycle.

Life Science Lessons

LIFE SCIENCE

Lesson Name	Life Science Content Standards	Grade Level	Activities
Plants			
Plant Parts and Needs	Characteristics of Organisms	K–4	Plant Dig • Eggshell Planters • Food Storage
Chlorophyll Production: Changing Leaf Color	Regulation and Behavior	2–4	Leaf Collection • Life of a Tree Drama • Leaf Press and Mobile
Osmosis and Capillary Action	Regulation and Behavior	5–8	Colored Carnations • Three-Way Split
Plant Photosynthesis	Population and Ecosystems	5–8	Radish Growth: Light versus Dark in a Bag • Radish Growth: Light versus Dark in Soil
Starch Exploration	Diversity and Adaptations	5–8	Microscopic Starch • Beans and Starch Grains
Animals			
Colors of Wildlife	Organisms and Environments	K–4	Animal Similarities and Differences • Create a Rainbow Animal
Shelter	Characteristics of Organisms	K–4	Shelter Drawing • Animal Homes
Wildlife and Domesti-cated Animals	Organisms and Environments	K–4	Animal Needs • Domestic versus Wild Charades
Habitat	Regulation and Behavior	2–4	Basic Needs Lap Sit • Animal Habitat Research
Crickets: Basic Needs of an Organism	Regulation and Behavior	5–8	Cricket Needs • Cricket Behavior
Animal Adaptations	Diversity and Adaptation	5–8	Mitten and Tweezer Beaks • Fish Adaptations
Owl Pellets	Populations and Ecosystems	5–8	Owl Pellet Dissection • Owl Research or Field Trip
Environment			
Humans and Trash	Organisms and Environment	K–4	Trash and Animals • Classroom Landfill and Recycling
Useful Waste	Populations and Ecosystems	5–8	Rating Garbage • Litter-Eating Critter • Making Paper
Litter in Our Waterways	Populations and Ecosystems	5–8	Sink-or-Float Litter • Plastic Food
Slogans and the Environment	Populations and Ecosystems	5–8	Slogan Categorization • Environmen-tal Slogans
Human			
Sense of Taste	Characteristics of Organisms	K–4	Buds and Tasters • Supertasters
Skeleton	Characteristics of Organisms	1–4	Bones Assembly Line • Newsprint Bone Bodies
Temperature Receptors on Skin	Structure and Function	5–8	Soaking Hands • Hot/Cold Receptor Mapping
Building Microscope Skills	Structure and Function	5–8	Microscope Use and Crystal Comparisons • Charcoal Crystals

Plant Parts and Needs

GRADE
K–4
DISCIPLINE
Life
Science

Concept to be invented

Main idea—The basic parts of a plant are roots, stems, and leaves.

Concepts that are important to expansion

Soil or some nutrient containing medium, air, water, and light is necessary for plant growth.

Materials needed

For exploration:

large paper or large plastic bags	resource books on plants
spoons for digging, or a spade or shovel	poster paint
	art paper
white paper	crayons
	markers

For expansion:

eggshells (halves or larger)	water
potting soil	sunlight or artificial light
mung beans	colored markers

➡ **Safety precautions:** Always have the proper adult:student ratio when taking the students away from the school campus. Make sure that the students are buddied up and that they are able to cross streets safely and know enough not to talk to strangers while walking to the dig site or while on the site.

Make sure all students can identify any poisonous plants at the dig site, such as poison ivy or poison oak. If large amounts of poisonous plants are in the area, it may be better to choose a different site.

Demonstrate to the students a safe method for digging up the plants and make sure they practice what was demonstrated. Remind the students never to put anything in their mouths unless the teacher gives prior approval. Do not eat the plants!

1. EXPLORATION: Which process skills will be used?

Observing, identifying, comparing

What will the students do?

Plant Dig

Take the students on a walking field trip to an area near the school where plants can be dug up without harming the environment. Identify the plants the students may dig up, and then allow them time to dig, making sure they get most of the root systems. Instruct the students to put their plants in bags and bring them back to school. Once back in class, ask the students to choose one of their plants and spread it out on a piece of white paper. Ask them to use the materials provided to draw pictures of their plants.

2. EXPLANATION/CONCEPT INVENTION: What is the main idea? How will the main idea be constructed?

Concept: The basic parts of a plant are roots, stems, and leaves.

Once the students have drawn their pictures, provide them with resource books that identify other plants. Ask the students the following questions: How are these plants different from the plant in front of you? How are they the same? What do all of our plants have in common? Continue with this line of questioning until the students understand that the basic parts of a plant are roots, stems, and leaves. Ask the students to return to the drawings they created of their plants. Ask them to label the roots, stems, and leaves in their drawings. At this time the teacher may provide the students with the common names for their plants, or ask the students if they already know what they dug up, or ask them to look through the resource books to identify their plants.

3. EXPANSION OF THE IDEA: Which process skills will be used?

Observing, gathering data, recording data, interpreting data, manipulating materials

How will the idea be expanded?

Eggshell Planters   Help the students collect eggshells (halves or larger). Ask the students to draw two eyes and a nose on their eggshells with colored markers. Provide potting soil so that the students can fill the shells with soil and sprinkle mung beans on top. Have them put a little more soil on top of the seeds. Sprinkle a small amount of water on the soil. Place the filled shells near the window. Challenge the students to observe the shells each day. When they discover bean sprouts appearing, have them draw a smile on the shell to complete the face.

Once the beans are well grown, ask the students to pull one of the sprouts out. Can you identify its root, stem, and leaves? Ask the students to describe what they did to help the plant grow from the bean seed to the sprout. What things were necessary for plant growth? Make a list on the board. Review with them why the items they identified are necessary for plant growth. Discuss the fact that leaves are necessary to plants because they are the place in the plant where food is created. The water and minerals are taken from the soil through the roots and brought up to the leaves. Gases from the air enter the plant through the leaf, and with the help of sunlight the leaves make food for the plant.

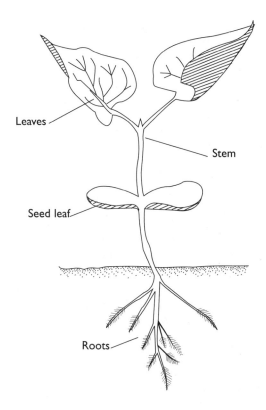

Additional ideas for expansion

Food Storage　The teacher can share with the students ways in which plants store food and what humans do with this knowledge. For instance, when food is stored, such as in nuts and seeds, the leaves drop off because they are no longer needed. Also, food is stored in various parts of plants. Provide the students with actual fruits, vegetables, and seeds (or pictures of them) to classify. Make a bulletin board of drawings done by students of roots, stems, leaves, flowers, fruits, and seeds eaten by humans. Hang the pictures near the appropriate term. Some possibilities are roots (beets, carrots, radishes, sweet potatoes), stems (asparagus, celery, green onions), underground stems (onions, potatoes), leaves (lettuce, spinach, cabbage), flowers (artichokes, broccoli, cauliflower), fruits (apples, pears, tomatoes, peaches, plums, apricots), seeds (nuts, peas, beans).

Science in Personal and Social Perspectives

- What would your life be like without plants? Why do you need to take care of plants?
- How might taking care of plants help you to develop responsibility?

- Ask the students if any of their parents or grandparents have a garden or grow plants indoors. Discuss the special care these plants need. Discuss how large fields of plants can be watered.

Science and Technology

- Why do plants sometimes need to be fertilized?
- Do all plants have to be in soil in order to grow? Hydroponic farming does not use soil. Can you think of what it uses instead of soil to grow plants?

Science as Inquiry

- Why do you need to know what plants need to grow?
- Why is research done on growing plants?
- What must we do to keep the plants healthy?
- During what part of a plant's life cycle can it grow without sunlight? Why?

History and Nature of Science

- Discuss with the students jobs or professions that involve caring for plants, such as gardening, working as a forest ranger, selling vegetables in a grocery store, or working in a nursery or flower shop.
- Growing and caring for plants takes a lot of work; some of the people who do this are agronomists, horticulturists, florists, botanists, and nutritionists.
- Ask the students to have their parents help them discover what Luther Burbank and Gregor Mendel did to help us understand plant growth better.

4. EVALUATION: How will the students show what they have learned?

Upon completing the activities the students will be able to:

- identify the root, stem, and leaf on a complete plant;
- name the four things most plants need to live;
- when given potting soil, sunflower seeds, water, and a cup, demonstrate the steps necessary to grow and care for a plant;
- when given a beet, spinach, and a piece of asparagus, identify which is a root, which a stem, and which a leaf.

Chlorophyll Production: Changing Leaf Color

GRADE
2–4
DISCIPLINE
Life
Science

Concept to be invented
Main idea—Living green plants produce chlorophyll for food.

Concepts that are important to expansion
Trees can be classified into two groups: those that lose their leaves and those that do not.

Materials needed

For the entire class: Sharon Gordon, *Now I Know Trees* (Mahwah, NJ: Troll Associates, 1983), or an equivalent; collection bags (one per student, paper lunch bag size), wax paper, electric iron, hole punch, yarn, scissors, towel.

➡ **Safety precautions:** Pair up the students with buddies before taking them outdoors. Go over safety rules when outside the school building: Stay with your buddy. Respect the other students who are still indoors by staying quiet. Do not talk to strangers who may come on the school grounds. Stay within eyesight of the teacher. Do not eat anything you find outside. Wash your hands after collecting the leaves. Do not poke each other with the scissors; use them only while seated. Stay away from the hot iron.

1. EXPLORATION: Which process skills will be used?

Observing, questioning, classifying, using time relationships, making assumptions, inferring, hypothesizing, drawing conclusions, communicating

What will the students do?

Leaf Collection

Begin the lesson by reading *Now I Know Trees* or any other book that introduces students to the idea of trees' losing leaves and the production of chlorophyll. Use the story to initiate a discussion about leaves on trees.

Give each student a collection bag. Take the students outside. Let them explore the area and use the bag to collect different kinds of leaves. Ask the students to look for signs that fall has arrived. Gather the students together to discuss their findings. Ask them to describe their observations in terms of colors, shapes, and sizes. Return to the classroom.

2. EXPLANATION/CONCEPT INVENTION: What is the main idea? How will the main idea be constructed?

Concept: Living green plants produce chlorophyll for food.

Ask the students the following questions to help invent the concept: How many different colors did you find? What do you think causes the leaves to change color? What do plants use as food?

All plants, including trees, make their food, called *chlorophyll,* using sunshine and water. The chlorophyll makes the leaves turn green. Why are the leaves green? Green is the color of the chlorophyll. What do you think would happen if the trees didn't get any water? any sunlight? When fall comes, the amount of sunlight decreases. As the ground hardens due to colder weather, it becomes more difficult for the tree to get water out of the ground and up to its leaves. As a result, the trees cannot produce as much food. Since food is scarce, the tree shuts off the food supply to the leaves in order to have enough for it-self. Without the chlorophyll, the leaves are no longer green.

What color are the leaves on the ground? Why are they no longer green?

Did all the trees you observed lose their leaves? Why or why not? Some trees stay green all year long. Does anyone know what these trees are called? There are two kinds of trees. The ones that lose their leaves are called *deciduous.* The second kind are called *conifers.* Most conifers remain evergreen, but some, like the larches, lose their leaves.

3. EXPANSION OF THE IDEA: Which process skills will be used?

Formulating models, experimenting, communicating

How will the idea be expanded?

Life of a Tree Drama

Have the students find their own space in the classroom with plenty of room to move. The students will dramatize the life of a tree. The teacher will narrate, talking through the seasons and the loss of the leaves. Free expression should be encouraged. Suggest using the arms for branches and hands for leaves.

Leaf Press and Mobile

Help the students to create leaf mobiles. The teacher will press the students' col-lected leaves between layers of waxed paper. The students can cut around the shape of the leaves, punch holes, and hang with yarn.

Science in Personal and Social Perspectives

- How does the approach of fall affect your life? How does the change of any season affect you?
- What do you think you would need if you could make your own food like a tree?
- Do you think we can trick a tree into never losing its leaves? What would we need to do in order for that to happen? How would this benefit society?

Science and Technology

- Can trees be grown in greenhouses? Will trees growing in greenhouses lose their leaves in the fall? Why or why not?

Science as Inquiry

- How and why do leaves change colors?
- What is chlorophyll?
- Do all trees lose their leaves in the fall?
- Are the needles on a pine tree leaves?

History and Nature of Science

- Whom might we ask to find out more about leaves and the change of the seasons?
- Would a Christmas tree farm owner have a job if Christmas trees were deciduous?

4. EVALUATION: How will the students show what they have learned?

Upon completing the activities the students will be able to:

- explain what chlorophyll does for plants,
- name the two groups of trees,
- dramatize how and why a tree loses its leaves.

Osmosis and Capillary Action

Concept to be invented
Main idea—Fluid is drawn up the stem of a plant by osmosis and capillary action.

Concepts that are important to expansion
Fiber membranes run throughout a flower from the roots to the petals.

Materials needed
For exploration (per student group):

two to three white, long-stem carnations	two clear cups or glass beakers
	water
food coloring	knife or sharp blade

➡ **Safety precautions:** Take care not to drop glass or beakers, thus increasing the likelihood of cuts. Use caution if using the knife or sharp blade.

1. EXPLORATION: Which process skills will be used?

Observing, predicting, reasoning, inferring, recording data

What will the students do?

Colored Carnations

Separate the class into groups of four to six students. Give each group two carnations and two beakers or clear cups. Fill the cups or beakers with water. Dissolve one color of food coloring in one cup and a different color in the other. Dark colors like red or blue work well. Take one of the carnations and cut a fresh end on the stem (this may be done by the teacher with students in each group assisting). After this cut, split the stem in half, starting a cut with the knife and further splitting it along the fibers without breaking them. Place each half of the stem in each beaker and observe the white flower. Record your observations over 3-minute time periods for a total of 30 minutes.

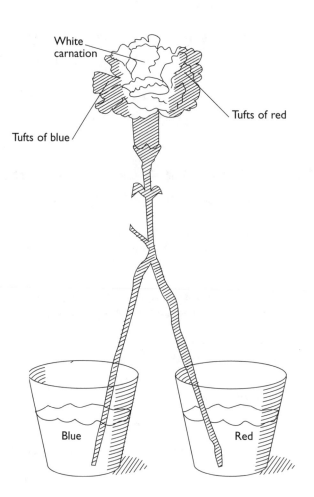

White carnation

Tufts of red

Tufts of blue

Blue

Red

2. EXPLANATION/CONCEPT INVENTION: What is the main idea? How will the main idea be constructed?

Concept: Fluid is drawn up the stem of a plant by osmosis and capillary action.

Ask the students questions such as the following to help invent this concept: What did you observe during the first 3 minutes of this experiment? How long did it take before you observed any changes in your flower? What were these changes? Why do you think they happened?

The stems of green plants support the plants and hold up the leaves and flowers. Some plants, like this carnation, have thin, green stems. Other plants, such as trees, have thick wooden stems. The trunk of an oak tree is its stem. It holds heavy branches and thousands of leaves. Water and food move up and down the plant through the stem. Water moves through special tubes in the stem. The water goes from the roots to the leaves and other parts of the plant. Other tubes carry food from the leaves to the roots and other plant parts. The colored water in our experiment is drawn up the stem of the carnation by osmosis and capillary action. The water molecules diffuse through the fiber membranes from a less to a larger concentration of plant sap (osmosis). The fibers are so tiny that the adhesive force of the water molecules to the fiber walls becomes very great. This capillary force in combination with the osmotic pressure sucks the water up the flower.

3. EXPANSION OF THE IDEA: Which process skills will be used?

Communicating, problem solving, experimenting, recording data

How will the idea be expanded?

Three-Way Split   When the stem is split three ways, it is very likely that the flower will be three colored. Ask the students to design an experiment to demonstrate this. This will show that the fibers must somehow run all the way from the stem to the petals of the flower. Encourage the students to experiment with how many ways they can get the stem to split to create as multicolored a flower as possible.

Ask the students to think about the following: What would happen if the stem were cut irregularly, such as diagonally? What if a cut was made that was jagged and cut across the fibers? How many other types of plants can be used to demonstrate this same phenomenon? Demonstrate this.

Science in Personal and Social Perspectives

- If you wanted to give someone a bouquet of carnations to celebrate the Fourth of July and could find only white ones, what can you do to those to get red and blue ones too? Do you think the same thing is done by florists?
- If you were to receive a bouquet of flowers and you wanted them to stay fresh for a long time, what should you do for them, and why?

Science and Technology

- How has knowledge of capillary action been used to create more efficient car engines?
- Artificial hearts and other organs are continuously being developed. How will osmosis and capillary action of blood affect the function of these artificial organs?

Science as Inquiry

- What force is pulling the colored solution up the stem of the carnation in this activity?
- What if the flower were placed in *clear* water? Would the liquid still be drawn up the stem? How could you tell?
- Could a plant live without a stem? Why or why not?

History and Nature of Science

- Can you name some people who work with plants?
- Why do you think it might be important for a farmer to understand plant growth? a florist? a grocer?

- Would you like to work in any of these occupations? Why or why not?
- How did the tradition of giving flowers on special occasions get started? Can you trace the history of this tradition? Can you trace the history of when flowers were artificially colored?

4. EVALUATION: How will the students show what they have learned?

Upon completing the activities the students will be able to:

- explain the purpose of splitting the stem in two during this lesson;
- demonstrate their knowledge of capillary action by explaining the process using a piece of celery, food coloring, a beaker, and water;
- observe several plants in various stages of watering (underwatered, over-watered, just right) and explain why the plant looks as it does.

Plant Photosynthesis

GRADE
5–8
DISCIPLINE
Life
Science

Concept to be invented
Main idea—Plants are capable of making their own food by a process called *photosynthesis.*

Concepts that are important to expansion
Seeds, moisture, chlorophyll, designing investigations.

Materials needed
For each student group:

radish seeds   one piece of aluminum foil
two Ziploc bags (large storage size)   paper towels
two paper towels   metric ruler

➡ **Safety precautions:** Do not put anything in your mouth. Avoid eating leaves or seeds of plants. Do not play with plastic bags; keep them away from your face.

1. EXPLORATION: Which process skills will be used?

Predicting, observing, inferring, controlling variables, experimenting, reducing experimental error, analyzing

What will the students do?

Radish Growth:
Light versus Dark
in a Bag

Provide each group of students with some radish seeds, two Ziploc bags, two paper towels, and one piece of aluminum foil. Challenge the students to design a way in which they could use these materials to compare the growth of radish seeds. Explain to them that the variable to be manipulated in this experiment is light. All other factors must remain constant. The students must write up the method they plan to use; do not be concerned if the students change too many variables. This will be a valuable lesson to them, as they will soon discover by their experimental results. Once they have designed and written up their experimental methods, including predictions of potential outcomes, give them time to act on their design. Check their uncovered bags each day. When leaves begin to grow in the uncovered bag, uncover the covered bag and compare the two environments.

2. EXPLANATION/CONCEPT INVENTION: What is the main idea? How will the main idea be constructed?

Concept: Photosynthesis is a process in which chlorophyll-bearing plant cells, using light energy, produce carbohydrates and oxygen from carbon dioxide and water. Simply put, it is a way in which green plants use the sun's energy to make their own food.

Have the students share the data they collected. Where did you place your bags in the room? Were they both put in the same place? Why is it important to make sure the bags were in the same area? What about the number of seeds you used? Was that kept constant? Is it important to keep the number of seeds the same? Why or why not? What happened inside both of your bags? Was it as you predicted? If so, can you explain why? If not, why not? Did the seeds sprout leaves in both the covered and uncovered environments? What color were they? Which environment appears more successful? Where did the green leaves come from? What gives your skin color? (Pigment.) Do plants have pigment?

Uncovered bag
(radish begins growing)

Covered bag
(with aluminum foil)

LIFE SCIENCE

Does anyone know the name of the pigment that gives plants their green color? (Chlorophyll.) Do you think, based on your experimental results, you can determine what the chlorophyll does for the plant? (It makes food for the plant.) What do we call the process whereby the chlorophyll makes use of light energy to make food for the plant? (Photosynthesis.)

3. EXPANSION OF THE IDEA: Which process skills will be used?

Experimenting, hypothesizing, predicting, observing, analyzing, controlling variables, inferring, recording data

How will the idea be expanded?

Radish Growth: Light versus Dark in Soil

Challenge the students to design another experiment, this time planting the seeds in soil instead of bags. Once again make light the manipulated variable. Predict the outcome, plan and record the methods, and act on your design. Once the seeds in the light begin to sprout, compare these results to the bag experiment. Were your predictions accurate? Why do you think you obtained the results you did? Did photosynthesis occur in the covered pot? the uncovered pot? Why? Continue to grow the plants and measure and record the results for one month.

Science in Personal and Social Perspectives

- How do plants help people survive on this planet?
- What would your life be like without plants?

Science and Technology

- Because they need land to live and grow things on, some people in Brazil are cutting down the tropical rain forests. Should this concern you? Do you think there is a technological solution to the problem of vanishing rainforests? Share your ideas.
- Of what advantage has hydroponic farming been to the people of the world?

Science as Inquiry

- New concepts for further inquiry include growth rates, leaf shapes, deciduous versus coniferous, and so on.
- Can photosynthesis occur if a plant does not contain chlorophyll?
- Does photosynthesis take place in plants that grow on the ocean floor?

History and Nature of Science

- What impact has the farming industry had on our daily lives? on the lives of people throughout the world today and in the past 100 years?
- Who was Gregor Mendel (1822–1884)? How did his knowledge of photosynthesis open up an entirely new field of genetics?
- Can just anyone become a landscape architect? What kind of background knowledge does a person in this field need?

4. EVALUATION: How will the students show what they have learned?

Upon completing the activities the students will be able to:

- when provided with two of the same plant, one grown in a shady environment and the other in a sunny one, identify which was grown where;
- observe plants growing around the classroom and accurately predict what will happen to the leaves if a small piece of paper is clipped over part of a leaf for one week;
- read a problem about a science exploration and accurately determine which variable should be manipulated and which should be controlled.

Starch Exploration

GRADE
5–8
DISCIPLINE
Life
Science

Concept to be invented
Main idea—Starches have a structure that is unique for each type of vegetable.

Concepts that are important to expansion
Starch grain, hilum, slide preparation, microscope use.

Materials needed
For each student group:

microscope
five slides
one scalpel
cover slips
tapioca

rice that was soaked in water for at
    least 4 hours
kidney beans
corn kernels
potatoes

➡ **Safety precautions:** Although the starches are edible, the students should be discouraged from tasting them. Caution should be used around electrical outlets for the electric microscopes. The bulb for the microscope will get hot. Students should be reminded of safety techniques when using the scalpel.

1. EXPLORATION: Which process skills will be used?

Observing, predicting, comparing, manipulating materials, recording data

What will the students do?

Microscopic Starch The students will prepare slides of each of the given vegetables by using the scalpel to gently scrape a newly cut surface of the vegetable. A very small speck of each should be placed on each slide with a drop of water. A cover slip should be applied. The students should make predictions before observing the different starch grains. Will all of them look alike, since they are all starches? What do you think? Record this prediction. The students should observe each prepared slide under the microscope and draw their observations of the starch from each vegetable.

2. EXPLANATION/CONCEPT INVENTION: What is the main idea? How will the main idea be constructed?

Concept: Starches have a structure that is unique for each type of vegetable.

Key questions to ask the students to help them come to these conclusions are: What did you observe as you looked at the potato grains? How were they different from the corn or rice? What did the bean and tapioca starch look like? Ask the students to compare their drawings to actual pictures of the various grains. Were you able to observe the detail these pictures show? Can you differentiate between parts of the grain?

Additional information to help develop the concept

The students should find countless oval, ellipsoidal, or even triangular shaped, almost transparent bodies that look like miniature oyster shells when they observe the potato starch grains. Since the grains are not flat, it may help if the students slowly rotate the fine adjustment on the microscope back and forth to get all the parts in focus. Usually on the narrower end the students will find a tiny dark spot that is not in the center of the grain. This is called the *hilum,* the oldest part of the starch grain, around which the remainder of the shell has grown layer by layer until fully formed. If you focus up and down at this point, you will find concentric lines or rings called *striations,* which indicate the layers where the grain has grown larger and larger.

Corn starch is different from potato. The grains may have an irregular globular shape or a very distinct polygonal shape. The shape will vary depending on the part of the kernel the students take their samples from—the horny or the floury portion. Corn starch has a central hilum that is usually a point but sometimes shows two, three, or four radiating clefts.

Rice starch grains are very small and many sided. They may be square, triangular, or pentagonal in shape. The hilum is not distinct, but in some grains a central portion appears brighter. This difference may be due to the drying of the grain. Ovoid or spherical shapes are usually due to a number of grains being compacted together.

Bean starch grains are usually ellipsoidal or kidney shaped. They have an irregular branching cleft running out from the center that appears black because of enclosed air.

Tapioca grains are usually circular or loaf shaped, depending on whether they sit on their flat surfaces or on their sides. The hilum is centrally located, usually coming to a point or small cleft. When students view the flattened surface, the hilum may appear triangular.

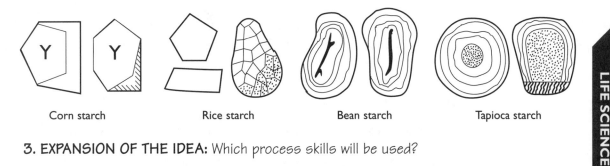

Corn starch   Rice starch   Bean starch   Tapioca starch

3. EXPANSION OF THE IDEA: Which process skills will be used?

Observing, predicting, comparing, manipulating materials, recording data, hypothesizing

How will the idea be expanded?

Beans and Starch Grains

- The students may brainstorm a list of other starch-containing foods. Obtain these foods, prepare slides, and check students' predictions by looking for evidence of starch grains. Are they similar to any of the grains previously identified? Are they different? What kind of starch do you think this food contains?
- The students may obtain several different kinds of beans. Pose a question: Will all beans contain the same kind of starch grains, no matter the type of bean? Allow the students to design an experiment to answer that question.

Science in Personal and Social Perspectives

- Do you think the differences in the starch grain will affect your ability to digest that starch? Why or why not?
- Are there any other kinds of plants that contain starch grains that humans do not eat? What are these? Why do you think we do not eat them?
- Why are starches important in a person's diet?

Science and Technology

- Why does the United States send starchy foods to underdeveloped countries? What kinds of conditions are necessary to grow starch-containing foods? Can modern technology do anything to help these underdeveloped nations to grow starches on their own?
- What kinds of products have modern industries created that make use of starches? How have these helped modern society? How have these hindered modern society?

Science as Inquiry

- Are all starch grains, no matter the plant they come from, the same? Will starch grains from many different varieties of potatoes look the same? Why or why not?
- What is the name of the oldest part of the starch grain? Does finding this structure under the microscope help in identifying the type of plant the starch grain came from?

- The process skills the students had to engage in to do these activities (predicting, manipulating materials, forming hypotheses, solving problems, recording data, making careful observations) enhance their overall academic growth.

History and Nature of Science

- Why do you think a person responsible for creating frozen dinners should understand that different vegetables have different starch structures?
- What kinds of jobs entail making careful observations and accurately recording what was observed?
- Do you think an insurance adjuster could benefit by learning the skills you utilized while participating in this lesson?

4. EVALUATION: How will the students show what they have learned?

Upon completing these activities the students will be able to:

- prepare a slide of starch grains,
- accurately draw starch grains observed under a microscope,
- identify with 80 percent accuracy the various starch grains and their sources,
- explain in writing or verbally why certain starches can be digested by humans while other starches cannot.

Colors of Wildlife

GRADE
K–4
DISCIPLINE
Life
Science

Concept to be invented
Main idea—Wildlife occurs in a wide variety of colors.

Concepts that are important to expansion
Camouflage allows an organism to blend in or hide in its environment.

Materials needed
For the entire class:
Magazines that have a wide variety of animal pictures, such as *National Geographic, Ranger Rick, National and International Wildlife, Audubon.* Try to have magazines that can be cut up.

Construction paper, crayons or markers, scissors, glue, felt, cotton balls, natural materials from outdoors (acorns, leaves, grass); an appropriate story book with a wide variety of different colored animals in it will also help introduce the topic. A book such as Richard Buckley and Eric Carle's *The Greedy Python* (New York: Scholastic Books, 1992) is a good selection.

➡ **Safety precautions:** Do not poke each other with the scissors; use them only while seated.

LIFE SCIENCE

1. **EXPLORATION:** Which process skills will be used?

Observing, comparing, generalizing

What will the students do?

Animal Similarities and Differences

Introduce the lesson by reading the students a book like *The Greedy Python.* Encourage the students to make note of the color of the python and of all the other animals it comes across. You will return to the ideas provided by the story later.

After the story and brief discussion about it, provide each student group with several wildlife magazines to look at. Ask the students to find pictures of animals, make observations about the animals, and compare the animals to one another. Create two lists on the board. Title one list *similarities,* the other *differences.* Ask the students to share their observations about the animals they found by providing information about the similarities and differences of the animals. Ask the students to each cut out three different animals.

2. **EXPLANATION/CONCEPT INVENTION:** What is the main idea? How will the main idea be constructed?

Concept: Wildlife occurs in a wide variety of colors.

Refer back to the story you read. For instance, if *The Greedy Python* was used, you might ask the following questions to help invent the concept: What animals did you see in the book? What colors were they? Why do you think the python was so successful in eating all the animals? Could a green python hide easily in a jungle?

Hold up a variety of different-colored pieces of construction paper. Ask the students to identify the colors. Then ask the students to raise their hands if they cut out animals that match the color of the paper you are holding. Assist them in concluding that animals appear in a variety of colors.

Let the students help in gluing the animals on to the construction paper that matches the animal's color. Hang these animal pages around the room. Ask the student farthest from each picture if is is difficult to identify the animal on the page, that is, a red animal on a red piece of paper. Ask why he or she thinks it is difficult. How would this coloration help it survive in the wild? Draw the students to the conclusion that camouflage allows an organism to blend in or hide in its environment.

3. **EXPANSION OF THE IDEA:** Which process skills will be used?

Observing, manipulating materials, generalizing, comparing, communicating

How will the idea be expanded?

Create a Rainbow Animal

Use the materials from the material list to have the students create their own animal. The animals may be real, or they can make them up. Encourage the generalization that wild animals appear in a wide variety of colors and that the animals' colors and markings help them survive. Encourage the students to look for rainbow animals—those that have three or more distinct colors on their bodies. Ask the students to share their creations with one another. Get them to communicate to one another how their animal can hide in its environment.

Science in Personal and Social Perspectives

- Where would you find _____? (Insert an animal name.)
- Do you think it is as important for a pet to blend in with its surroundings as it is for wild animals? Why or why not?
- Do we need to protect the environment where some animals live? Why?
- What are some things society can do to protect animal environments?

Science and Technology

- Hunters used to wear only clothing that blended into the environment when they hunted. Today we see hunters wearing bright orange vests and bright orange hats. Why do you think the design of their clothing changed?

Science as Inquiry

- Where could you learn more about a particular animal?
- What are some ways that color helps animals survive?
- Besides color, what other kinds of things can animals use for camouflage?

History and Nature of Science

- Can you think of any jobs in which people work with or study animals?
- Can you think of any jobs in which people work with aquatic animals?
- Can you think of any animals that work? (Police dogs, seeing-eye dogs, sled dogs, horses, pigeons, animals that help on a farm.) How are these animals trained?

4. EVALUATION: How will the students show what they have learned?

Upon completing the activities the students will be able to:

- construct an animal using a variety of colors when given materials,
- explain how a cartoon animals relates to a real animal,
- make a graph of animals that have one, two, or more colors.

Shelter

GRADE
K–4
DISCIPLINE
Life
Science

Concept to be invented
Main idea—Shelter is a necessary condition for the survival of many animals.

Concepts that are important to expansion
Food, water, and space are other conditions necessary for the survival of an animal.

Materials needed

For each student:

Construction paper and crayons or markers.

➡ **Safety precautions:** Remind the students to use crayons and markers properly and not to place them in their mouths.

1. **EXPLORATION:** Which process skills will be used?

Inferring, predicting, analyzing, comparing, generalizing, communicating, manipulating materials, recording data

What will the students do?

Shelter Drawing   Ask the students to draw a picture of the place they live in. Upon completion, allow each child to hang his or her picture in the classroom. Be sure all the drawings can be easily viewed by the students. Ask the students to determine what each has in common. Possible answers include roofs, ceilings, walls, floors, doors, windows. Ask the students to determine how each is different. Suggestions may include apartment, trailer, house, size, color, materials dwelling is made of.

Ask the students to draw another picture of items found inside their home. To simplify, ask them to focus on their favorite room in the house. Once again, display the pictures. Ask the students to view the pictures and decide what items a home may have more than one of, such as refrigerators, beds, lamps, pictures in frames. Ask the students to identify the things they must have, such as food, water, space, clothing. Ask the students to identify the items that make living in the home more fun or easier, such as television, radio, chairs.

2. **EXPLANATION/CONCEPT INVENTION:** What is the main idea? How will the main idea be constructed?

Concept: Shelter is a necessary condition for the survival of many animals.

Carry on a discussion with the students centered around this question: What would happen if we didn't have a place to live? Be sure to mention that we would be affected by the weather, we could get sick, be harmed by animals, get dirty, and so on.

Focus again on the first pictures drawn. Be sure the following idea comes out during discussion: All homes may not be the same, but they serve the same purpose—protection.

Ask the children if they think anything beside humans need homes. Lead the discussion toward animals. Why do animals need a shelter? Is it for the same reason as humans? Help the students to conclude that shelter is necessary for the survival of many animals, humans included.

3. EXPANSION OF THE IDEA: Which process skills will be used?

Observing, communicating, problem solving, formulating models, classifying, questioning, hypothesizing

How will the idea be expanded?

Animal Homes

Ask each child to choose an animal and draw a home for that animal. Display these drawings. Discuss how the animals' homes are the same and how they are different. Compare the animals' homes with the drawings of the children's homes. Discuss with the students the answers to the following questions: Do animals live in bigger or smaller homes than humans? Where do animals get their food? Where do humans get their food? Do animals have furniture in their homes? How many people live in your home? How many animals live in their homes?

Be sure the students understand that although animals do not live in houses, trailers, or apartments, they do live in homes in nature where they are protected from the weather and other animals, where they sleep, eat, and care for their young. Food, water, and space in a suitable arrangement are basic needs that every animal has. This arrangement is different for different animals; for example, humans live in neighborhoods that may meet all of their basic needs.

Science in Personal and Social Perspectives

* If you had to choose only three items from your home to keep, which items would you choose? Why did you choose these items? Do you need these things to stay alive?
* If you found a bird's nest, would you pick it up or leave it alone? Why?
* How can humans make homes for animals? What kinds of things must humans use to make animals' homes?
* What do you think happens to animals when humans tear down forests (where many animals live) to build human homes or office buildings? Do you think this kind of action is responsible human behavior?

- If you were a community developer and you were offered a large space of land to build an amusement park if you cut down a forest, would you cut down the forest to build the park? Why or why not? What if you could build homes for people on that same land; would you do it?

Science and Technology

- Why do you think the shelters that humans build can survive the forces of nature better than the shelters that animals build? How are these structures different?
- Modern technology has created many useful products like microwave ovens, electric shavers, and bread machines. Do you think these are necessary for survival?

Science as Inquiry

- What kinds of things do humans and animals need in their homes to survive?
- Where can animals' homes be found?
- Can animals live in human homes?
- What kinds of animals live with people?

History and Nature of Science

- What kinds of supplies do construction workers use to build homes for people? How are these supplies like those that animals use?
- Interview someone born before 1950. Ask this person to share with you what homes were constructed of when he or she was your age. Is there much difference between then and today? If so, why?

4. EVALUATION: How will the students show what they have learned?

Upon completing the activities the students will be able to:

- choose from various items found in a home those that are necessary for living;
- classify homes according to human or animal homes when given several pictures,
- explain similarities and differences between human and animal homes and explain why humans and animals need shelter,
- list the four items necessary for life: food, water, shelter, and space.

Wildlife and Domesticated Animals

GRADE
K–4
DISCIPLINE
Life
Science

Concept to be invented
Main idea—Wildlife includes animals that are not tamed or domesticated.

Concepts that are important to expansion
Endangered animals, extinct, threatened, safe.

Materials needed

For exploration:

Pictures of both wild and domesticated animals, attribute blocks.

➡ **Safety precautions:** Do not throw attribute blocks; use care when acting out animals in expansion activity so as to not hit any other student.

1. EXPLORATION: Which process skills will be used?

Observing, hypothesizing, inferring, categorizing, recording data

What will the students do?

Animal Needs

Using attribute blocks, ask the students to place these blocks into two different groups. This activity will ensure that the students understand the concept of grouping. Next, ask the students to look around the room at the pictures hanging up. What do you observe in the pictures? (Animals.) Divide the class into groups of four to six. Provide them with pictures of both wild and domesticated animals (at least as many pictures as there are students in a group). Each student in the group will pick up an animal and record characteristics of the animal that make it different from any other. Some prompting questions could be: Where do they live? How do they get their food? Are they dependent on humans for their survival? Once each child in the group has listed the characteristics of the animal he or she chose, ask the students to decide how they could put their animals into two different groups. Once they make that decision, then divide the animals.

2. EXPLANATION/CONCEPT INVENTION: What is the main idea? How will the main idea be constructed?

Concept: Wildlife includes animals that are not tamed or domesticated.

Ask the students questions such as the following to help invent this concept: How did your group decide to divide your animals? What characteristics of your animals led you to this decision? How do the animals in one of your groups get their food? How do the animals in your other group get their food? Do either of your groupings separate the animals into whether they rely on humans for their survival?

Animals that do not rely on humans for survival and that are neither tame or owned are called *wild*. *Domesticated* animals rely on humans for their survival.

3. EXPANSION OF THE IDEA: Which process skills will be used?

Observing, classifying, analyzing, inferring, communicating

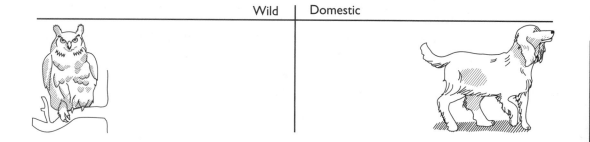

	Wild	Domestic

How will the idea be expanded?

Domestic versus Wild Charades

Ask the students to choose an animal, and without telling anyone else in the class, write down the name of that animal. The students may choose one from a picture in the room or think of one on their own. Divide the class in half, and collect their listed animals in two groups. Explain to the students how the game of charades is played. Have students from one half of the class pick from a pile of animals that came from the other half of the room, and vice versa. Ask the students to look at the name of the animal on the card, and without saying what is written on the card, act out the behaviors of that animal for the students on your side of the room to guess. Write the words *domestic* and *wild* on the board. Once the students guess which animal was acted out, ask the student who just acted out the animal to decide whether that animal should be listed as domestic or wild. Make sure all of the students agree on the listing before acting out the next animal.

Science in Personal and Social Perspectives

- Name some domesticated animals that we could find in your neighborhood. What would the neighborhood be like if these animals were wild?
- What do you think life would be like if any of the wild animals we acted out no longer existed, that is, they became extinct?
- What do you think would happen if you tried to tame a wild animal?
- Why is a wildlife preserve important to our society?
- Can the study of wildlife give us any ideas about how people behave?

Science and Technology

- Propose a method to change an animal from wild to domestic.

Science as Inquiry

- What important facts must we remember when dealing with wildlife?
- What things are important to remember when taking care of pets?
- What is the difference between a wild and a domesticated animal?

History and Nature of Science

- What type of job requires knowledge of wildlife or requires someone to work with wild animals?
- Interview a zookeeper. What special skills does someone in this line of work need?

- What kind of jobs would have to be created if wildlife started taking over our community?
- Choose a domesticated animal. Search throughout history to determine when it first became domesticated and why.

4. EVALUATION: How will the students show what they have learned?

Upon completing the activities the students will be able to:

- give two examples of a wild animal,
- give two examples of a domestic animal,
- list the characteristics of a wild and a domestic animal,
- draw a picture of an animal and identify it as wild or domestic by drawing an appropriate habitat for it.

Habitat

**GRADE
2–4
DISCIPLINE
Life
Science**

Concept to be invented
Main idea—An animal's *habitat* is an environment in which there is a suitable arrangement of its basic needs—food, water, shelter, and space.

Concepts that are important to expansion
Niche.

Materials needed
For each student:

one large sheet of newsprint
scissors, glue
markers, crayons
old magazines to cut up

construction paper of various colors
resource books that provide information on different animals' habitats
and their niches in those habitats

➡ **Safety precautions:** Remind students about the safe use of scissors.

1. EXPLORATION: Which process skills will be used?

Predicting, hypothesizing, inferring

What will the students do?

*Basic Needs
Lap Sit*

Begin the session by asking the students to think about the last meal they ate. Could they have gotten by without it? How long could they have gone without eating? Why is food necessary? Could you survive without it? After a discussion on food, move on to a similar line of questioning, getting at the necessity of water and shelter. After there is consensus through effective questioning techniques on the necessity of food, water, and shelter, ask all the students to get out of their seats and direct them to some small space or corner of the room. Encourage all of them to crowd into a small space. Keep encouraging them to get as close to one another as possible. After they have spent a few moments crowded into a small space, if there is not too much protest, begin your line of questioning about how they feel right now. If they really begin to complain, allow them to return to their seats; then continue a discussion about the importance of suitable space. How necessary is it?

Once the students have reached agreement on the importance of food, water, shelter, and space in their lives, move the class to a room or outdoor setting where they will have plenty of space to stand up and form a circle. The teacher should stand at the center of the circle and lead a discussion about the importance of food, water, shelter, and space, not just for humans, but for all living organisms. Assign each student in the circle one of the four necessities—food, water, shelter, or space. When assigning the students, make sure that you try to assign at least three students in a row the same necessity. Take, for example, these ten students, who were standing in the circle in the following order: John, water; Kevin, food; Mary, shelter; Carol, space; Colette, food; Charlie, food; Pat, food, Trudy, water; Joshua, shelter; Calvin, space; José, water; Yolanda, shelter. This assignment of necessities will be used later to invent part of the concept.

As the students are facing you in the center of the circle, ask them to turn to their right and place their hands on the shoulders of the person in front of them. Encourage them to get as close to one another as possible while still maintaining a circle formation. They may have to take one or two steps toward the

middle of the circle to close their ranks. Once *they* believe their circle is tight enough, ask the students at the count of three to sit down slowly on the knees of the person behind them. (Note: Some shuffling and rearranging of bodies may occur to tighten the circle some once the students hear this direction. If this does not happen or the circle has a lot of empty space between bodies, do not tell them to tighten up the circle. The students will soon realize this on their own after one try at the lap sit. They may even decide that their sizes will affect the success of the lap sit and try to arrange themselves before the sit so that the tallest student is not expected to sit on the lap of the shortest student.) If the lap sit falls apart, encourage the students to get up and try it again. Once it is successful, the students are ready to help invent the concept.

2. EXPLANATION/CONCEPT INVENTION: What is the main idea? How will the main idea be constructed?

Concept: An animal's *habitat* is an environment in which there is a suitable arrangement of its basic needs—food, water, shelter, and space.

As the students are sitting in a successful lap sit, remind them that each student represented a basic necessity—food, water, shelter, or space. Tell them that some terrible natural disaster came along, like a flood, that wiped out most of their food source. Ask three fourths of the students who represented food to leave the lap sit. What happened to the lap sit once those students left? Could the lap sit survive? In a circle where several students next to one another represented the same necessity, it is virtually impossible to maintain the lap sit. It quickly falls apart. The teacher should lead a discussion by asking the students why they think the lap sit fell apart. What could have kept the lap sit together? Could they have arranged themselves differently in the lap sit so that it would not fall apart if a few people from one type of necessity were asked to leave? Could animals survive if only one of the areas where they get food (or water, shelter, space) from was wiped out? Can they survive if all of their food (or water, shelter, space) is in one place and it gets wiped out? Help the students conclude that food, water, shelter, and space are all needed in a *suitable arrangement* to help ensure the animal's survival. This area where there is a suitable arrangement of the animal's basic needs is called its *habitat.*

3. EXPANSION OF THE IDEA: Which process skills will be used?

Observing, gathering data, recording data, interpreting data, manipulating materials

How will the idea be expanded?

Animal Habitat Research   Ask each student to choose an animal in which he or she has a particular interest. Encourage the students to be creative, to suggest a variety of animals, not just dogs and cats for everyone. If necessary, assign animals. Provide the students with the materials listed above. Ask the students to do some research on the animal they chose using the resource books provided; books they find through a library research time; or computer software on animals. During their research they should find out as much as possible about that animal's habitat. What are its needs for food, water, shelter, and space? What role does it play or *niche* does it occupy in its environment? Encourage them to find one other interesting fact about their animal.

Once they have completed their research, ask them to use the materials to create a pictorial representation of the animal's habitat. This can be done as a diorama, collage, drawing, or other medium. On the back of their creation, they should provide in writing a brief description of the animal's habitat indicating how its basic needs are met.

Science in Personal and Social Perspectives

- How are your basic needs similar to those of the animal you studied? How are they different?
- In what ways have humans been able to alter their habitat?
- Do you think there will come a time when even humans will not have their basic needs met? Do you think some humans are already at that point? Why or why not?

Science and Technology

- What is the Biosphere II Project in Arizona all about? What can be learned by creating artificial habitats?
- Of what importance is our understanding of the concept of habitat to the success of a space station?
- Should logging be allowed in a national forest that is the only known habitat for a particular species of owl?

Science as Inquiry

- What are the basic needs for a human?
- Can an organism survive in a habitat where one of its basic needs is low or missing?
- Can two different animals with basically the same habitat survive in an area if the role they play in the environment (their niche) is different?

History and Nature of Science

- What do you think a wildlife officer does?
- Does an animal behaviorist discipline animals? If not, what kind of a job does this person have?
- Can a social worker apply the idea of a *suitable arrangement of basic needs* to his or her job? Why might he or she want to, and how would it be done?

4. EVALUATION: How will the students show what they have learned?

Upon completing the activities the students will be able to:

- describe the *basic needs* for a human,
- draw a picture of an ideal habitat for an organism of their choice,

- engage in a healthy discussion of where in society they think humans have applied their understanding of habitat to cure a social problem,
- explain the difference between a habitat and a niche.

Crickets: Basic Needs of an Organism

GRADE
5–8
DISCIPLINE
Life
Science

Concept to be invented
Main idea—All organisms, no matter the size, have a basic need for food, water, shelter, and space in a suitable arrangement.

Concepts that are important to expansion
Living organisms respond to stimuli from their environment. Animals in captivity must be able to adapt to their environment in order to survive.

Materials needed
For each group of students:

one terrarium

one plastic pint container with
   screen top

one hand lens

one piece of black construction paper

seeds (six each of clover, grass,
   wheat, radish, and bean)

For the entire class:
Eric Carle's *The Very Quiet Cricket* (New York: Philomel Books, 1990); four plastic bags, each containing eighteen crickets; felt pen, paper clips, tape or staples, chart paper.

➡ **Safety precautions:** Remind the students to wash their hands after handling the crickets. Do not eat the seeds or put them in your mouth. Do not poke each other with the staples or paper clips.

1. EXPLORATION: Which process skills will be used?

Observing, recording data, experimenting, drawing conclusions

What will the students do?

Cricket Needs

Begin the lesson by doing something that students of this age level would never expect. Read very animatedly *The Very Quiet Cricket,* by Eric Carle. Although not age appropriate, the story is very effective in getting students to think about the task to come. Divide the class into research groups of four. Allow library time for the students to find answers to the following questions: What is necessary for the survival of a cricket? Are their needs similar to human needs? What requirements do they have for food, water, and shelter? Can many crickets live in a small space? How many can live comfortably together?

2. EXPLANATION/CONCEPT INVENTION: What is the main idea? How will the main idea be constructed?

Concept: All organisms, no matter the size, have a basic need for food, water, shelter, and space in a suitable arrangement.

Ask the various student groups to report on the results of their inquiries. Through their reporting, continue to question them to clarify the results of their research efforts. Help the students to draw the conclusion that all organisms, no matter the size, have a basic need for food, water, shelter, and space in a suitable arrangement.

3. EXPANSION OF THE IDEA: Which process skills will be used?

Observing, communicating, problem solving, formulating models, classifying, questioning, hypothesizing

How will the idea be expanded?

Cricket Behavior   Set up a terrarium with a few crickets living in it. Encourage the students to make observations about the crickets in the terrarium as they are collecting their data. Assign each of the different research groups from the exploration phase of this lesson one of the following tasks so that they will understand the behavior of a cricket:

- Take a cricket from the terrarium. Place it on a smooth surface and then on a rough surface. Watch the cricket for 3 to 5 minutes on each surface. Record your observations. Which surface causes the greater obstacle to movement? Why do you think this is so? Try manipulating the environment in other ways: hot versus cold surface or light versus dark conditions. Return the cricket to the terrarium.
- Obtain a shoebox. Cut a hole on one side about the size of a small flashlight. Cut a hole on the other side just big enough for your eye to peep inside. Take a cricket from the terrarium. Place the cricket in the dark end of the shoebox (opposite end from the flashlight hole) and put on the lid. Cover the flashlight hole with your hand in an effort to make the box as dark as possible inside. Watch the cricket's behavior for 5 minutes. Record your observations. Now place a small flashlight in the hole and turn it on. Observe the cricket for another 5 minutes. Record your observations. Were there any differences in the cricket's behavior when the lights were on versus when they were off? If so, why do you think this occurred? Return the cricket to the terrarium.
- Take a cricket from the terrarium and place it in a shoebox. As a group, decide on three different kinds of food you think a cricket might like to eat. Place the three types in front of the cricket. Make sure you keep accurate records about the amount of food placed in the box. It may be important to weigh each food choice. Put the lid back on the box. Place the box in a dark, quiet place in the classroom. Ask the group members to make predictions

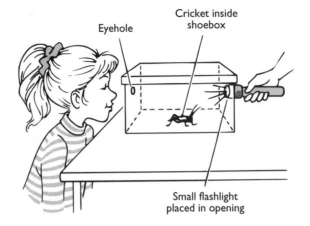

Eyehole

Cricket inside
shoebox

Small flashlight
placed in opening

about which food type they think the cricket will choose. Make and record observations every 30 minutes for one school day. Did the cricket choose the food you predicted? Why or why not? Do you think more than one cricket should be used in this experiment? Why or why not? Return the cricket to the terrarium.

Ask each of the different research groups to report on their findings. Encourage all the students to communicate to one another exactly what they did, why they did it, and what they discovered as a result. Help them in their discussion to come to the following conclusions: Living organisms respond to stimuli from their environment. Animals in captivity must be able to adapt to their environment in order to survive.

Science in Personal and Social Perspectives

- What legends exist about crickets? How and why have these been handed down through generations?
- What could you do for an animal if it has lost its mother? How could you help it survive without removing it from its environment?
- Why would it be important for you to know how to care for an animal in a situation like that?

Science and Technology

- Do you think fluctuations in cricket populations could tell us something about what people are doing to their environment? How would you design an experiment to determine what humans are doing to their environment?
- Do you think it is important that humans understand something about other animals no matter what their size? Why or why not?

Science as Inquiry

- Why does a terrarium need to have soil in it?
- Can a cricket drink water out of a bowl? Why does a cricket rub its wings?
- What are the basic needs of a cricket?

History and Nature of Science

- What kinds of occupations deal with a variety of animal species? (Game wardens, zookeepers, wildlife officers.)
- What would it be like if there was no one who understood the basic needs of certain animals? Was there ever a time in history when our lack of understanding affected the life of an animal? Provide an example.
- What does an entomologist do?

4. EVALUATION: How will the students show what they have learned?

Upon completing the activities the students will be able to:

- design and build their own terrarium for a cricket, making sure that it is designed to meet all of the cricket's basic needs;
- pick one animal and determine its basic needs for food, shelter, water, and space;
- pick a domesticated animal such as a chicken, dog, or hamster and describe the adaptations necessary for that animal to survive in the wild;
- participate in a discussion of how humans would have to adapt in order to survive in the wild.

Animal Adaptations

GRADE
5–8
DISCIPLINE
Life
Science

Concepts to be invented
Main idea—The shape of a bird's beak determines the type of food it will eat. This is one form of an adaptation.

Concepts that are important to expansion
Many animals have developed specialized adaptations in order to survive in their environments. Fish utilize adaptive coloration, body shape, and mouth placement to help them survive in different aquatic environments.

Materials needed
For exploration:
Enough tweezers and mittens so that each student in the class has one or the other of these. Numerous pipe cleaners, paper wads, and strips of construction paper to serve as "food" for the birds. Place pictures of various kinds of birds with different feeding habits all around the classroom.

For expansion:
Pictures of various kinds of fish placed around the room. The fish should demonstrate such differences in coloration as light-colored belly, dark upper side, mottling, vertical stripes, or horizontal stripes. Differences in body shape

could be flat bellied, torpedo shaped, horizontal disc, vertical disc, or hump-backed. The mouth shapes may be an elongated upper jaw, duckbill jaws, an elongated lower jaw, an extremely large jaw, or a sucker-shaped jaw. A fish tank with fish that live at different levels of the tank would also serve to emphasize the secondary concept. Art materials like crayons, markers, scissors, scrap material, construction paper, chalk, old buttons, yarn, pieces of felt, and so on are also needed.

➡ **Safety precautions:** Remind the students to walk, not run, while participating in the bird-feeding activity. Use caution with scissors in the expansion activity.

1. EXPLORATION: Which process skills will be used?

Observing, inferring, experimenting, analyzing

What will the students do?

Mitten and Tweezer Beaks

Distribute the pipe cleaners, paper wads, and paper strips throughout the room. Place some on the floor and some of them in harder-to-get-to places. Each student will choose the type of "beak" (mitten or tweezers) that he or she wants to use. The students will explore a bird's eating habit by trying to pick up the different types of food using the beak they chose.

2. EXPLANATION/CONCEPT INVENTION: What is the main idea? How will the main idea be constructed?

Concept: The shape of a bird's beak determines the type of food it will eat. This is one form of adaptation.

Ask the students questions such as the following to help invent this concept: Why was it easier for _____ (student's name) to pick up the paper strips than _____ (a different student's name)? Do you see any pictures of birds in this room with a beak that would work like the tweezers? Can you think of any others? What do you think they use these beaks for? What types of food can a bird with a beak like a pair of mittens eat? Birds have a variety of adaptations that help them survive in their environment. Their beaks are one such adaptation.

3. EXPANSION OF THE IDEA: Which process skills will be used?

Hypothesizing, observing, questioning, classifying, analyzing, inferring, manipulating materials, communicating

How will the idea be expanded?

Fish Adaptations The students will look at pictures of different types of fish and try to categorize them in three different ways: coloration, mouth shape, and body shape. A discussion should ensue on how these three classifications are important adaptations to ensure the fish's survival in its environment. After the discussion, the teacher should assign each student or group of students a particular combination of adaptations from each of the three groups, such as mottled coloration, torpedo body shape, and sucker-shaped jaw. Ask the students to use the art materials provided to create fish with those three types of adaptations. Ask them to create environments in which fish with those adaptations could survive. Have the students share their creations.

Science in Personal and Social Perspectives

- What are some ways in which people have adapted to their environment?
- What are some ways in which we share our environment with the birds? fish?
- What has society done to improve the lives of animals in their habitat?

Science and Technology

- If you were to make a hummingbird feeder, would it be useful to know the type of beak this bird has, and why?
- What are some disadvantages of taking an animal out of its natural habitat?
- Could an animal adapt quickly enough to survive in a new environment? Why or why not?
- Choose an animal. Outline all of the problems that would need to be overcome for that animal to survive in a different habitat.

Science as Inquiry
- Can an animal's inability to adapt to rapid changes in its environment lead to its extinction? What other events may lead to the extinction of an animal?
- Is there any one species of bird that has a beak that allows it to winter in an area with a relatively cold climate? What advantage does this beak shape have over any other?
- If you were to buy a fish from a pet store and wanted one that would clean the food off the gravel in the bottom of your fish tank, what kind of a mouth shape would it have?

History and Nature of Science
- How important is it for a zookeeper to understand the special feeding adaptations many animals have developed? Why?
- If you were working at a nature center and were responsible for creating an aquarium that made use of fish found at a local lake, what would you need to know about the local fish to make your display enjoyable for center visitors?

4. EVALUATION: How will the students show what they have learned?

Upon completing the activities the students will be able to:

- identify bird beak adaptations and explain how these contribute to the survival of the bird;
- design an ideal habitat for an animal of their choice, emphasizing that animal's special adaptations for survival in its environment;
- explain why several species of fish can live together in one lake without competing with one another for food.

GRADE
5–8
DISCIPLINE
Life
Science

Owl Pellets

Concept to be invented
Main idea—Owl pellets contain undigested parts of animals eaten by the owl, such as hair and bones.

Concepts that are important to expansion
Digestion, eating habits.

Materials needed
For each student group:
One owl pellet, which may be obtained through a local department of natural resources wildlife division for the state. Sterilized pellets can be ordered through a supplier. One dissecting kit, glue, handouts of the skeleton of a vole, mouse, or rat.

⮕ **Safety precautions:** Remind the students to use caution when handling the sharp dissecting tools.

1. EXPLORATION: Which process skills will be used?

Observing, predicting, inferring, hypothesizing

What will the students do?

Owl Pellet Dissection

Provide each pair of students with an owl pellet and a dissecting kit. Ask the students what they think this is. How was it created? What do you think you will find in here as you carefully pick the matted hair away from the owl pellets? After student predictions are shared, instruct the students to keep everything they find as they pick away carefully at the pellets. Try to reconstruct a skeleton of a rodent, using the picture as a guide.

2. EXPLANATION/CONCEPT INVENTION: What is the main idea? How will the main idea be constructed?

Concept: Owl pellets contain the undigested parts of animals eaten by the owl, such as hair and bones.

Ask the students questions such as the following to help invent this concept: What kind of rodent do you think your owl ate? Did you find the remains of more than one kind of rodent? What do these findings tell you about the type of food an owl eats? What is an owl capable of digesting?

3. EXPANSION OF THE IDEA: Which process skills will be used?

Observing, communicating, problem solving, formulating models, recording data

How will the idea be expanded?

Owl Research or Field Trip

- Take the students on a field trip to an area where owls are known to nest. Look carefully on the ground around the area. What do you expect to find to indicate to you that owls may be in the area? How are pellets different from owl scats?
- Invite a wildlife specialist to bring an owl to visit your classroom to discuss its characteristics and habitat. Ask your class to prepare in advance sound questions to ask the visitor about the owl.
- Assign each student team to write a report about a different species of owl. This report should include such things as where it is found and its life span, habitat, and food preferences.

Science in Personal and Social Perspectives

- What might happen to owls if humans disrupt their habitats?
- What are some ways that owls are adapted to their environment?

Vole Skelton

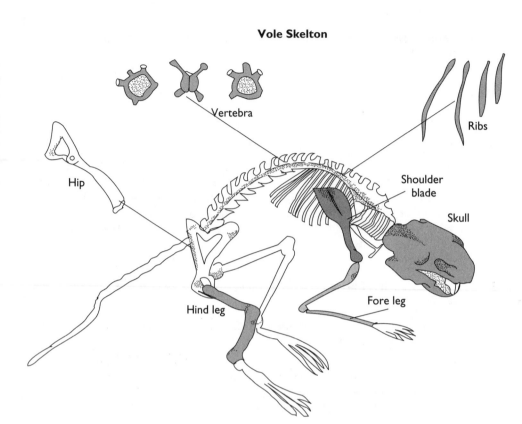

Other Animal Skulls Found in Pellets

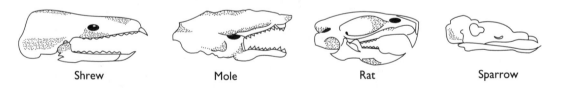

Shrew   Mole   Rat   Sparrow

- How are we adapted to our environment?
- What has technology done to improve the lives of animals in their habitats? What could society do?

Science and Technology

- What are some disadvantages of taking an animal out of its natural habitat and placing it in another environment?
- If you came across some bones of an animal, how could you go about identifying which animal they came from?

Science as Inquiry
- What special needs does an owl have in order to survive in any habitat?
- Why were the bones and hair of the rodents not digested by the owls?

History and Nature of Science
- What kinds of professions are dedicated to ensuring animal safety? What kinds of careers endanger animals?
- In this activity you found the bones of a rodent and reconstructed them to determine which rodent it was. Do any other careers expect you to take evidence and reconstruct it to find answers? Which ones?

4. EVALUATION: How will the students show what they have learned?

Upon completing the activities the students will be able to:

- construct a food chain, placing the owl at the highest level,
- dissect an owl pellet and use the bones found to reconstruct the skeleton of a rodent,
- speculate on how information provided through owl pellet dissection can assist people in raising the survival rate of many owl species.

Humans and Trash

GRADE
K–4
DISCIPLINE
Life
Science

Concept to be invented
Main idea—Human-made trash affects all living matter.

Concepts that are important to expansion
Recycling can decrease the amount of waste created by humans.

Materials needed
For exploration:
Selected (clean) trash, drawing paper, crayons, glue, stapler. Enough of these materials should be collected so that each child in the class can actively participate in the lesson. One large box filled with a piece of trash for each child, five or six medium-sized boxes that can be labeled for glass, paper, plastic, aluminum, tin, and so on.

Safety precautions: Remind the students to use caution when handling trash. Do not put fingers in mouth. Wash hands thoroughly after handling trash.

1. EXPLORATION: Which process skills will be used?

Questioning, inferring, predicting, hypothesizing, communicating, manipulating materials.

What will the students do?

Trash and Animals   Before doing this lesson with the class, collect enough trash so that each child in the class may have several pieces to choose from. Be sure that any trash chosen is free of rough edges, broken glass, or sharp points so that the children will not be harmed during the lesson. Wash out any plastic bags and cans used as trash.

Ask each student to think of an animal and draw a picture of it.

Supply the students with a large selection of trash. Ask the students to choose one piece that particularly intrigues them. Ask the students to draw a picture of how that piece of trash would hurt their animal if the animal came across that piece of trash while outside. Ask the students to attach the piece of litter to their picture. Each student should be allowed to share the picture with the class, explaining how their animal was harmed by the piece of trash they chose. Encourage the students to act out how the animal moved both before and after the trash affected them.

2. EXPLANATION/CONCEPT INVENTION: What is the main idea? How will the main idea be constructed?

Concept: Human-made trash affects all living matter.

Ask the students questions such as the following to help invent this concept: What's wrong with leaving our garbage just anywhere? How do you think trash can hurt animals besides the ways each of you just shared? The teacher can give such examples as: How many of you have been fishing? What happens when your line gets stuck? Just as it tangles up in the weeds, if you simply cut the line and leave it in the water, it can get tangled on ducks' necks, legs, and beaks. It can keep them from walking, flying, and swimming. Sometimes it may become wrapped around their beak, and they starve to death.

Hold up a ring from a six-pack of cans. Could this hurt an animal? How? Explain how fish or birds can get tangled up in it. Check the local wildlife office for pictures of tragedies like these. Show the students how to break up the plastic rings before they place them in the garbage. Explain to them that even though they put them in the garbage, eventually that garbage bag will break down and that plastic ring will be left to cause possible harm to some animal. If they cut it up before placing it in the trash, there is less of a chance of it harming an animal.

In what ways do people get rid of their trash? Do you think the way in which we get rid of our trash harms animals? What do you think we can do to get rid of litter? (Pick up litter alongside the road, reduce our use of materials in excessive packaging, recycle, and so on.)

3. EXPANSION OF THE IDEA: Which process skills will be used?

Observing, communicating, problem solving, formulating models, classifying, questioning, hypothesizing

How will the idea be expanded?

Classroom Landfill and Recycling Refer back to the explanation phase of this lesson. Remind the students of the conversation they had in which you asked about the ways people get rid of their trash. Perhaps some students mentioned that their garbage is hauled away by a service. Ask them to think about where that trash goes after hauling. Introduce the term *landfill* (the place where trash gets hauled to be buried in the ground) if they are not already familiar with it. Ask them to suggest alternatives to taking trash to a landfill. As they make suggestions, list them on the board.

After the students have created a list, show them a large box in the front of the room labeled *landfill*. (Note: The teacher should have filled this box with a piece of trash for every child in the class.) Have each child pick out one item. Ask them if they think it can be recycled. If so, they should place it in the appropriately labeled medium-sized box. Sum up this activity by getting the children to surmise that recycling can decrease the amount of waste created by people.

Science in Personal and Social Perspectives

- What can you do to help eliminate excessive trash?
- Do you know what to do with recyclable materials where you live? If not, why not ask your parents to help you work on recycling some of your trash?
- What are some ways businesses can cut down on their trash?
- How can companies that make different products help the environment?
- Do you think businesses have a responsibility to reduce the amount of trash they create?

Science and Technology

- Do you think twice about buying a toy that is not only boxed but then wrapped in paper and then in plastic? Do you think the practice of excessive packaging affects our environment?
- Create a map of what happens to a toy's packaging from the time the toy is packaged until the packaging no longer exists.

Science as Inquiry

- What kinds of household items can be recycled?
- How does trash harm animals?
- How does trash harm plants?
- It has sometimes been said that one person's trash is another person's treasure. After doing these activities, how true do you think that statement is?

History and Nature of Science

- Who is responsible for making sure that animals are not harmed by human trash?
- Who is responsible for making sure that plants are not harmed by human trash?
- Do you think you could make a career out of collecting recycled trash? Can people make money from recycling?

4. EVALUATION: How will the students show what they have learned?

Upon completing the activities the students will be able to:

- separate recyclables into appropriate groups,
- state three ways in which trash harms animals,
- draw pictures of our environment before trash was recycled and after it was recycled. The students will be able to explain the difference between the two drawings.

Useful Waste

GRADE
5–8
DISCIPLINE
Life
Science

Concept to be invented
Main idea—A great majority of human-made waste can be recycled or reused.

Concepts that are important to expansion
Recycle, reuse, water, litter, useful and nonreusable waste, landfill, hazardous waste.

Materials needed
For exploration:

aluminum can	bug spray can	bottle cap
glass bottle	orange peel	blender
newspaper	art supplies (crayons,	water
plastic soda bottle	markers, scissors,	old piece of screen
tin can	construction paper,	rolling pin
cigarette butt	glue, scrap paper)	
rope		

➡ **Safety precautions:** Be careful of the sharp edges and glass. Exercise care when carrying and using the scissors and blender.

1. EXPLORATION: Which process skills will be used?

Observing, questioning, hypothesizing, predicting, reasoning, recording data

What will the students do?

Rating Garbage   Separate the class into groups of four to six students. Give each group the materials listed above (except for the art supplies) concealed in a brown grocery bag. Ask the students to remove the items from the bag, make observations, and rate or arrange the items in order from the most usable to the least usable. The students' reasoning behind their rating scheme should be recorded.

2. EXPLANATION/CONCEPT INVENTION: What is the main idea? How will the main idea be constructed?

Concept: A great majority of human-made waste can be recycled or reused.

Ask the students questions such as the following to help invent this concept: What did you find in your bags? How did you rank these items from most usable to least usable? Why did you put _____ (name item) as the most usable? Why did you put _____ (name item) as the least usable? Refuse is often regarded as useless waste and ends up in landfills and pollutes our environment. Although not all human-made materials can be recycled, they can be reused in a number of ways not originally intended. Why is it important for us to recycle and reuse? What is the difference between recycling and reusing? What can you do to see that materials such as those found in your bags are recycled or, if possible, reused?

3. EXPANSION OF THE IDEA: Which process skills will be used?

Communicating, problem solving, interpreting data, classifying, making assumptions, drawing conclusions, manipulating materials

How will the idea be expanded?

Litter-Eating Critter

Ask the groups of students to decide what kind of litter-eating creature they could create using the materials found in their grocery bags and the art supplies you make available. After they create plans for their creatures, allow them sufficient time to make and explain to the class just how their litter-eating creatures function.

Hold up the bug spray can in order to introduce hazardous wastes that are found in the home. Ask the students if they can think of any household items that cannot be disposed of in a regular fashion. Some examples of items that are dangerous and need to be disposed of properly are paint thinners, paints, and motor oils. Ask the students if they are aware why these items cannot be dumped in regular landfills. Explain in detail the impact these items have on the environment.

Making Paper   Encourage the students to learn how to recycle paper by doing the following activity with them: Collect different types of paper scraps, and using a blender, cut the paper into very small pieces. Mix the fine paper to a pulp mixture with water. Pour out of the blender and roll flat. This can be done on an old piece of screen using a rolling pin. Place an old towel over the pulp as you roll it flat to help squeeze out some of the excess water. Allow the new piece of paper to dry before use.

Science in Personal and Social Perspectives

- Do you think you have a responsibility to future generations to reduce the amount of waste you create? Why or why not? Do you think your parents and grandparents thought about the amount of waste they generated in the past and how it affects the quality of your life?
- How can reducing, reusing, and recycling our resources ensure that future generations will have a lifestyle comparable to or better than ours?

Science and Technology

- How does a landfill function? Who is responsible for selecting a site for the landfill? How long can we continue dumping our waste into the same landfill?
- What technological advances have decreased the amount of waste we put into our landfills? What technological advances have added to the problem of overflowing landfills?
- What things can you do to reduce litter in your home? What plans do you have for reducing, reusing, and recycling waste materials you generate?

Science as Inquiry

- How can a product be recycled or reused?
- Can all waste products be recycled? If not, is there anything else that can be done with that waste product first before you throw it away?
- Should cost factors prohibit you from recycling waste products? Why or why not?

History and Nature of Science

- How many different jobs are involved in the recycling of any product?
- Aside from using natural resources, what other sources can manufacturers go to in order to obtain materials to create their products?

4. EVALUATION: How will the students show what they have learned?

Upon completing the activities the students will be able to:

- differentiate between litter and waste in terms of definitions and usefulness,
- rank a pile of materials according to which are the most to least recyclable and which are the most to least reusable,
- identify and collect from home one clean waste item, one clean recyclable item, and one clean reusable item,
- start a recycling project for the entire school.

Litter in Our Waterways

**GRADE
5–8
DISCIPLINE
Life
Science**

Concept to be invented
Main idea—Irresponsible actions by people are causing the earth's waterways to become littered. This upsets the ecological balance of the water.

Concepts that are important to expansion
Beaches, floating, lakes, litter, oceans, recycling, rivers.

Materials needed
For exploration:

aquarium
plastic six-pack holder
empty tin can
empty plastic 2-liter soda bottle
metal bottle cap

water to fill aquarium three-fourths
   full
empty aluminum soda can
empty glass soda bottle
metal can opener

➡ **Safety precautions:** Be careful of the sharp edges and glass. Keep hands away from the aquarium.

1. EXPLORATION: Which process skills will be used?

Observing, questioning, hypothesizing, predicting, experimenting, recording data

What will the students do?

*Sink-or-Float
Litter*

- Display the seven litter items listed under "Materials Needed." Ask the students to predict which items will sink when placed in the water. Record their predictions. Allow student volunteers to place each item in the water (one at a time) and observe what happens. Record the results and compare with the initial predictions made by the students.
- Ask the students if they think any of the items that floated could sink eventually. After soliciting several answers, point out that some empty containers may fill with water and sink. The time they take to sink may vary based on certain conditions, such as rough water or human manipulation.

- Ask the students to generate a list of litter they think may be underwater in lakes and rivers. Ask the students how they think it got there.

2. EXPLANATION/CONCEPT INVENTION: What is the main idea? How will the main idea be constructed?

Concept: Irresponsible actions by people are causing the earth's waterways to become littered. This upsets the ecological balance of the water.

Ask the students questions such as the following to help invent this concept: What types of litter sank to the bottom of the aquarium? What types of litter floated on top? Do you think that those that floated may eventually sink? How do you think litter such as this could end up in a lake or river? What do you think happens to the litter after it sinks? How do you think this affects water life, such as aquatic plants and animals? What do you think will happen to an aquatic animal if it eats a piece of litter such as a plastic bag?

Litter that floats is easily mistaken for food by many aquatic animals. It is not uncommon for sea turtles to mistake plastic bags for jellyfish and eat them. When this happens, the sea turtle thinks it is full because the plastic bag is stuck in its stomach. It eventually starves to death. Ducks and some fish get their beaks or bodies tangled in six-pack rings. This prevents them from eating, and they starve to death. Litter that sinks is not always considered a nuisance. Some sunken ships become places for coral reefs to grow upon.

3. EXPANSION OF THE IDEA: Which process skills will be used?

Communicating, problem solving, interpreting data, classifying, making assumptions, drawing conclusions

How will the idea be expanded?

Plastic Food

Ask the students to collect and save every piece of plastic waste used in their homes for one week, clean the waste, and bring it to school. Divide the class into groups of four to six. Ask them to pool their plastic collection. Ask the students to classify the waste according to how an aquatic animal might look at that plastic as a source of food. The categories might be definitely, somewhat likely, unlikely. List some animals that would go for the food in each of the categories. Share these divisions with the class. Once they have discussed their divisions, ask the students to divide the plastic waste according to whether an animal could get tangled up in it. Again, discuss the classification scheme the students developed and why. Ask the students as a summary activity to state one positive thing they could do to prevent further pollution of a waterway.

Science in Personal and Social Perspectives

- Does litter affect your everyday life? If so, how?
- What could you do to cut down on litter?
- Why should someone who lives far from a major waterway be concerned with litter in our waters?

- Do you and your family recycle? If so, what and how?
- Who in our community should be responsible for cleaning up our waters?
- What are some projects in your neighborhood that deal with litter control?
- What are some different litter control agencies operating in your community?

Science and Technology

- Contact a local hospital. Determine how its medical waste is disposed of. Do you think its disposal methods will keep that waste out of our waterways? Why or why not?

Science as Inquiry

- Are pollutants that float in a waterway just as dangerous as pollutants that sink? Why or why not?
- Are people in danger if they play on beaches near polluted water? Why or why not?
- Can a sunken ship ever be beneficial to aquatic organisms?

History and Nature of Science

- Are there any special precautions one must take if his or her job is to clean up a waterway?
- How could an oceanographer use his or her knowledge of ocean currents to help the Coast Guard to identify businesses or cruise ship lines that pollute the waterways?
- Do health care workers have a responsibility to the rest of us to know exactly where their garbage will be disposed? How can they prevent it from ending up in the nation's waterways?

4. EVALUATION: How will the students show what they have learned?

Upon completing the activities the students will be able to:

- explain how plastic bags could cause the death of a sea turtle,
- give an example of a piece of plastic litter that can be harmful to aquatic life and propose a solution about how this product could be eliminated from the environment without harming wildlife,
- write a letter of concern to a product manufacturer that they believe uses excessive amounts of plastic packaging on their products.

Slogans and the Environment

GRADE
5–8
DISCIPLINE
Life
Science

Concept to be invented
Main idea—Slogans are used to get a message across.

Concepts that are important to expansion
Campaign slogans, public service slogans, advertising slogans, media, target audience.

Materials needed
For exploration:
Slips of paper with slogans written on them, an overhead transparency with the definition of a slogan on it and examples of slogans, scrap paper for all students, and slogan planning sheets such as the one at the top of page 73.

➡ **Safety precautions:** None needed.

1. EXPLORATION: Which process skills will be used?

Observing, inferring, categorizing, experimenting, recording data

What will the students do?

Slogan
Categorization

Give each table several slips of paper with one message printed on each. Choose messages with advertising your students are familiar with. As a group, arrange the messages into two or more categories. One suggestion is to read all of the messages and then to decide the criteria they will use to separate them. This will make it easier to put them into categories. Ask the students to record their categorizations.

2. EXPLANATION/CONCEPT INVENTION: What is the main idea? How will the main idea be constructed?

Concept: Slogans are used to get a message across.

Name: _____   Date: _____

Important Issue:

_____

_____

_____

Form of Advertising:

_____

_____

Selected Audience:

_____

How will your audience get the message?

_____

_____

Rough Draft for Advertisement:

Ask the students questions such as the following to help invent this concept: What are some ways in which slogans are advertised? Can you think of any slogans for which you are the target audience? For one of the slogans that your group discussed, what is the slogan's purpose? How did you classify the slogans? What important things do all of these slogans include?

Slogans are short phrases used by businesses, public parties, or the like to advertise their purposes. They are meant to influence a certain group of people (target audience) in some way. The following information can be placed on a transparency:

Slogans:
Short phrases used over and over again in advertisements.
Good slogans are easy to remember and tend to stick in people's minds.

Examples:
Product slogan: *Just for the taste of it* (Diet Coke)
Restaurant slogan: *Have it your way* (Burger King)
Company slogan: *I love what you do for me* (Toyota)
Political slogan: *Make peace not war* (Peace)
Environmental slogan: *Reduce, reuse, recycle* (Recycling)
Public service slogan: *Just say No!* (Drugs)

3. EXPANSION OF THE IDEA: Which process skills will be used?

Hypothesizing, observing, questioning, classifying, analyzing, inferring, manipulating materials, communicating

How will the idea be expanded?

Environmental Slogans

Encourage the students to create a list of important environmental issues that affect their area. Ask the students to work in small groups to do the following: (1) choose an issue from the list generated by the class; (2) create a slogan pertaining to this issue using the slogan planning sheet. Is your slogan one that people could easily remember? Is the purpose clearly stated?

Science in Personal and Social Perspectives

- Do you think you can be affected by slogans without even realizing it? Can you give any examples of this happening? (Subliminal messages.)
- Do you think the use of subliminal messages is ethical?
- Are slogans always truthful? How do you know when to trust the message of a slogan?
- What are some effective environmental slogans that have been used to improve the world we live in?

Science and Technology

- Do you think the number of billboards on highways should be limited? Do they serve a purpose? If so, what is it? Can this purpose be served in a different manner, without the use of a billboard? Propose a plan to limit the number of billboards within your area. Share your plans with local community leaders.

Science as Inquiry

- What is the purpose of a slogan? What is it intended to do?
- Can your slogan be used to influence the other students in your school about their actions toward the environment? Design a way in which your message could reach a large proportion of the students in this school.

History and Nature of Science

- Which occupations rely on one's ability to create slogans quickly that send powerful messages?
- How do the following occupations utilize slogans to sell their product: media executive, political adviser, restaurateur, beautician, vitamin manufacturer, construction company executive, soft drink bottlers?
- Identify an environmental group. When did it begin? For what purpose?

4. EVALUATION: How will the students show what they have learned?

Upon completing the activities the students will be able to:

- cooperatively create a slogan on an important local issue,
- choose a medium to advertise the slogan,

- suggest a target audience for the slogan,
- choose a different environmental issue, create a slogan, and design a t-shirt with the slogan on it.

Sense of Taste

GRADE
K–4
DISCIPLINE
Life
Science

Concept to be invented
Main idea—A person can taste sweet, sour, salty, and bitter on every single area of the tongue that has taste buds.

Concepts that are important to expansion
People with more taste buds taste things more strongly than those with fewer taste buds.

Materials needed
For each pair of students:

lemon juice	four paper cups	blue food coloring
cocoa powder	wax paper	10 cotton-tipped swabs
brown sugar	magnifying glass	hole puncher
salt		

Preparation:
For each pair of students, label four cups A, B, C, and D. Fill three of the paper cups with water. Dissolve in cup A the salt, cup B the cocoa, and brown sugar in cup C (corn syrup may be used instead of brown sugar). Pour some lemon juice in cup D. Create an outline of a tongue on a sheet of paper, and duplicate it for each pair of students.

➡ **Safety precautions:** Before distributing the cotton-tipped swabs, remind the students that they are to be used carefully and cautiously to avoid eye injury. Also, to avoid contamination of the unknowns and to inhibit the spread of germs, students should be reminded not to put used cotton-tipped swabs back into the cups after they place them on their tongue.

1. EXPLORATION: Which process skills will be used?

Observing, predicting, experimenting, evaluating, generalizing, inferring, recording data

What will the students do?

Buds and Tasters Ask the students to choose partners or assign partners yourself. Each set of partners should be provided with four paper cups labeled A through D, each filled with a different liquid. Ask the students to make predictions as to what kinds of tastes they think they have and where on the tongue they think they will taste them. Once predictions are recorded, have one student dip a clean cotton swab into the paper cup labeled A, then touch the cotton swab to the tip of his or her partner's tongue. He or she will then touch the back and the sides of the tongue. Record how your partner thought liquid A tasted. Was it as predicted? Mark on the tongue map the places on the tongue where liquid A was tasted. Repeat this procedure for liquids B and C. Do the same for each partner. Remember that a *clean swab* should be used for each cup and by each student.

2. EXPLANATION/CONCEPT INVENTION: What is the main idea? How will the main idea be constructed?

Concept: A person can taste sweet, sour, salty, and bitter on every area of the tongue that has taste buds.

Ask the students questions such as the following to help invent this concept: How did your partner think each liquid tasted? Did you agree with your partner? Did you find any special places on the tongue where these tastes could be detected?

There is no single area on the tongue where each of these tastes can be detected more so than the other. Your tongue is the organ that gives you your sense of taste. If you observe it closely starting at the tip, you will notice thousands of tiny bumps that make you tongue look rough. The tiny bumps are called *filiform papillae*. They are responsible for grabbing onto your food as you chew. The roundish *buttons* you find interspersed within the filiform papillae are called *fungiform papillae*. Anywhere from five to seven taste buds can be found on each fungiform papilla. The taste buds are made up of a bundle of cells, each containing special sensors or receptors that can pick out the four basic tastes of sweet, sour, bitter, and salty. The *circumvallate papillae*, found in the back of your tongue, are larger than the other papillae. Found within deep furrows of the circumvallate papillae are taste buds that also can detect the four basic tastes.

In order to taste your food, you must chew it. Chewing grinds up your food. It also wets the food by mixing it with saliva, the liquid made by small organs in your mouth. When your food is well mixed with saliva, your taste buds can pick up messages about its flavor. Nerves take these messages to taste centers in each side of your brain. Your brain then decides what you are tasting.

Your senses of taste and smell work closely together. The taste of many foods is really a mixture of taste and smell. Food often seems to have no taste when you have a cold. The cold stops up your nose and dulls your sense of smell. When you cannot smell the food, a part of its taste seem to be missing.

3. EXPANSION OF THE IDEA: Which process skills will be used?

Observing, problem solving, recording data, inferring

How will the idea be expanded?

Supertasters Ask the students to go back with their partners to perform the following task:

- Cut a piece of wax paper 1 inch square. Punch a hole using the paper puncher in the middle of the 1-inch-square piece of wax paper.
- Place the piece of wax paper on the tip of your partner's tongue just slightly off center. Be sure the tongue is slightly wet so the paper will stick.
- Using a cotton-tipped swab, dab blue food coloring where the hole is. Be careful not to use too much coloring. For accurate data collection, you want just the dot of tongue exposed to be dyed.
- Use the magnifying glass to count the number of larger, raised dots that did not turn blue. These will be the *fungiform papillae.*
- Take the number of fungiform papillae you discover and multiply by six. This will give you an estimate of the number of taste buds your partner has.
- Repeat this procedure for the other partner.

Were you able to find the same number of fungiform papillae on your partner as your partner found on you? Did everyone have the same number of taste buds?

You will discover that the fewer the raised dots, the less likely the person tasted the four basics tastes all over his or her tongue. Some people are *supertasters* because they have a large number of fungiform papillae, whereas those with just a few are considered *nontasters.*

Science in Personal and Social Perspectives

- Where on the tongue did your partner taste the sweet liquid and the sour, salty, and bitter? Was it the same place as yours?
- Why do you think many adults tolerate flavorings like hot pepper sauce that a baby cannot?

Science and Technology

- Do you think that people from countries other than your own have different amounts of taste buds on their tongue? How do you explain that many cultures tolerate food much spicier than typical American fare? Does the number of taste buds have anything to do with it? How might you design an experiment to determine the answers to these questions?

Science as Inquiry

- How do the filiform papillae differ from the fungiform papillae or the circumvallate papillae?
- What do the fungiform papillae and the circumvallate papillae have in common?
- Where on the tongue can the circumvallate papillae be found?

History and Nature of Science

- Ask the students to generate a list of spices used in cooking. Assign each student a spice. From which country does it originate? How does it grow? How is it harvested? How important is that spice to the society of the country in which in grows? When was it first used as a spice?

- Do you think someone with permanent damage to his or her nose resulting in the loss of the sense of smell would have a promising career as a professional chef? Why or why not?

4. EVALUATION: How will the students show what they have learned?

Upon completing the activities the students will be able to:

- list the four major tastes that can be picked out by receptors on the tongue,
- design a method for separating the class into nontasters, regular tasters, and supertasters,
- describe the role of the filiform papillae, fungiform papillae, and the circumvallate papillae.

Skeleton

GRADE
1–4
DISCIPLINE
Life
Science

Concepts to be invented
Main idea—The internal support system for muscles in mammals is the bones. All the bones arranged together make up the skeleton.

Concepts that are important to expansion
Joints help skeletons move.

Materials needed
For each student:
One large sheet of newsprint, markers, crayons, several brass paper fasteners, a packet of paper bones that when put together will create a replica of a human skeleton.

➡ **Safety precautions:** Explain to the students how to use the brass fasteners. Remind them that they could hurt themselves if they poked themselves or others with the pointed edge.

1. EXPLORATION: Which process skills will be used?

Observing, questioning, manipulating materials, analyzing

What will the students do?

Bones Assembly Line

Introduce the lesson by reading two poems from *A Light in the Attic*, by Shel Silverstein. The poems are "Day After Halloween" and "It's Hot!" Begin a discussion with the students about the ideas behind the poems. Ask questions

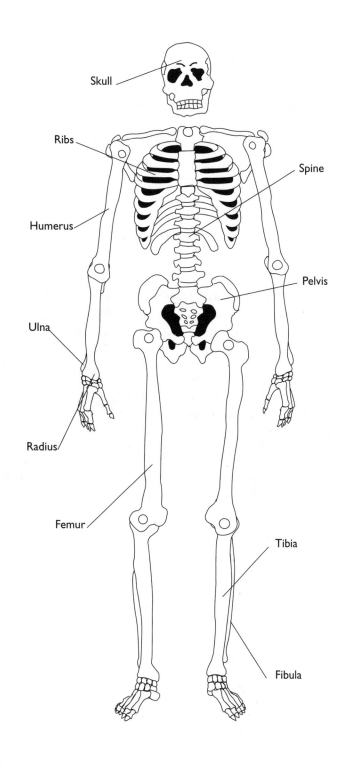

Skull

Ribs

Spine

Humerus

Pelvis

Ulna

Radius

Femur

Tibia

Fibula

such as: What would it be like if we didn't have a skeleton? Why do we need bones in our bodies?

Give each child several brass fasteners and a packet containing paper bones cut into the different major bones of the body using the figure on pages 81–82. Ask the students to empty the packets and to manipulate the materials in any way they wish in an effort to determine what they can create with all the bones. Encourage them to use the brass fasteners to assemble the bones. Walk around the room asking questions like: What do you think all of these different parts make up? Do you think you know where all the parts go? What could the brass fasteners represent in a real body that helps us to move? How do the bones in our body connect for real?

2. EXPLANATION/CONCEPT INVENTION: What is the main idea? How will the main idea be constructed?

Concept: The internal support system for muscles in mammals is the bones. All the bones arranged together make up the skeleton.

Using a picture of a skeleton and a life-size skeleton, ask the children if they know the nonscientific names of the bones. Write these on the board. If students offer the scientific names, list those as well; compare them to the common name. Show a picture of the muscle system of the human body. Explain to the students how the bones help give the muscles support.

Walk around the classroom very stiffly. Encourage some or all of the students to do the same. Really play it up. Tell them they cannot bend their elbows or knees. You used brass fasteners to connect the bones in your skeleton. Do you think those are used in our bodies? Of course not; what do we have? (Joints.)

Ask the children to demonstrate what would happen to them right now (as they are standing) if they did not have bones in their body. The students should drop to the floor. Summarize that the skeleton supports our muscles.

3. EXPANSION OF THE IDEA: Which process skills will be used?

Observing, classifying, recording, manipulating materials

How will the idea be expanded?

Newsprint Bone Bodies

Pair up the students and provide each child with a large sheet of newsprint and a pencil. Ask the students to spread the paper out on the floor. The paired children should take turns. One child should lie flat on the paper with his or her face down. The other child should outline the body. Let each child switch roles. After they have created their outlines, have each child fill in the outline with the bones of the body.

Science in Personal and Social Perspectives

- Do you think it is good to know what is inside our body? Why?
- How do joints help us move?

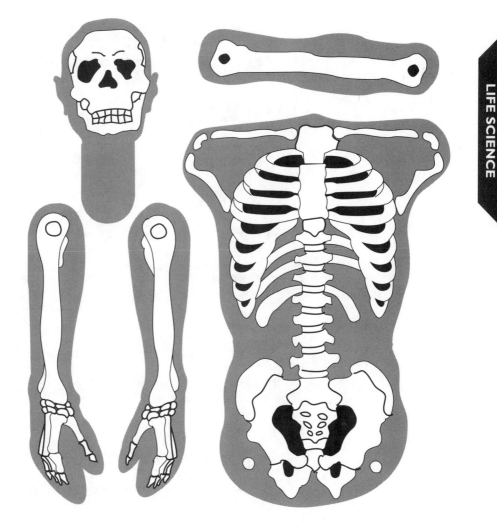

- Could you do the same activities you do on a daily basis if you didn't have a skeleton?

Science and Technology

- What do you think scientists do with bones found in nature?
- Do you think bones found by scientists tell them anything about the organism and the environment it lived in?
- How do you think we see our bones inside our body? What is that picture called?

Science as Inquiry

- How do bones connect together?
- Why do you think it is good to understand how our bodies move?
- Why do you think we have two bones in our forearms and lower legs?

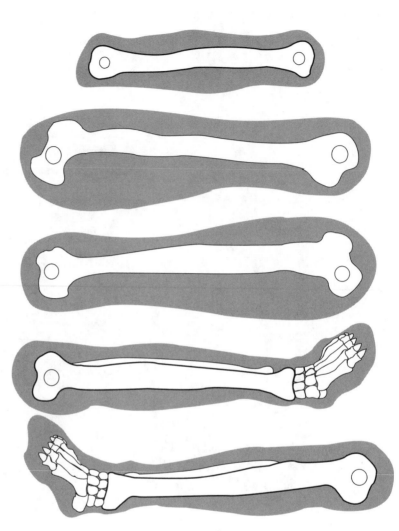

History and Nature of Science

- What is the name of the person who shows you pictures of your bones inside you?
- If you had some back problems and you wanted your spine readjusted, what type of professional would you go to?
- What would you call a person who went to different locations to dig up buried bones and artifacts?
- What does a doctor do if you have a broken bone? How do you think the first doctors figured out how to mend broken bones?

4. EVALUATION: How will the students show what they have learned?

Upon completing the activities the students will be able to:

- assemble a paper skeleton,
- identify at least five bones in the body with common names,
- understand why we need joints in our bodies and explain what they do,
- play Hokey-Pokey Skeleton; that is, do the Hokey-Pokey, but use the common names of bones rather than body parts.

Temperature Receptors on Skin

**GRADE
5–8
DISCIPLINE
Life
Science**

Concept to be invented
Main idea—Our bodies have separate spots, called receptors, for feeling temperatures that are hotter or colder than body temperatures.

Concepts that are important to expansion
Water can feel hot and cold to our bodies at the same time.

Materials needed
For each student group:

a source of hot and cold water
three bowls
six nails

two fine-tipped pens, each a different
color
paper towels

➡ **Safety precautions:** Do not poke each other with the nails. Use care around the water: If it is knocked over, be sure to clean it up immediately. Make sure hot water is not so hot that it will scald.

1. EXPLORATION: Which process skills will be used?

Observing, questioning, designing an experiment, recording data, predicting, generalizing

What will the students do?

Soaking Hands   Divide the students into cooperative working groups of four. Ask the materials manager to obtain three small bowls. Fill one with hot water, one with cold water, and the third with warm water. The groups' mission is to find out how hands feel when placed in water of different temperatures. Encourage the groups to design an experiment to solve this problem. Ask them to record their data. Their experimental designs may look something like this: Each student in the group will take turns placing one hand in hot water and the other in cold. Hands should be left for several minutes in the water. Remove hands from those bowls and immediately immerse them in the warm water. They should be able to describe what happened next. There may be some variations to this plan. Teachers may find that some groups first put both hands in cold and then in hot. They all should be able to help invent the concept, no matter the experimental design.

2. EXPLANATION/CONCEPT INVENTION: What is the main idea? How will the main idea be constructed?

Concept: Our bodies have separate spots, called *receptors*, for feeling temperatures that are hotter or colder than body temperatures.

To help invent this concept, ask each of the student groups to report on the experiment they designed. What did you do? What results did you get? Did the water feel hot and cold at the same time? How can that be? Does it have to do with the temperature of the water your hand was in first or just the temperature of your hand? The students should be able to conclude that it has to do with the temperature of the water their hand was in first. On their skin are receptors that sense temperatures different from normal body temperature.

3. EXPANSION OF THE IDEA: Which process skills will be used?

Observing, classifying, recording, predicting

How will the idea be expanded?

Hot/Cold Receptor Mapping   Ask each student to use one of the pens provided to the groups to draw a square on the back of his or her hand. Place one nail in the bowl of cold water and another in the bowl of hot water. Ask the group members to pair up. Ask one student from each pair to take the nail from the cold water and touch the tip of the nail to any spot in the square of his or her partner's hand. If it feels cold, mark that spot with the pen (marking all the cold ones in the same color). Now switch so that each partner has cold receptors marked. Other student pairs in each cooperative group can be doing the same thing with the hot water and a nail. Be sure to use a different color pen for hot spots. Now exchange bowls and make marks for the opposite water type. Are you surprised at where you find the hot and cold receptors?

Science in Personal and Social Perspectives

- People say that to test bath water you should use your elbow or to test a baby's bottle you should use your wrist. Why do you think they chose those particular body parts?
- Which would you test your bath water with, your hand or your toes? Why?

Science and Technology

- On a hot summer day it is nice to enter an air-conditioned building. After you've been in the building for an hour, you begin to think the air-conditioning has been shut off. Why do you think you feel this way?
- How has technology allowed us to exist comfortably in the winter and the summer? Can you design a way to keep cool during hot weather without using an air-conditioner or fan?

Science as Inquiry

- Could you find a way to pick up a snowball and not feel the cold?
- Which part of your hand is most sensitive to hot things?
- What is a receptor?

History and Nature of Science

- Why do people who work in meat lockers wear gloves?
- Do you think it is important for someone involved in child care to make sure that his or her heat receptors are not damaged? Why or why not?
- In 1853 Georg Meissner described a corpuscle that became known as *Meissner's corpuscle*. What is this, and what did Meissner do to discover it?

4. EVALUATION: How will the students show what they have learned?

Upon completing the activities the students will be able to:

- identify the different hot and cold receptors on each hand,
- explain how water can feel hot and cold at the same time,

LIFE SCIENCE

- identify the child with the cold hands when looking at a picture of children involved in building a snow fort (the one without gloves),
- view a picture of working firefighters with and without fire coats and identify which ones will feel hot. Why is this not the same as pictures of children in the winter with and without coats?

Building Microscope Skills

GRADE
5–8
DISCIPLINE
Life
Science

Concept to be invented
Main idea—A microscope is used to identify objects not visible to the naked eye.

Concepts that are important to expansion
Identifying a compound by its characteristic crystal shape, slide preparation.

Materials needed
For exploration:

noniodized salt	water	microscope
iodized salt	eye droppers	scale
sugar	cups	graduated cylinder
alum	slides	pictures of crystals
borax	slide covers	

For expansion:

water	laundry bluing
noniodized salt	household ammonia

➡ **Safety precautions:** Avoid placing hands near eyes or mouth while working with materials to prepare slides. When using an electric microscope, be sure to use proper safety measures near electrical outlets. The microscope lamp may be hot to touch. Apply the usual safety standards when working with such chemicals as bluing and ammonia.

1. **EXPLORATION:** Which process skills will be used?

Observing, classifying, recording data, diagramming, comparing, manipulating instruments

What will the students do?

Microscope Use and Crystal Comparisons

Measure out 5 grams of each solid. Dissolve each in a separate cup containing 25 ml of water. Be sure to label the cup with the name of the material dissolved in the water. As the solution is forming, label a slide for each solute. Place a drop of each solution on its assigned slide. Allow the water to evaporate. Carefully place the cover slip over the remaining crystals on the slide. Focus each slide under the microscope and record your observations for each at low power. Focus under a higher power and again record observations.

2. EXPLANATION/CONCEPT INVENTION: What is the main idea? How will the main idea be constructed?

Concept: A microscope is used to identify objects not visible to the naked eye.

Key questions to ask students to help them come to this conclusion are: What shapes did you observe on the slide? How does it compare to a drawing of the crystal shape? Can you share a diagram of those shapes with the class? How are these shapes similar? How are they different? How did the microscope help you to observe the crystal?

3. EXPANSION OF THE IDEA: Which process skills will be used?

Graphing, classifying, experimenting

How will the idea be expanded?

Charcoal Crystals
- Use the results of the previous crystal comparison activity to graph the crystal shapes versus the number of substances that have that particular shape.
- The students should be encouraged to brainstorm a list of other possible substances that contain crystals. Observe these under the microscope.
- The students will grow a crystal garden in a Styrofoam egg carton by first placing pieces of charcoal into the egg sockets. In a separate container, mix the following substances:

6 tablespoons of water	6 tablespoons of laundry bluing
6 tablespoons of noniodized salt	2 teaspoons of household ammonia

Once this solution is prepared, the students should carefully pour it over the pieces of charcoal in the egg container. The students can then place these in an area in the classroom where they will not be hit or bumped. The crystals will grow for several days. If the students want colored crystals, they may place a few drops of food coloring on the charcoal after the solution is poured on them. The students may wish to make each egg socket a different color. Once the crystals have grown, the students may safely carry them home in their egg cartons. If the crystals do get bumped in transit, sometimes they can be revived by putting a little water on them.

Science in Personal and Social Perspectives
- While rummaging through your kitchen for a salt shaker, you come across a container you think will work. After placing the salt into the container, you find that no salt comes out of the holes when you shake the container. Why

do you think this happened? Will the size of the salt crystals determine the size of the holes that should be on top of a shaker?

- Do you think there are any other areas of your life where the skills you learned in this lesson can be applied? If so, where?
- How do you think your increased knowledge of crystal shapes will help you become a better consumer? Would you buy ice cream that contained frost crystals? Why or why not?

Science and Technology

- Knowing that salt or sugar can be placed in solution allowed past generations to preserve foods more easily, thus ensuring their survival. How have our present-day technologies expanded on these early ideas?
- Think about the frozen food industry. How does it make use of their knowledge of crystal formation?

Science as Inquiry

- What scientific concepts did you discover while participating in these activities?
- What problem-solving techniques did you employ?
- What procedures were used with the microscope?

History and Nature of Science

- How important is it for a gemologist to understand the differences between crystal shapes? Why?
- In addition to knowledge about crystals, what other kinds of skills would a geologist need? a gemologist? a hospital laboratory technician?
- Antoni van Leeuwenhook is credited with creating one of the earliest microscopes. What kind of discoveries was he able to make with his primitive microscope?

4. EVALUATION: How will the students show what they have learned?

Upon completing these activities the students will be able to:

- demonstrate proper slide preparation techniques,
- prepare a slide of a crystal and focus it under a microscope,
- identify on a diagram the basic crystal shapes,
- state why different compounds may have different crystal shapes.

Physical Science Lessons

Lesson Name	Physical Science Content Standards	Grade Level	Activities
Waves: Sound and Light			
Sound versus Noise	Position and Motion of Objects	K–4	School Sound Search • Magazine Sound Search
Sounds Are Different	Position and Motion of Objects	2–4	Megaphones and Vibrating Straws • Bell Ringers
Vibrations Causing Sound	Position and Motion of Objects	2–4	Sound Makers • Waxed Paper Kazoo
Loudness and Pitch	Position and Motion of Objects	2–4	Soda Bottle Orchestra • Cigar Box Strings • Fish Line Harps • Home-made Music
Sound Movement as Waves	Position and Motion of Objects	2–4	Vibrating Fork • Striking Rod • Clapping Blocks • Sound Producers? • Tapping Tank • Paper Cup Telephone
Sound Waves	Position and Motion of Objects	2–4	Soup Can Reflectors • Slinky Waves • Sound Waves and the Ear
Sound Production	Properties of Matter	5–8	Noise and Sound Identification • Sound Movement • Sound Game: "What Is Sound?"
Matter			
Characteristics of Matter	Properties of Matter	5–8	Plastic Bag Chemistry • Marble Matter
Physical Properties of Matter	Properties of Objects and Materials	K–4	Egg-citing Observations • Chocolate Chip Exploration
Changing Matter	Properties of Matter	5–8	Physical and Chemical Paper Change • Polymer-Rubber Balls
Identification of an Unknown	Properties of Matter	5–8	Physical Properties of an Unknown • Chemical Properties of an Unknown
Using the Scientific Method to Solve Problems	Properties of Matter	5–8	Exploring with Efferdent Tablets • Exploring with Cornstarch
Heat Energy	Light, Heat, Electricity, and Magnetism	1–4	Liquid Birthday • Liquids to Solids
Physics			
Structure Strength	Motion and Forces	5–8	Simple Construction • Triangle Construction
Mirrors and Reflection	Transformations of Energy	2–4	Mirrors and Reflectors • What's a Mirror?
Paper Chromatography	Properties of Matter	5–8	Moving Black Ink Dots • Moving Colored Ink Dots and Snowflakes
Toys in Space	Motion and Forces	5–8	Toy Behavior in Zero Gravity • Toys and Newton
Simple Machines: The Lever	Motion and Forces	5–8	Lever Creations • Spoons and Nuts • Lever Scavenger Hunt

Sound versus Noise

GRADE
K–4
DISCIPLINE
Physical
Science

Concept to be invented
Main idea—Sound can be considered useful or simply noise.

Concepts that are important to expansion
Sound can be pleasant or unpleasant.

Materials needed

whistle   tape recorder (if possible, one per group)
magazines for cutting up   one blank audiotape per group

➡ **Safety precautions:** The students should be reminded of the importance of
walking, not running, as they move through the school to find a place to listen
to different sounds. They should use care when carrying pencils or pens to
record their observations. Exercise caution when using the scissors in the expansion activity.

Discrepant event
While the students are working quietly at their desks, make sure no students
are looking, and then take out a whistle and blow it loudly. Ask the children
what they first thought when they heard the whistle. Record some of their
thoughts on the board.

1. **EXPLORATION:** Which process skills will be used?

   Observing, classifying, predicting, describing, recording data, communicating

   What will the students do?

*School Sound
Search*

   Divide the class into four groups. Send each group to different parts of the
   school building, such as the janitors' work room, the playground, the gym or
   music room, their own classroom. Ask them to go to these areas quietly. Have
   them sit quietly in their areas for 3 minutes. Create a list of all of the sounds
   they hear in those areas. Return to the classroom. Instruct the students to work
   with the people in their group to decide if there is any way they could group
   the sounds. When all of the groups have analyzed their lists, share the categories of sounds with the rest of the class. Ask the students if any of the groups
   came up with categories their group never thought of.

2. **EXPLANATION/CONCEPT INVENTION:** What is the main idea? How will the main idea
   be constructed?

   Concept: Sound can be considered useful or simply noise.

Place on the board in separate columns the terms *useful, noise, pleasant,* and *unpleasant.* Ask the students if any of these terms fit the feelings they had when you blew the whistle unexpectedly. Do any of these terms fit the categories you placed your sounds under? If so, which of your sounds would go under the different headings? Encourage members of the group to write their sounds under the appropriate headings. Do all sounds fall *only* into one classification? Fire alarms, whistles—where do they fall? Sounds can be useful or noise depending on circumstances. Sound can be harmful. We need ear protection from some sounds.

3. EXPANSION OF THE IDEA: Which process skills will be used?

Observing, classifying, communicating, inferring, manipulating materials, interpreting data

How will the idea be expanded?

Magazine Sound Search

The children will work in groups, looking through magazines, cutting out possible sources of sound. Each group will create an audiotape, mimicking the sounds that the different items they collected make. Each group will place its pictures on a poster, then play its tape to the other groups. The members of the other groups will guess which item the sound goes with, and then determine if it is useful or noise, pleasant or unpleasant, or any combination of these. They must be able to explain why they would classify the item that way.

Science in Personal and Social Perspectives

- When listening to a radio with headphones on, is it wise to have the volume so loud that those around you can hear it?
- If you were asked to create a sound that would serve as a warning for some devastating disaster like a tornado, what would this sound be like? How would you categorize it? How unique would it have to be?

Science and Technology

- Why was it necessary for the Occupational Safety and Health Administration (OSHA) to set standards for an acceptable noise level in work areas?
- Personal computers have changed our lives in many ways. While they have been a help, they have also created problems. How have they contributed to the problem of noise pollution, and what has the computer industry done to eliminate some of this noise?
- Many airports near major cities were built in areas long considered migratory routes for some animals, mating habitats for others. The constant roar of jet engines affects the behavior of these animals. What have people done to eliminate some noise hazards brought upon these creatures? What must we continue to do?

Science as Inquiry

- How would you classify the sound best suited for quiet study time?
- Can sounds be classified into more than one category?

History and Nature of Science

- Which type of work do you think would be most affected by noise pollution? least affected? Which type of work would you choose? Why?
- Do you think it is important for a music critic to distinguish between a useful sound or noise, a pleasant or unpleasant sound?

4. EVALUATION: How will the students show what they have learned?

Upon completing the activities the students will be able to:

- listen to an audiotape of various sounds and classify them according to useful/noise and pleasant/unpleasant,
- take one of the assigned categories—useful/pleasant; useful/unpleasant; noise/pleasant; noise/unpleasant—and over a week find some music that they think fits into their assigned category and explain why they believe it does. They are encouraged to get their families involved in their search. If they cannot find some music that fits their category, they can create their own sound.

Sounds Are Different

GRADE
2–4
DISCIPLINE
Physical
Science

Concept to be invented
Main idea—Sounds vary in loudness and pitch.

Concepts that are important to expansion
Loudness is determined by the strength of the vibration. Pitch is determined by the length of the vibrating object. Magnification of sound is achieved by megaphones and speakers.

Materials needed
several large and small bells
pieces of at least 8-inch × 8-inch
   square paper
tape
paper straws
scissors

➡ **Safety precautions:** Be careful when using the scissors. Remember basic scissors safety. Be careful when placing the straws into your mouth. During the expansion activity, do not ring a bell in anyone's ear.

Discrepant event
Find a time when the students are working quietly in their seats. Take a large and a small bell and ring them at the same time. Ask the students: "Did I get your attention? Did you hear just one noise or two? Did one sound softer than the other? higher than the other?"

1. **EXPLORATION:** Which process skills will be used?

Observing, communicating, inferring, predicting

What will the students do?

Megaphones and Vibrating Straws   Ask half the students to shout "hello" to you from their seats. Now ask them to cup their hands around their mouths and shout "hello" again. Ask those who did not yell if they noticed a difference in the sound produced. Now let the other half try it. Give the children pieces of paper and have them roll them into cones. Tape the sides together to maintain the cone shapes. Use the scissors to cut away about 1 inch of the pointed end of each cone. Once again have half the class shout "hello," and then shout again, holding the cut ends of the cones by their mouths. Once again ask the listeners if they noticed a difference in the sound produced each time. Allow the other half to test their cones too.

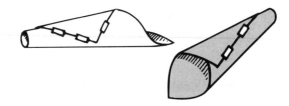

Give the students one straw each. Ask them to cut a little piece off both sides of one end so that what remains looks like an inverted V. Ask them to predict what will happen when they blow into the cut end of the straw. What do they need to do to get the cut V-shaped pieces to vibrate? As they hold the straws in their mouths, they should continue to blow into the straws and start cutting off pieces at the ends of the straws. What is happening to the sound as the straw gets shorter?

2. **EXPLANATION/CONCEPT INVENTION:** What is the main idea? How will the main idea be constructed?

Concept: Sounds vary in loudness and pitch.

When did the "hellos" sound the loudest? When you used nothing, your hand, or your school-made megaphone? What does a megaphone do? It magnifies sound. It increases the strength of the vibration, thus making the sound louder. What happened to the sound produced by the straw as you cut it? Was the loudness of the sound the same? What property of sound changed? The pitch got higher. *Pitch* is determined by the length of the vibrating object.

3. **EXPANSION OF THE IDEA:** Which process skills will be used?

Predicting, designing an experiment, communicating, controlling variables, experimenting, observing, recording data, hypothesizing, inferring

How will the idea be expanded?

Bell Ringers   Divide the students into groups. Give each group at least four different-sized bells. Before ringing each bell, ask the students to create a prediction sheet identifying the loudness and pitch of the bell. Have each group design a way that will most fairly and accurately ring the bells. Emphasize the importance of keeping all other variables constant when comparing the four bells, such as having the same person ring the bells for each trial, or having each person in the group ring each bell to see if the person doing the ringing affects the loudness or pitch. After filling out their prediction sheet and designing a way to ring the bells without letting their predictions prejudice them, they should ring the bells. Record your results. Did your results match your predictions? Is there any way you can alter the bell to magnify the sound coming from it?

Science in Personal and Social Perspectives

- What harm can the earphones on headsets have on your eardrums? What does the magnification of sound do to your eardrums?
- Would the magnification of sound be useful at a baseball or football game? Why or why not? Would everyone at these games appreciate sound being magnified?

Science and Technology

- How has knowledge of loudness, pitch, and magnification led to the creation of devices that are important for crowd control? for large group communication? for the production of music?
- Why do you think a baseball stadium needs to be designed differently from a concert hall? In which would you want the sound to be louder? to be magnified?

Science as Inquiry

- How could you control the loudness of the sound created by a piano?
- How could you change the pitch of a guitar?

History and Nature of Science

- In what careers would you need to understand that loud sounds could set objects vibrating, which could cause structures to collapse? (Safety engineers, contractors, civil engineers, hotel/motel managers, high-rise office building workers.)
- How can a cheerleader save his or her voice by knowing about sound, loudness, pitch, and magnification?

4. EVALUATION: How will the students show what they have learned?

Upon completing the activities the students will be able to:

- infer, when given a set of pictures (large bell, small bell, siren, whistle), which would create a loud or soft sound;

PHYSICAL SCIENCE

- infer, when given another set of pictures (long and short guitar strings, large bell, small bell, man's voice, child's voice), which would create a high or low sound;
- give at least three ways in which one could magnify one's voice.

Vibrations Causing Sound

Concept to be invented
Main idea—Vibrations are caused by the movement of air molecules due to a disturbance.

Concepts that are important to expansion
There are many ways to produce sounds. You may not be able to see all vibrations.

Materials needed
For exploration:
Prerecorded tape of classroom sounds, tape player, string, wire, meter stick, drum and beans, tuning forks and rubber mallet, pans of water, kitchen fork.
For expansion:
Combs and waxed paper squares.

➡ **Safety precautions:** Remind students of the importance of using the rubber bands as instructed. Any other use may result in injury to eyes or faces. Exercise caution when carrying the kitchen forks during the exploration activity.

Discrepant event
Ask the students to listen carefully as you play the tape recording of classroom sounds. Try to guess what these familiar sounds are. Can you give any descriptive terms to remember them by?

1. **EXPLORATION:** Which process skills will be used?

Observing, communicating, recording data, experimenting, predicting, inferring

What will the students do?

Sound Makers
- Have the students place their hands on their throats and make sounds. Record what it feels like.
- In groups, ask the students to stretch and pluck rubber bands and strings. Record their observations.
- Have the students place the handle end of a kitchen fork between their teeth. Quickly flick the other end of the fork. What do their teeth feel like?
- In groups, ask the students to tap pans of water and observe.

- In groups, have the students tap tuning forks with rubber mallets and observe. Ask them to predict what will happen if they strike a tuning fork and quickly thrust it into a pan of water. Have them check their predictions.

2. EXPLANATION/CONCEPT INVENTION: What is the main idea? How will the main idea be constructed?

Concept: Vibrations are caused by the movement of air molecules due to a disturbance.

What did it feel like when you placed your hands on your throat and made sounds? Did your hands begin to tingle? What happened to the rubber bands when you stretched them out and plucked them? How did your teeth feel when you flicked the kitchen fork? What path did the water create when the pan was gently tapped? Did the tuning fork tickle your hand when you struck it with the rubber mallet? What happened when you thrust the tuning fork into the water? Was it as you predicted? Elicit the idea that sound is produced by movement. If no one says "vibrate," introduce this term now.

3. EXPANSION: Which process skills will be used?

Inferring, experimenting, hypothesizing, communicating

How will the idea be expanded?

Waxed Paper Kazoo

Have each student make a comb-and-waxed-paper kazoo by folding a piece of waxed paper over the teeth of a comb. Instruct the children to place their lips on the wax paper and to hum a tune. How is the sound being produced? What is vibrating?

Science in Personal and Social Perspectives

- How is sound made? Can you avoid sound?
- Do sounds affect the way you feel and act?

- Would you want to attend a concert or go to a movie where the sound kept echoing off the walls? Why or why not?

Science and Technology

- The quality of speakers and sound systems relies heavily on sound vibrations; how has modern technology eliminated a lot of excess vibrations?
- How important a role does the design of a room play in carrying sound vibrations?
- How did an understanding of sound vibrations help in the creation of the microphone, the phonograph, the telephone, underwater depth sounding, and ultrasound? How have these inventions changed the world?

Science as Inquiry

- Knowing that sound is produced by a vibrating object, do you think you can make a bell ring under water? Try it.
- Some birds, like loons, can dive under water for their food and stay down for an extended period of time. Do you think they call to one another while they are under the water? Can they hear each other? What could you do to determine whether your answer is correct?

History and Nature of Science

- Who was John William Strutt, also known as Baron Rayleigh? What role did he play in helping us understand how sound behaves? (For second grade, the teacher could give a brief biography of Baron Rayleigh. He was born in England in 1842. While many people before him expressed opinions about the nature of sound—Pythagoras, Galileo, Mersenne, Chladni ("the founder of modern acoustics"), Colladon and Sturm, and von Helmholtz—Baron Rayleigh was the first to put it all together in a book titled *Theory of Sound*, which he published in 1877. A second edition was published in 1894. In 1904 Rayleigh won the Nobel Prize for physics, mainly for his work that led to the discovery of argon and other inert gases. Baron Rayleigh died in 1919.)
- Sound production is important in entertainment. Develop a list of entertainment careers that utilize sound.

4. EVALUATION: How will the students show what they have learned?

Upon completing the activities the students will be able to:

- predict from a given set of objects which will vibrate and produce sound (Nerf ball, drum, taut rubber band, loose rubber band, ruler, feather).
- spend one week in which they will be expected to test various wall surfaces to determine which ones allow for maximum and for minimum sound vibrations. They will share their findings with the class and, based on these findings, accurately predict which type of wall surface would be best for a movie theater or a concert hall.

Loudness and Pitch

**GRADE
2–4
DISCIPLINE
Physical
Science**

Concept to be invented
Main idea—Sounds vary in loudness and pitch.

Concepts that are important to expansion
Size and strength of vibration will affect loudness and pitch.

Materials needed

drinking glasses	wooden board with eye hooks and fish line
large nail	oatmeal boxes
empty soda bottles	wood blocks
water	pan lids
cigar box	guitar or piano
rubber bands	

➡ **Safety precautions:** Care should be taken when handling any of the glass containers used in many of the activities. Protect eyes against flying rubber bands—wear goggles!

Discrepant event
Ask the students to predict what will happen to the sound as you tap an empty glass with a nail and gradually add water as you tap. Once all predictions are given, begin to tap the glass and fill it as you do so. Did the sound behave as you predicted? What happened to the sound as more water filled the glass? Do you have any ideas why this happened?

1. EXPLORATION: Which process skills will be used?

Observing, manipulating materials, predicting, communicating, recording data, inferring, hypothesizing

Soda bottles filled with water at varying levels

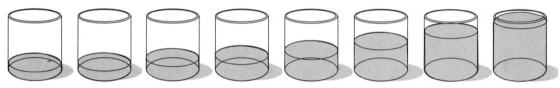

Glasses filled with varying levels of water

What will the students do?

Divide the class into four groups. Have each group rotate through the following activities:

Soda Bottle Orchestra

Soda bottles, glasses, water, nails: Set up a center with glasses and bottles filled with water at varying levels. Have children explore sound variation with water levels in both glasses and bottles. Ask them to record their observations, taking special note of the relationship between the sound produced and the amount of water in the different containers.

Cigar Box Strings

Rubber bands of varying widths and lengths, open cigar box: Stretch the different-sized rubber bands over the open cigar box. Pluck the rubber bands. What kinds of sounds do they make? Record the sounds made by the different-sized rubber bands.

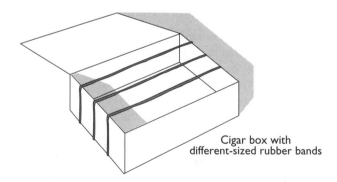

Cigar box with
different-sized rubber bands

PHYSICAL SCIENCE

Fish Line Harps   Make a fish line harp by cutting at least eight different lengths of fish line. String each line through two eye hooks that are screwed into a foot-long piece of board (a 1 × 8 will do) the same distance apart as the string length. (The teacher can make this harp ahead of time.) Pluck the strings. What do you observe about the relationship between the string length and the sound produced? Is there a relationship between the sound produced and the tightness of the string?

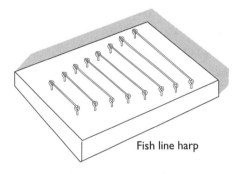

Fish line harp

Strum a guitar, or play a piano in which the guts are exposed. If you are using a guitar, what relationship do you observe between the size of the guitar string and the sound it produces? For the piano, what relationship do you observe between the size of the piano string and the sound it produces?

2. EXPLANATION/CONCEPT INVENTION: What is the main idea? How will the main idea be constructed?

Concept: Sounds vary in loudness and pitch.

What did you observe when you tapped the various glasses and bottles? What happened to the sound if you used a lot of force to strike the nail to the container? In which containers were the sounds higher?

How were you able to make the rubber band sound loud when plucked? What types of sounds were produced with very skinny, tightly stretched rubber bands? very fat, loosely stretched ones?

When you played the harp, which length string gave you the highest sound? the lowest? Did you try loosening the strings? What happened to the sounds when the strings were loose?

When you played the guitar or piano, what did you do to create a very loud sound? How were you able to get a very high sound? a low sound?

Summarize all the answers by reinforcing the following: Loudness is determined by the strength of vibration. Pitch is determined by the length of the vibrating object.

PHYSICAL SCIENCE

3. EXPANSION OF THE IDEA: Which process skills will be used?

Predicting, communicating, experimenting, interpreting data

How will the idea be expanded?

Homemade Music   Based on your conclusions from the previous activities, choose a song familiar to everyone in your group and try to play that simple melody on the glasses, the bottles, or any of the other instruments. Each group will take a turn performing for the other groups.

Science in Personal and Social Perspectives

- The ability to produce music enriches the lives of children and can lead to a lifetime skill. The ability to control sound enhances self-concept.
- How could you use sound to help you determine how much soda you have left in a can? or how much milk is left in a carton? or how much laundry detergent is left in its container? or if a new bottle of perfume or aftershave is totally full?

Science and Technology

- Many video games use sound to heighten the suspense and action of the play. Do you think these games would be as popular if all sound were eliminated?
- What effect does the loudness and pitch of music have on moviegoers? Would scary movies be as effective without the sound effects?
- How has the computer industry made use of the loudness and pitch of sounds in personal computers?

Science as Inquiry

- What properties affect the pitch of a sound? the loudness of a sound? Can you create an instrument with high pitch and soft sound? with low pitch and loud sound?

History and Nature of Science

- Children enjoy music for listening and movement and may look to a future as an entertainer. Ask the students to trace the history of an instrument. Who designed it? How does it produce sound?
- Where do you think someone with a background in music production, sound engineering, or the creation of musical instruments could use his or her talents?

4. EVALUATION: How will the students show what they have learned?

Upon completing these activities the students will be able to:

- predict whether a high or low pitch will be produced by looking at pictures of various-sized strings or columns of water,
- predict loudness and softness of sound when given pictures of thick or thin strings of the same length,

- create a high-pitched sound when given a straw,
- create a low pitch with a soda bottle.

Sound Movement as Waves

Concepts to be invented

Main idea—Sounds move in the form of waves through air, water, wood, and other solids.

Concepts that are important to expansion

Sound waves must strike your eardrum for you to hear sound; sound waves weaken with distance.

Materials needed

Set up the following as activity centers:
(1) fork and string chime, (2) metal rod, (3) meter stick, wood blocks, (4) pieces of cloth, cotton balls, feathers, cork, Nerf ball, (5) 10-gallon fish tank filled with water.

Per student pair:
Two paper cups and two paper clips per student; string for telephone; tin can and fish line telephone for comparison with paper cup telephone.

➡ **Safety precautions**: Care should be taken when handling the kitchen fork and tuning forks; keep them away from your own eyes and those of your friends. Be careful where you place your fingers as you bang the two wood blocks together; avoid crushing them between the blocks.

Discrepant event

Ask the students to listen as they tap the sides of their desks. Now ask them to lay their ears on their desk tops while tapping the sides of the desks with the same force as before. Have them describe the sounds they hear. Are there any differences? Why?

1. EXPLORATION: Which process skills will be used?

Observing, recording data, predicting, inferring, describing, communicating, measuring, defining operationally

What will the students do?

Divide the class into five groups. Have each group record its observations while rotating throughout the following activity centers.

Vibrating Fork   Tie about a 12-inch length of string to the handle end of a fork. Allow it to bang on the side of a desk or a wall as you set it in swinging motion. Write a description of the sound it creates. Can you manipulate the string or fork in any way to change the pitch or loudness of the sound? Can you feel the vibrating fork through the string?

Striking Rod   Hold the metal rod and strike it against a wall, a book, a desk, a variety of surfaces. Is sound produced? Which striking surface will make the rod sound the loudest? the softest? Why do you think this is so?

Clapping Blocks   Take turns with members of your group clapping the two wood blocks together. Use the meter stick to measure at what distance the clapping blocks sound the loudest. How far can you move away from the clapping blocks and still hear them?

Sound Producers? Using the cloth, cotton, feathers, cork, and Nerf ball, try to produce a sound. Is it possible to create a sound if you simply drop the items on your desk? What if you strike them with your hand? Are these items capable of producing sound? Why or why not?

Tapping Tank   Place your ear to one end of the filled fish tank. Have another student gently tap the glass on the other side of the tank. Can you hear this sound? Did the sound travel through the glass or through the water? This time place your ear so that it is directly above the tank. Have a friend gently drop a quarter into the fish tank when you are not looking. Could you hear when the quarter hit the bottom of the tank?

2. EXPLANATION/CONCEPT INVENTION: What is the main idea? How will the main idea be constructed?

Concept: Sounds move in the form of waves through air, water, wood, and other solids.

Were you able to make the fork sing? How did you do this? Did the hand that was holding the string feel anything as the fork sang? What about the metal rod? How did you get it to sound the loudest? Could you see the rod moving as it made sound? What about the wood blocks? Were they very loud? How did your hands feel as you banged the blocks together? What about the cloth, cotton, feathers, cork, and Nerf ball? Were you able to get them to make a sound when they were dropped? Why or why not? Do these items behave like the fork, metal rod, or wood blocks? What can those items do that the cloth items cannot? (Help students realize that objects that vibrate will set the air in motion to create a sound.) Could you hear sound through the water? When was it the easiest to detect? Why is it important that your ear be facing the source of the sound? Sound waves must strike your eardrum for you to hear sound.

Based on your observations from these five activities and when we put our ears to our desks and tapped, can you tell me through which media sound waves will travel? Sounds move in waves through air, water, wood, and other solids.

3. EXPANSION OF THE IDEA: Which process skills will be used?

Communicating, experimenting, interpreting data, reducing experimental error

How will the idea be expanded?

Paper Cup Telephone

Provide each student with two paper cups and any length of string (minimum 2 feet). Instruct the students to poke a small hole in the end of their paper cups and thread the string through them. Tie the end of the string to a paper clip to prevent the string from slipping out of the cup. Ask the students to work in pairs trying out their paper cup telephones. Experiment with loose string versus tight string, long versus short string. Compare results. Touch the string as they talk to dampen the sound. Ask each pair to try using the tin can–fish line telephone. Is there any difference between this phone and the one you made? Which telephone sets up more vibrations? What can you say about how sound travels?

Science in Personal and Social Perspectives

- Where in your house would be the best place to set your stereo speakers: on a metal table or a cloth-covered bench? or would neither of these be good? Can you suggest a good place?
- Why do you think most homes have doorbells? How are these better than just yelling for our friends?
- Do you think it is fair for people who are fishing to use a fish echo-locator to determine where the fish are before they begin fishing?
- Do you think it is ethical for someone to use knowledge of sound to eavesdrop on other people for such purposes as collecting military intelligence, listening in on criminals, or listening to others talk about himself or herself?

Science and Technology

- What materials would you use and how would you go about building a soundproof room? Can you create a plan that would be easy to follow that takes all variables into account in building this room? Work with your parents to create a working model of your design.

Science as Inquiry

- A knowledge of the conductivity of sound helps develop further concepts of controlling sound loudness, quality, and usefulness.
- Do you think you could design a tin can phone that lets three or more people use it at once? Try it. Draw a diagram of your design.

History and Nature of Science

- How have marine biologists used their knowledge of sound to study the humpbacked whale? Why should we be concerned with the singing behavior of the humpbacked whale?
- Why would a pilot be concerned with how sound travels? If you were the pilot of the Concorde, would you have a problem trying to get permission to land your plane in Columbus, Ohio? Why?
- How did Alexander Graham Bell apply his understanding of sound? Identify one of his inventions and describe how it works.

4. EVALUATION: How will the students show what they have learned?

Upon completing the activities the students will be able to:

- rank-order a given set of materials from good to poor conductors of sound: air, wood, metal rod, cotton string, wire, water, cotton balls;
- take an object that is capable of creating sound when struck and alter it so that when it is struck, the loudness of the sound is decreased.

Sound Waves

GRADE
2–4
DISCIPLINE
Physical
Science

Concepts to be invented
Main idea—Sound travels in waves. Waves consist of areas of compression and rarefaction. Waves move through the air.

Concepts that are important to expansion
Sound waves cause vibrations as they hit the eardrum, causing us to hear sounds.

Materials needed
For each group of students:
soup can open at both ends   Slinkies

balloon
rubber band
small rectangular piece of mirror
flashlight

a model of the ear (one for the
  whole class)
a labeled diagram of the ear

➡ **Safety precautions:** Be sure that all rough edges are filed off soup cans before providing them to student groups. Make sure there are no sharp edges on the mirrors; file if necessary. Encourage the students to use caution near edges of mirror and soup can.

Discrepant event

Stretch a piece of the balloon over one end of the soup can. Secure it tightly with the rubber band. Glue a small piece of mirror on the balloon membrane, slightly off center. Shine a flashlight onto the mirror so that its reflection shows up on the chalkboard. Ask the students to observe the mirror's reflection on the board. Ask one student to come up and speak into the open end of the can. What happens to the mirror's reflection on the chalkboard when someone speaks into the can?

1. EXPLORATION: Which process skills will be used?

Observing, experimenting, predicting, hypothesizing, inferring

What will the students do?

*Soup Can
Reflectors*

Divide the students into groups depending on class size. Have one soup can reflector for each group. Provide each group with a flashlight. Ask the students to predict and then record what happens to the soup can reflectors as they vary the loudness of the sound. What do you think is causing the mirror's reflection to move? Think of this as you begin to play with a Slinky. Stretch and shake the Slinky, and record what the Slinky looks like as you do this. A diagram may be useful at this point. Try to label where the Slinky looks mashed together and where it looks thin on your diagram.

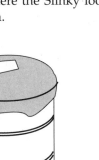

2. EXPLANATION/CONCEPT INVENTION: What is the main idea? How will the main idea be constructed?

Concept: Sound travels in waves. Waves consist of areas of compression and rarefaction. Waves move through the air.

What do you think caused the mirror to move? Can you actually see the balloon moving as someone speaks into the open end of the can? Speaking into the can set the balloon membrane vibrating. Can you feel the vibration of the balloon if you lightly touch it as someone speaks into the open end? What type of pattern does the moving mirror make on the board? How is this pattern similar to the movement of the Slinky?

What would be a good name to describe the path sound travels in? (Waves.) Ask for a volunteer to share his or her drawing of Slinky movement with the class. Reproduce this drawing for all to see. As you moved the Slinky, were you able to detect areas where the Slinky was mashed together? Were you able to detect areas where it was more spread out? These Slinky movements are similar to sound waves. Areas where sound waves are mashed together are called *compression*; areas that are spread out are called *rarefaction*.

3. EXPANSION OF THE IDEA: Which process skills will be used?

Observing, manipulating materials, inferring, predicting, communicating

How will the idea be expanded?

Slinky Waves

Ask the students to take turns laying their heads on their desks while another student stretches the Slinky out on top of the desk and releases it rapidly, or have another student hold a ruler over the edge of the desk and strike it quickly. Ask the student with his or her head on the desk what this felt like. What did your ear detect?

Sound Waves and the Ear

Provide the students with diagrams of the inner ear. Ask them to label what they believe is the path that sound takes as it reaches our ears. Use the ear model to trace this path for the students. Allow them to check their labeled predictions with the model you are tracing. Remind them that sound waves vary in strength. As the sound waves hit the eardrum, they cause it to vibrate in rhythm with them, causing sound messages to the brain. The human ear can interpret sound waves with frequencies ranging between 16 and nearly 20,000 vibrations per second. Those vibrations above 20,000 are termed *ultrasonic*.

Science in Personal and Social Perspectives

- Why is it important that you never put anything in your ear smaller than your elbow? What kind of ear-cleaning products do you think are the safest to use?
- Have you ever tried to talk to your friends while you are under water swimming? Is it easy to understand someone talking under water? Why or why not?

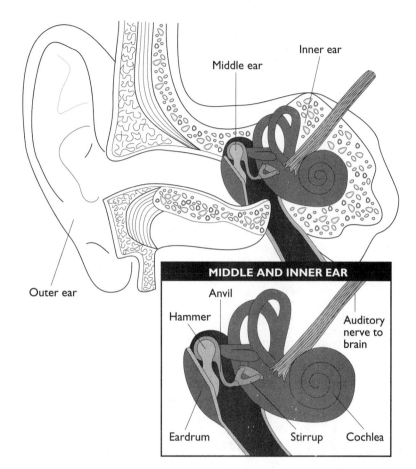

- Interview people in different lines of work who use ear plugs, such as factory workers, road construction crews, or building contractors. What types of ear plugs do they use? How well do they think their ear plugs work?
- Is it a good idea to wear headphones while riding your bicycle? Why or why not?

Science and Technology

- How effective are ear plugs in preventing potentially damaging sounds from reaching your eardrum?
- Write to the manufacturers of the various ear plugs. What materials do they use to make their ear plugs? Is any one material better than another? What is the most widely used brand of ear plugs? (A teacher can assign this question as homework or as another expansion activity for the class to investigate.)

Science as Inquiry

- At a track meet, why do you think you see the spark and smoke from the starter's gun before you hear the sound made by the gun? Can you explain this phenomenon in terms of sound waves?
- If someone in the room was speaking to you and you could detect only faint, muffled sounds, what might be the probable cause for your loss of hearing? How is sound supposed to travel from your ear canal to your brain?

History and Nature of Science

- What do you think would happen to you if you had a job working at an airport loading cargo onto planes and you did not wear protective headphones?
- Would a piano tuner need to be aware of compression and rarefaction of sound waves? How could he or she apply this knowledge in his or her work?
- Interview a local audiologist. What does his or her job entail? What kind of knowledge is needed to perform the job? Ask if he or she could share with you any cases where a person's job affected his or her hearing. Share the interview with the class.

4. EVALUATION: How will the students show what they have learned?

Upon completing the activities the students will be able to:

- identify areas of rarefaction and compression on a diagram of sound waves,
- trace the path of the sound waves from its source through the ear when given a worksheet with a diagram of the ear. The students should be able to label the ear canal, eardrum, bones of the middle ear, and nerve to the brain.

Sound Production

GRADE
5–8
DISCIPLINE
Physical
Science

Concept to be invented
Main idea—Sounds are produced by vibrations.

Concepts that are important to expansion
A vibrating object has an energy source. Moving energy is referred to as *kinetic*. Vibrations that cause sound can be produced by hitting, plucking, stroking, or blowing an object.

Materials needed
For each student group:

pencil	one balloon
paper	small pieces of mirror
percussion instruments	one flashlight
one soup can with both ends cut out	chalkboard

➡ **Safety precautions:** Remind the students to exercise caution when making sounds with the instruments. They should be reminded not to hold them up to a friend's or their own ear when the sound is loud or piercing. During the expansion activity they must use care when handling the mirrors, and watch for sharp edges on the cans as well.

1. EXPLORATION: Which process skills will be used?

Observing, recording data, predicting, hypothesizing, experimenting

What will the students do?

Noise and Sound Identification

Activity 1. Ask the students to close their eyes, sit perfectly still, and not speak. Tell them to listen carefully to all the noises they can hear, even the slightest sounds that they normally ignore. After a few minutes ask them to open their eyes and write descriptions of every noise they heard and, if possible, identify what they believe is the source of those sounds. Students should describe noises in terms ordinarily used for sounds, such as high, low, loud, soft, hissing, rumbling, piercing, musical.

Activity 2. Tell the students that they are going to play a listening game. Ask the students to close their eyes while the teacher makes a sound and then try to guess what the sound was. The first one to guess what the sound was will make the next sound. Make sure everyone gets a turn.

Activity 3. Present various percussion instruments to the class, such as drums of various sizes, cymbals, pots, pot lids, and xylophones (toy ones will work as well). Ask the students to guess how you can get each one to produce a sound. Ask the students to predict what causes each one to make a sound. Allow the students to experiment with the various instruments, asking them to take note of how sound is produced on each instrument. Ask the students to describe what it feels like. After students have done this, have them strike the instrument again and then hold it tightly. Ask them if the sound stopped. Why did it stop?

2. EXPLANATION/CONCEPT INVENTION: What is the main idea? How will the main idea be constructed?

Concept: Sounds are produced by vibrations.

Activity 1. Ask the students to go back to the first list they made. Make two columns on the board, one labeled *descriptive words* and the other *sound sources.* Ask the students to help fill in the chart from the lists they created. The class will be referring back to this list after they discuss the other two activities.

Activity 2. Ask each student: What type of sound did you make for everyone to guess? How was the sound made? What energy source did you use to make it? Add these sounds to the list on the board already; include a third column, *how made,* to the chart.

PHYSICAL SCIENCE

Activity 3. When you hit your instrument, what did you set up? How did you get the sound to stop on your percussion instrument? Go over the list on the board and stress that sound is a type of energy. To make sound, one form of energy is changed to another form of energy. Energy causes movement. Sounds can be produced by hitting, plucking, stroking, and blowing. All of these actions use energy to create vibrations. Vibrations are the source of sound.

3. EXPANSION OF THE IDEA: Which process skills will be used?

Experimenting, predicting, inferring

How will the idea be expanded?

Sound Movement   Divide the class into groups. Have each group stretch a piece cut from a balloon over one end of a soup can, using a rubber band to hold it tightly in place. Glue a small piece of mirror slightly off center. Darken the classroom, and hold the can at an angle to the blackboard. Using a flashlight, shine the beam so that it strikes the mirror and reflects on the board. Ask the group to predict what will happen to the mirror's reflection on the board as someone speaks into the open end of the can. Ask someone in the group to talk into the open end of the can. Ask the other members of the group to take note of what happens to the mirror's reflection as the person speaks into the can. Do your observations match your predictions? What do you think causes the changes in the reflection? What source of energy causes the balloon to vibrate?

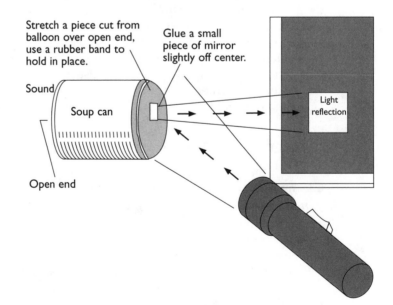

Sound Game:
"What Is Sound?"

Home assignment

This assignment may be done alone or with other family members.

1. Go home and sit down in your bedroom or the room of your choice, close your eyes, and be very quiet for 3 minutes. Listen carefully. Do you hear anything? Write down the sounds you hear and describe them.
2. If you have heard new sounds, what are they, and why do you think you haven't heard them before?
3. How did the quiet make you feel? (To show how the quiet made you feel, you may write a descriptive paragraph, write a poem, or draw a picture.)

"How well can you match sounds?"

Students will construct a game for younger students. After the students have made the game, they will take it to a primary class and supervise the younger students playing it.

Materials needed

At least twelve 6-ounce unmarked metal cans, small objects (materials used in cans to make noises could include dried rice, beans, peas, marbles, BBs, gravel, sand, bits of Styrofoam, puffed rice, or any other small objects found around the house), tape.

Preparation:

Place small objects in a pair of cans and then seal the cans with tape. Be sure children cannot see in the cans and that the cans are prepared in pairs with approximately the same amount of material in each set of cans.

Procedure:

1. Shake the cans and listen to the noise they make.
2. Can you hear the different sounds they make?
3. Do any of the cans make the same sound?
4. If you find cans that sound alike, put them next to each other.
5. Have a friend listen to the cans and see if he or she agrees.
6. You may want to make more cans with different sounds to see how well your friends can tell the difference.

Science in Personal and Social Perspectives

- What would your life be like without sound?
- What are some sounds that you hear around you and how are they made?
- How have people made use of their knowledge that a vibrating body will produce a sound? What types of signals have we created because of this? (Fire alarms, smoke detectors, burglar alarms, fog horns.)
- When you wake up in the middle of the night and hear creaking bed springs or creaking stairs, knowing what you now know about sound, how could you explain away any fears that you might have?

Science and Technology

- How do vibrating strings allow us to create a violin, a guitar, or a bass fiddle? Why is it that some of the sounds created by these instruments sound soothing to some, while others may think of them as simply obnoxious noise?
- How do we record and transmit the sounds we make or the sounds that are made around us? Choose something that records sound or something that sound is recorded on. Draw a diagram explaining how it works.

Science as Inquiry

- Explain how it is possible to create a percussion instrument. Make one and describe how it works. Use terms like *vibration* and *energy* in your explanation.
- Why do you think you enjoy certain types of music? Survey people of different ages as to their choices in music. Create a pie chart or bar graph to describe your results. Would you have predicted these results?

History and Nature of Science

- Why do you think it is important that a car mechanic is able to distinguish one sound from another? How does his or her job depend on recognizing engine sounds?
- Do you think Beethoven was able to continue his musical career after he became deaf? Do you think it is possible for deaf people to "feel" sounds?
- What other occupations can you think of in which reliance on sound is essential?

4. EVALUATION: How will the students show what they have learned?

Upon completing these activities the students will be able to:

- describe sources of sound, explaining how a vibration is set up and the energy source for that vibration;
- report on their home assignment "What Is Sound?" and share with the class their poems, paragraphs, or drawings about the sounds they observed;
- work successfully with the younger students when they play the "What Is Sound?" game they made, helping the younger students invent the concept of vibration.

Characteristics of Matter

GRADE
5–8
DISCIPLINE
Physical
Science

Concept to be invented
Main idea—Anything that occupies space and has mass is called *matter*. Matter can be found in a solid, liquid, or gaseous state.

PHYSICAL SCIENCE

Concepts that are important to expansion

Physical versus chemical change, solutions versus mixtures, chemical symbols, chemical formulas, matter can be neither created nor destroyed.

Materials needed

For exploration (per student group):

Two Ziploc plastic bags (label one A and the other B); 1 teaspoon sodium bicarbonate (place in bag A and seal closed); 1 teaspoon calcium chloride, sold as ice melter during winter months (place in bag B and seal closed); magnifying glass; small medicine cups with 10 ml of water in each; 5–10 drops of bromothymol blue (number of drops may vary due to the alkalinity of local water supplies; when it is placed in the water, make sure the water stays blue); wood splint; matches.

For expansion:

Three clear cups or plastic beakers, marbles, sand, water, graduated cylinder, and weighing scale.

➥ **Safety precautions:** Remind students that safety goggles must be worn at all times. Since this is a guided discovery lesson, they are to listen to the teacher at all times before they begin to manipulate the materials—this is for their safety! Tell students not to taste anything during these activities.

Advanced organizer used to set the stage for this guided discovery activity: Which process skills will be used?

Observing, analyzing, inferring, hypothesizing

What will the teacher and students do?

The teacher should enter the classroom with a lit candle. Ask the class the following: Why does it burn? What helps it burn? How can I make it go out? Act on student suggestions. Why does the candle go out when I place it under a glass? What is it lacking? Could I try to grow plants under glass? Could animals, like a hamster, live under this glass? Why or why not? Through questioning, the teacher should bring out the idea that a way to test for the presence of oxygen in a gas would be to see if a flame stays lit in the gas. If the flame goes out, that would tell us that a gas like carbon dioxide may be present. (If the students are not already aware of fire safety skills, please review them at this time.)

1. **EXPLORATION:** Which process skills will be used?

Manipulating materials, collecting and recording data, communicating, observing, hypothesizing, predicting, inferring

What will the students do?

Plastic Bag Chemistry

Make and record their observations of two unknown white powders found in bags A and B. Use the magnifying glass to make careful observations of the two

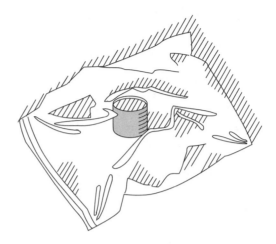

unknowns. Draw pictures of unknown white powders. (Stress the importance of keeping bags sealed and not tasting the unknown substances. Encourage the students to make observations about the shape of the unknown white powders).

Make observations of the unknown liquid placed before them; record these (work on getting students to realize that the liquid takes the shape of the container).

Introduce the mystery solution and ask students to predict what will happen when the solution is placed in the unknown liquid before them. Have them record the amount of mystery solution that was placed in the unknown liquid and the results of the mixing. (The "mystery solution" is bromothymol blue. Conceal its name on the container and move from group to group asking the students for their predictions of what it is. Then place the 5 to 10 drops of mystery solution in the students' cups.)

Ask the students to open bag A, taking care not to touch or eat the substance, and pour it into bag B. Seal the bag, and record their observations once the two unknown powders are combined together. After they record their observations, ask the students to place the bag on its side and open it. Without mixing the unknown liquid with the unknown powders, place the container with the unknown liquid into the bag and seal it.

Ask the students to design a way in which they can mix the powders with the liquid without actually picking up the bag and shaking it. They should discuss this with the students closest to them. While they design their plan, remind them that they have been provided with a wood splint and some matches (the students should already be aware of appropriate fire safety skills). Ask the students to recall the previous candle demonstration. Do you think a gas will be given off when you mix the unknown powders with the liquid? How will you know? What can you do to determine which gas it is? Encourage the students to incorporate these suggestions into their experimental design.

After sufficient time has been allowed for the students to design their experiment, have them act on their plans. Record their observations. Encourage them to observe the bags with the magnifying glasses, make some careful observations (not only looking at the bag but also holding it to feel for any changes in temperature and using the burning wood splint to check for evolution of a gas—remember we observe with all of our senses), perhaps even drawing what they see.

2. EXPLANATION/CONCEPT INVENTION: What is the main idea? How will the main idea be constructed?

Concept: Anything that occupies space and has mass is called *matter.*

By working with the unknown white powders, students can make observations in which they realize that the unknown substances are in a *solid* state of matter. By observing the unknown *liquid* and the mystery solution, also in a *liquid* state, they can see they are using another state of matter. Upon mixing the *solid* with a *liquid,* they can see the bag expanding, thus observing the third state of matter, a *gas.* Careful use of questions will also get the students to realize that *solids* always retain their shape, no matter the container. *Liquids* take up the shape of the container, and a *gas* will take up as much space as you give it.

Ask the students the following questions to help get to the ideas stated above: You drew pictures of the unknown white powders in bag A and in bag B. When you mixed them together, did they change their shape? (Work on the children's understanding of the concept of a solid, which does not change in shape. Physical change can be observed if they crush the solids; what was created is a *heterogeneous mixture*—a combination of two or more substances each distinct from one another.) If so, how or why? What shape was the liquid in when it was inside the cup? What about when you poured it out? Why? What happened to the liquid when the mystery solution was added? Could you tell where one liquid began and the other ended? (Work on the concept of liquids taking the shape of their container and only within the limit of the volume that the sample occupies. Also work on developing the concept of a solution). What happened when you mixed the solids with the liquids? What did you observe? (Listing all of their observations will allow you to expand on specific secondary concepts you want the students to understand, such as physical versus chemical change, heat of reaction, acid formation.) Why did your bag get bigger? How did you find out what gas evolved? If you used a bigger plastic bag, would it be blown all the way up, too? Why? (Work on the concept of a gas taking the shape of its container.)

If you are interested, use this activity to introduce the students to chemical nomenclature. Provide students with the chemical formulas for the unknowns involved in the activity (older students may help derive these formulas and help balance the equation).

PHYSICAL SCIENCE

$$CaCl_2 + NaHCO_3 + H_2O + \text{bromothymol blue}$$
$$\rightarrow NaCl(aq) + HCl(aq) + CaCO_3 + H_2O$$
$$CaCO_3 + H_2O \rightarrow H_2CO_3 + CaO$$
$$H_2CO_3 \rightarrow H^+ + HCO^-_3 \rightarrow CO_2(g) + H_2O$$

3. EXPANSION OF THE IDEA: Which process skills will be used?

Measuring, predicting, hypothesizing, observing, recording data

How will the idea be expanded?

Marble Matter   Provide each student group with three clear cups or plastic beakers, marbles, sand, and some water. Ask the students to weigh a cup, then fill the cup with marbles. Record their weight and number of marbles. Ask them questions such as the following: How many marbles did you put in the cup? Do you think you can put in any more marbles? Did the marbles take the shape of the cup? (Work here to make sure they understand that the marbles did not change their shape.) What was the weight of the cup? What state of matter are the marbles?

Ask the students to weigh another cup. Fill the cup with sand and then weigh it. Have them place a mark on the cup indicating the top of the sand. Use the same line of questioning as for the marbles.

Now ask the students if they think both cups are full. Ask the students if they think they can pour any of the sand into the cup filled with marbles. Solicit

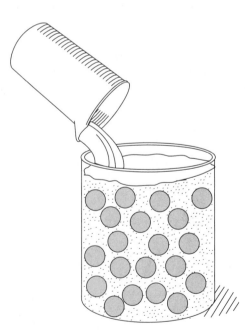

responses. React to responses: I thought you told me the cup with the marbles in it was full; how can you possibly put anything else into this cup?

Have the students pour some sand into the cup of marbles. Mark the new level of sand on the sand cup. What happens? Were you able to add sand into an already-filled cup of marbles? Why? What is the weight of your new mixture? What is the weight of the sand remaining in the cup? Subtract this remaining weight of sand from the original weight of sand. How much sand did you lose? Subtract the original weight of the marbles from the new weight of the marble and sand mixture. Is this amount gained equal to the amount lost from the sand cup? (Reinforce the concept of matter—anything that occupies space and has mass; concept of states of matter—two different solids. Secondary concept—physical change, matter was not created or destroyed, it still has the same weight; nothing was lost, just placed in different containers.)

Weigh a third cup and fill it with water. Weigh this. Ask the students if they think it is possible to put water into an already-filled cup of sand and marbles. Why? Why not? What state of matter is the water? What do you know about liquids? (For older students, instead of weighing the water in a cup, introduce them to a graduated cylinder; have them measure out so many milliliters of water and record the volume of water in milliliters that they pour into the marble-sand cup.)

Was your prediction true? What happened when you tried to add water to the marble-sand cup? Why could the container that was already filled with marbles still hold more sand and water?

Do you think we could have started with the water, then the sand and marbles? Why? What does this tell you about the sizes of molecules of different materials or substances? (The concept of solids versus liquids leads into a discussion of the size of particles. Smaller-size particles can slip between the larger ones. Make an analogy of molecules. Introduction of this new term may lead into a new unit on atoms and molecules.)

Science in Personal and Social Perspectives

- Which would you rather take a bath in: water mixed with sand or water mixed with bath bubble beads? Why?
- What would happen if you burned a dollar bill? Could you tape it back together and still have a dollar?

Science and Technology

- How has knowledge of chemical changes allowed the food industry to create cake mixes that can be made in a microwave rather than a regular oven?
- Getting matter to change its shape has allowed us to create many large buildings, like the Sears Tower in Chicago. How is this so?

Science as Inquiry

- The students engage in manipulative skills during the activities.
- For understanding the concept of physical versus chemical change, ask the students to explain why they can heat snow and get water, or why they can

PHYSICAL SCIENCE

mix flour, water, baking soda, and sugar together, heat the mixture, and taste not these separate ingredients but a cake.

- Why can't you put a round peg in a square hole?

History and Nature of Science

- Using a list of all of the concepts discovered in the activities, ask the students to survey their parents and other adults to see if they make use of any of these concepts in their work. Where do they see them utilized? Are these people in typical scientific careers? Can anyone use these science concepts?
- Early scientists called *alchemists* thought they could turn simple elements into gold. Did everyone believe them at that time? Why or why not? Do you believe them? Why or why not?

4. EVALUATION: How will the students show what they have learned?

Upon completing the activities the students will be able to:

- demonstrate a physical change and then a chemical change when given a piece of paper;
- provide examples of solid matter, liquid matter, and gas;
- demonstrate how to capture a gas;
- name five chemical elements;
- name and write the chemical symbols for five elements (intermediate grades). Primary grades should be able to state simple chemical symbols such as hydrogen and oxygen.

Physical Properties of Matter

GRADE
K–4
DISCIPLINE
Physical
Science

Concept to be invented
Main idea—Physical properties of matter help distinguish one kind of matter from another.

Concepts important to exploration and expansion
A cooked egg will spin freely, whereas a raw egg will be difficult to spin. It will have a slight wobble as it spins. The term *best* is arbitrary; members of a group must decide criteria for judging an object the best.

Materials needed
For exploration:
Cook enough white eggs for half the class. Place randomly in a bowl the cooked eggs and an equal number of raw eggs. Allow each student to pick an egg out of the bowl.

one can of broth or any canned   one can of dog food
   liquid   clear container/bowl
paper towels

For expansion:
Three or four different brands of chocolate chip cookies, paper towels.

For each student group:
one ruler   paper for recording data
five to ten toothpicks

➡ **Safety precautions:** Remind students that although you encourage them to make as many observations as possible, they should never taste anything without your permission. Discourage the students from licking the eggshells. Remind them to wash their hands after the exploration activity, especially before they begin the expansion activity.

1. EXPLORATION: Which process skills will be used?

Observing, manipulating materials, collecting and recording data, communicating

What will the students do?

Egg-citing Observations

Enter the classroom carrying the bowl of eggs and acting as if you are greatly troubled. Explain to the students that you boiled some eggs last night for a dinner party and placed them in the refrigerator. When you went into the refrigerator this morning, you found that someone took the cooked eggs and combined them with the raw eggs in this bowl. Now you have to determine which are cooked and which are raw without breaking any of them. Ask the students if they can help you solve your problem.

Ask each student to choose an egg from the bowl. Ask them to make as many observations about their egg as possible. Remind them not to break the egg! Allow sufficient time for the students to collect their data. Encourage them to record their observations. For very young students, ask them to draw their observations. Once they have made their observations, move to the concept invention phase of this lesson.

2. EXPLANATION/CONCEPT INVENTION: What is the main idea? How will the main idea be constructed?

Concept: Physical properties of matter help distinguish one kind of matter from another.

As the students are making their observations, move among them, encouraging those students who appear to be stumped to think of ways in which observations can be made. Ask questions like: When I make an observation, am I

PHYSICAL SCIENCE

using only my eyes? What other things can I use to make an observation? Encourage the students to think about ways they can manipulate the egg without dropping or breaking it. Remind the students to record the information they are discovering.

Once the students have made their observations, solicit them from the class. Make a list on the board. Once you have received an observation from each of the students, go back to your original question and ask the students: Now, which of these observations will help me solve my problem? Ask a student to restate the problem (which eggs are raw and which are cooked).

Through the process of elimination, the students will find that some physical properties are more distinguishing than others. For instance, simply observing that the egg is white is not going to help solve the problem, since all of the students have white eggs. However, an observation that it sounds as if something is moving inside when I shake my egg or that my egg will spin or stand on end are observations that will help the problem. Ask the students: Is one distinguishing characteristic enough to decide if an egg is cooked or raw? If some students think so, then ask them to make their prediction about whether their egg is cooked or raw based on that one distinguishing characteristic. Let one student crack an egg only to find that the prediction was incorrect. (Make sure that the student chosen to bring out the idea that one characteristic is not enough has in fact made a wrong decision.)

As you progress through the list of student observations, keep referring back to the original problem. As you narrow down their observations to those that help solve the problem, you may find that the students eventually come to an observation that stumps them: Some eggs spin easily and other sort of wobble but don't spin well. The students aren't sure if it is the raw or cooked eggs that spin easily. At this point the teacher should bring out the cans of broth and dog food. (Two cans of each may be helpful.) Open the can of broth and pour it into a clear container. Ask the students what state of matter the broth is in.

Now ask for a student volunteer to try to spin the unopened can of broth. Ask the student if it is easy or hard to get the can to spin.

Now open a can of dog food. Empty that into a clear container. Ask the students what state of matter the dog food is in. Now ask for a student volunteer to try to spin the unopened can of dog food. Ask the student if it is easy or hard to get the can to spin.

Ask the class to determine if the broth is similar to a raw or cooked egg. What about the dog food? Once they have decided that the raw egg is similar to the broth and the cooked egg is similar to the dog food, ask them to tell you how you can determine if an egg is cooked or raw. Encourage them to list all the criteria that helped them come to their conclusions. The students should conclude that the cooked eggs will spin freely and the raw eggs will wobble like the broth can when spun. Through careful observation you can sense movement in raw eggs when you shake them.

3. EXPANSION OF THE IDEA: Which process skills will be used?

Designing an experiment, observing, measuring, predicting, hypothesizing, recording data

How will the idea be expanded?

Chocolate Chip Exploration

This expansion activity is more appropriate for students in grades 3–6. For K–2 students, you may want to lead a guided discovery activity using the following ideas:

Remind the students about the concept learned from the exploration activity: Physical properties of matter help distinguish one kind of matter from another. Explain to the students that you would like them to design an experiment using just physical properties to determine which brand of chocolate chip cookies is the best. Allow sufficient class time for groups of students to brainstorm ways in which they could use only physical properties to determine the best brand of chocolate chip cookies. Ask the students to submit a copy of their planned experiment and a materials list to you so that they can perform their experiment in the next class meeting. Suggested materials are included in the materials list at the beginning of the lesson. Be sure to read over the designed experiments to be sure that they are using only physical properties and also that appropriate safety standards are maintained.

On the second day, allow the students to act on appropriately planned lessons. On the third day, ask the different student groups to share the methods they used for determining the *best* cookie and the results of their experiment. Once all of the groups have had a chance to share their results, and especially if the results were different, ask the students if it is necessary to set some criteria for determining which cookie is *best*. The students should conclude that the term *best* is arbitrary—the members of the group must decide criteria for judging an object the *best*.

As a final discussion question, ask the students why you asked them to design their experiment around physical properties. Why could they not taste the cookie to determine the best?

Science in Personal and Social Perspectives

- If you had to describe your best friend to another student, how would you do that? Would a description such as, "He or she is really nice and cute," be enough? Why or why not?
- If you were talking with a group of people about the best movie you ever saw, do you think everyone in the group would agree with you? Why or why not?

Science and Technology

- How does the mineral industry determine which mineral is which?
- Why has the auto industry gone from metal bumpers to plastic bumpers? What do properties of matter have to do with this decision?

Science as Inquiry

- Students engage in manipulative skills during the activities.
- How can you accurately describe an object?
- How can you tell the difference between a raw and cooked egg without cracking the egg open?

History and Nature of Science

- Pretend you want a new sidewalk in front of your house. You need to hire a cement contractor to do the work. One contractor you interviewed said it didn't matter what kind of material he or she used to pour your sidewalk. Does this person know much about distinguishing physical properties of matter? Would you be willing to hire that contractor? Why or why not?
- Who do you think should be aware of the many different physical properties of matter for their work? What kind of skills are needed for that profession? Have the necessary skills changed in the past twenty years?

4. EVALUATION: How will the students show what they have learned?

Upon completing the activities the students will be able to:

- determine, when given an egg, whether it is cooked or raw,
- design an experiment to determine the best brand of paper towels,

• list the physical properties of three or four different things (the teacher can choose any number of items to set before the student: a rock, flower, penny, button, or anything else will work).

Changing Matter

Concepts to be invented
Main idea—An alteration of the composition or the properties of matter is called a *chemical change*. An alteration of the shape of matter without a change in its chemical composition is called a *physical change*.

Concepts that are important to expansion
Small, single units of matter are called *monomers*. A substance that will speed up a chemical reaction without being affected itself is called a *catalyst*. A bond linking the chains of atoms in a polymer is a *cross linker*. A compound formed by adding many small molecules together in the presence of a catalyst or by the condensation of many smaller molecules through the elimination of water or alcohol is a *polymer*.

Materials needed
Per student:
one piece of scrap paper
one clear cup
matches

one stirring rod or popsicle stick
one lunch-size Ziploc bag

For entire class:
one aluminum pie pan
three large containers of glue (enough
  to give each student 30 ml)
food coloring
liquid starch

borate solution (50 g borax
  with 100 ml of water)
beaker or graduated cylinder for
  measurements
paper towels for clean-up

The following items are used to introduce the problem:
Teflon frying pan
compact disc
plastic baby bottle

football helmet
pair of nylons

➡ **Safety precautions and/or procedures:** During the exploration phase, when the paper is burned, the teacher should make sure there is adequate ventilation in the classroom. The teacher should also be sure the matches are kept away from the students and use care when an open flame is present: sleeves must be pushed up, hair pulled back, and eyes protected. During the expansion phase,

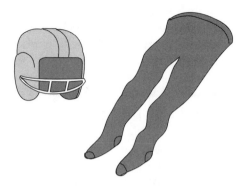

the students should be discouraged from putting their hands in their mouths. Be sure they wash their hands as soon as they are finished with the activity.

1. EXPLORATION: Which process skills will be used?

Observing, predicting, inferring

What will the students do?

Physical and Chemical Paper Change

Introduction: The teacher will allow the children to examine the following items: compact discs, baby bottles, Teflon pan, nylons, and a football helmet. As the students view the items, tell the students that you would like them to think about each item, and that by the time they finish the activities, they should be able to tell you what each item has in common.

Student Activity: Give each student a piece of paper. Ask each of them to make it look different in some way. Then ask each to share what they did to make it look different.

2. EXPLANATION/CONCEPT INVENTION: What is the main idea? How will the main idea be constructed?

Concept: An alteration of the composition or the properties of matter is called a *chemical change.* An alteration of the shape of matter without changing its chemical composition is called a *physical change.*

Ask such questions as: What did you do to make the paper look different? If they tore it up, ask, "If I taped it back together, would I still have a piece of paper? By changing its shape, did I do anything to change the molecules that came together to make that piece of paper?" Be sure to allow the students to share their comments with one another. Explain that a change in shape with no loss of molecules is called a *physical change.*

If students suggest burning the paper, ask if they think they will still be able to use the paper once you change it by burning it. Then burn it over the aluminum pie pan. Is the paper still in a usable form? Why not? Explain that the paper underwent a *chemical change*. When it burned, carbon atoms were lost.

3. EXPANSION OF THE IDEA: Which process skills will be used?

Observing, measuring, recording data, predicting, inferring

How will the idea be expanded?

Polymer-Rubber Balls

Do all chemical changes result in the creation of useless matter? Think about that question while you try the following activity. Ask the students to use the graduated cylinders to measure out 30 ml of glue. Pour it into the clear cup. Choose a color from the food coloring and mix it with your glue (use popsicle sticks for stirring). Do you still have glue in front of you? What kind of change did the glue undergo?

What do you think will happen if you mix the colored glue with the liquid you have in front of you? (The teacher should place in front of half of the class the liquid starch, in front of the other half a borate solution). Please make some predictions, and share them with one another on each side of the room. What do you think will happen when you mix the glue with the unknown liquid in front of you? Make your predictions and record them.

Ask the students to measure out 30 ml of either the starch or the borate solution. Encourage the students to make predictions about how much of the solution they will need to bring about a change in the glue. Since they do not know for certain how much starch or borate solution they will need, encourage the students to add one of these slowly, stirring all the time, until they see a change. Record how much starch or borate solution was necessary to bring about a change in the glue. Record any new observations you may have made about the colored glue.

Did you create anything new, or can you still tell the glue from the starch or borate solution? Can you pick up this new piece of matter? (Encourage the students to do so—the more they manipulate it in their hands, the more the water will come out, and eventually they will have created their own rubber ball.) What do you think you can do with it? What kind of change do you think you created by combining the glue with the starch or the borate solution? Why do you say this?

Go back to the original question: Do all chemical changes result in the creation of useless matter? How many of you think you created a new form of matter that is useful? What did you do differently from your classmates? What do you think you can do with your newly created piece of matter? How useful is it? As a teacher, you may encourage the students from the different sides of the room to compare their newly created rubber balls. Do they bounce the same? Roll the same? Feel the same? Here, two different catalysts were used to create this special kind of chemical change called a *polymerization reaction*. After they finish, the students may place their balls in a Ziploc bag, where they will stay fresh for a few weeks.

Do you think that other inventions could have been discovered just by people mixing things together in the lab and making careful observations about how much and of what materials they mixed together?

Teflon, used to coat pans, is one of these accidental chemical combinations that was discovered in a lab when scientists weren't looking for it. Chemists realized that it was possible to get small pieces of matter to link up chemically when a catalyst was used to force the reaction to occur. Sometimes these smaller pieces of matter, called *monomers,* add together in one long chain to create *polymers.* Saran wrap, Lucite, Plexiglas, and Teflon are polymers formed by this additive process. Polymers can also be formed by bringing monomers together, removing water or alcohol through a condensation reaction, and forcing the monomers to link together. This is what happened to form nylon, and this is what happened here to create a new form of matter—rubber balls! In addition to these synthetic polymers, silk, cellulose, and rubber are naturally occurring polymers.

Go back to some of the first items shown to the students: the football helmet, the baby bottle, the CD, the nylons, and the Teflon pan. Encourage the students to think about the activities they just participated in as they try to answer the very first question you asked: What do all of these things have in common?

They were all created by a chemical change in which small pieces of matter, called monomers, were linked together to form polymers. These polymer reactions created new kinds of matter that have proven to be very useful.

Science in Personal and Social Perspectives

- You're tired of the color of your bedroom, and you want to change the color of your walls. Will your room undergo a physical or chemical change?
- Can you name any products created because of a polymerization reaction that have directly affected your life?
- There is much controversy over the use of Teflon bullets. Police unions bitterly oppose their use. Why do you think this product, formed from a polymerization reaction, is of serious concern to our society?
- Knowledge of chemical changes has led to the invention of many products that have greatly changed society. Can you think of any products that were created as the result of a chemical change?

Science and Technology

- A technological advancement for many parents is the disposable diaper. Describe the materials used to make a disposable diaper. How has this technological advancement created more problems for society? Suggest possible solutions.

Science as Inquiry

- Can you demonstrate the difference between a physical and a chemical change?

- Explain how a polymer can be created. How is this a unique type of chemical change?
- Can you name some monomers or polymers that are found in nature? How about some synthetic ones?

History and Nature of Science

- Do you think a cement finisher or a beautician needs to understand how a chemical change can occur? Why or why not?
- Are physical or chemical changes common in the type of work your parents do? Identify one of the changes, and explain where it occurs.
- Interview a female over age sixty. Ask her to describe what nylon stockings were like when she was twenty. How and why did they change?

4. EVALUATION: How will the students show what they have learned?

Upon completion of the activities the students will be able to:

- appreciate the need to think about a problem first, and then use clear, concise language to communicate the action taken on the problem;
- demonstrate the differences between physical and chemical changes;
- make predictions based on previous experiences;
- utilize the scientific method to solve a newly designed problem;
- explain how certain chemical reactions, such as polymer formation, can result in the creation of useful materials;
- explain what a football helmet, a compact disc, a Teflon pan, a baby bottle, and a pair of nylons have in common.

PHYSICAL SCIENCE

Identification of an Unknown

GRADE
5–8
DISCIPLINE
Physical Science

Concept to be invented

Main idea—Physical properties alone are not always sufficient characteristics to identify an unknown.

Concepts that are important to expansion

Indicators are used to bring about a physical or chemical change in an unknown. Common indicators are iodine, vinegar, and heat.

Materials needed

For exploration (for class of 24):
The following items make up the secret powders: 4 pounds of granulated sugar, two boxes of table salt, 4 pounds of baking soda, 4 pounds of cornstarch, 4 pounds of plaster of Paris.

The following items are necessary for all parts of the lesson: twenty plastic spoons, one box of toothpicks, ten eyedroppers, twenty small cups or containers.

Some optional materials are newspapers, paper towels, broom and dust pan, black construction paper, hand lenses or microscopes.

For expansion (for class of 24):
To perform indicator tests the following items are necessary: 1 quart of vinegar, one roll of aluminum foil, 1 ounce of tincture of iodine, crackers, potatoes, one bucket of water or a water source in room, birthday candles (one per student group), small lumps of clay (one per student group), wooden clothespins (one per student group).

➡ **Safety precautions:** Never taste any of the unknown substances unless given teacher permission. Goggles must be worn at all times! Wash hands between testing different unknowns and immediately after the lab is completed. Remove all combustible material from the area of the flame during the heat tests during expansion. Roll up sleeves and tie back hair when using an open flame.

1. EXPLORATION: Which process skills will be used?

Observing, manipulating materials, inferring, collecting and recording data, communicating

What will the students do?

Physical Properties of an Unknown

Start off the lesson by asking the students the following: Have you ever thought about some of the common substances we use in our homes? For instance, how many of you can name some common white powder substances we may use in our homes? (List these on the board. If the ones used as secret powders are not suggested, make suggestions that will help the students think about those possibilities.) What are they used for? How do we know that what it says on the container is really what is inside? The following activity will provide you with skills to help identify unknown substances.

Provide each student group five small cups numbered 1–5 and containing five different secret powders. The students will also receive five toothpicks to use as stirring sticks, some black construction paper to dump their powders on, and a hand lens. Ask the students to try to determine what the unknowns

PHYSICAL SCIENCE

are, based on their observations of physical characteristics. The following questions should serve as a guide to encourage the students to focus on physical properties: How are the powders alike? How are they different? Do they feel the same? Does any powder have an odor? Are they the same shade of white? Can you list three properties of each powder? Can you list more than three? Using the hand lens, can you discover anything new about the powders? Are all the powders really powders? Can you describe the particles that make up each powder? Do you think a powder can be identified by the shape of its particles? Describe which properties of the powders seem to be the same and which seem to be different. Which properties are helpful in describing a particular powder?

2. EXPLANATION/CONCEPT INVENTION: What is the main idea? How will the main idea be constructed?

Concept: Physical properties alone are not always sufficient characteristics to identify an unknown.

Ask the students to share answers to questions asked during the exploration phase. Refer back to the original list of common white powders from home. Ask the students to match up the unknowns to knowns based on physical characteristics they observed. Salt and sugar are made of cube-shaped particles, but salt is much more uniform and less broken. Cornstarch, baking soda, and plaster of Paris are similar in appearance, and it is hard to distinguish one from another simply on the basis of physical characteristics.

3. EXPANSION OF THE IDEA: Which process skills will be used?

Designing an experiment, observing, measuring, predicting, hypothesizing, recording data, evaluating, controlling variables, interpreting data, reducing experimental error

How will the idea be expanded?

Chemical Properties of an Unknown

Discussion before the activity: Ask students if they know why canaries were used in coal mines years ago, or what good it is to know the pH of pool water, or why a gas gauge in a car is useful. Once you obtain answers to these questions, ask what these three questions have in common. Work at getting to the idea that all of these are indicators of some sort: Canaries indicate the quality of the air, pH indicates the acidity or alkalinity of water, and a gas gauge indicates the amount of gas in the car.

Indicators can be used to conduct tests on the secret powders to assist in a more accurate determination of the unknown. These indicators may bring about a physical or chemical change in the secret powder. (Be sure the students already know the difference between a physical change—one in which a change of shape can occur, but the chemical composition of the original material is not

altered, such as freezing of water or shredding paper—and a chemical change—
a change in the composition of the original material in which molecules are lost
and cannot be put back into the material to return it to its original composition,
such as burning sugar or mixing vinegar and baking soda.)

During a discussion of the indicators, ask the students the following, to see
if they can determine how the indicators can be used in determining the identity of the secret powders: What do you think might happen when water (or iodine, vinegar, or heat added) is mixed with the secret powder? How might you
go about doing this without contaminating your secret powder sample? Why
is it important to avoid contamination?

Action: Observe the reactions of the five secret powders when acted on by
the water, iodine, vinegar, and heat. Reaffirm the notion of contamination at this
point. Have the students use separate eye droppers for the water, iodine, and
vinegar. Be sure they use different toothpicks and clean containers to mix the
unknown with the indicator. The students should record their results.

Water: What happens to each powder when you put a few drops of water
on it? Did each powder mix with the water? Did any of the powders disappear?
Did you put the same amount of powder in each cup? Is this important? What
will happen if you add twenty drops of water? Fifty? Eighty? Does additional
water affect the powders? Did any powders disappear? Where did they go? Did
the powder leave the cup?

As students work with the water, they will discover that sugar, baking soda,
and salt are soluble in water. By comparing the number of drops needed to dissolve these powders, some students may conclude that sugar is more soluble in
water than baking soda and that salt is the least soluble of the three. Both cornstarch and plaster of Paris are insoluble in water. Plaster of Paris will harden if
permitted to stand for a short period of time. After hardening, plaster of Paris
cannot be changed back into its original state. The concepts of solubility and
evaporation, as well as the differences among solution, suspension, and mixture, can be highlighted through this portion of the activity if necessary.

Iodine: Place small amounts of secret powders in five separate cups. Add a
few drops of iodine. Do all the powders react to iodine in the same way? How
can iodine be used to distinguish one powder from another? Take a cracker and
a piece of potato; how do these react with the iodine? Was this reaction similar
to any of the secret powders' reactions? What do the cracker and potato have
in common?

The cup containing cornstarch will show a striking blue-black color when
iodine is added. A deep blue or blue-black color on contact with iodine is the
standard test for the presence of starch. The starchier the food, the more obvious and deep the blue color will be.

Vinegar: Place small amounts of secret powders in five separate cups. Add
a few drops of vinegar. What happens when you put a few drops of vinegar
on each powder? Did any powder react more than others? Do you think that
powders that dissolved in water will also dissolve in vinegar? Which powder

do you think will take the least amount of vinegar to dissolve? the most? How can you find out? How can vinegar be used to distinguish baking soda from the other powders? If you place vinegar on an unknown substance and it bubbles, can you be sure that the substance is baking soda? Could it be another substance?

Baking powder fizzes actively when vinegar is added, while other powders fizz only slightly or not at all. Other powders can be tested with vinegar. A solution of powdered milk is curdled by vinegar.

Heat: Support a small candle in a lump of clay. This will supply sufficient heat to test the effects of heat on the powders. Fashion the aluminum foil into a small dish to be used to heat the secret powders. Use the clothespin as a handle for your aluminum dish when holding the dish over the flame. Be sure to make a separate dish for each powder.

Remove combustible litter from the area where the candle will be used. Roll up loose sleeves and tie back long hair while working with the burning candle. It is extremely important to use dry powder when performing this activity, to prevent spattering. Never use powders that have been mixed with any liquid. Place a small amount of powder in the dish and heat it.

Did any of the powders change when heated? Was an odor given off during heating? Do all the powders look the same after cooling? Compare them with samples of powders that were not heated. Were any new substances formed by heating?

When heated, baking soda and plaster of Paris seem to remain unchanged, while salt snaps and crackles. Starch turns brown and smells like burned toast. Sugar melts, bubbles, smokes, smells like caramel, turns brown, turns black, and finally hardens. The heat test, then, is a good way to detect sugar, since sugar is the only one of the secret powders to melt and turn shiny black when heated. The same reaction occurs to sugar even when it is mixed with any of the other powders.

After using the indicators, ask the students to share their results to help determine the identity of the unknown powders. Which powder turned black when iodine was added? Can you name the powder or powders that are soluble in water? Which liquid added to which powder caused bubbles? How can a hand lens help you to identify a powder? Is a hand lens helpful in identifying all substances?

Science in Personal and Social Perspectives

- Why is it important for you to wash your hands before you eat any food?
- Has this activity changed your mind on decisions you make about whether you like a certain food? What about decisions on whether you want a certain person as your friend; do you base that choice on looks alone?

Science and Technology

- Do you think an automobile manufacturer could be competitive if it based a car's performance ability on results from one test? Why or why not?

PHYSICAL SCIENCE

Encourage interested students to research the performance tests that cars undergo.

- Which properties of coal or oil make them a useful form of energy for our power plants: physical or chemical?

Science as Inquiry

- Students engage in manipulative skills during the activities.
- You are given one of five powders. When tested with vinegar, it bubbles. Can you identify the powder? Can you be sure of its identity?
- You are given one of the five powders. It dissolves in water. Can you identify the powder? Are additional tests needed? Can you eliminate any powders?

History and Nature of Science

- Can you think of any jobs in which avoiding contamination of materials is important?
- What care should be taken when mixing unknown substances with known substances? What good is knowing possible reactions? In what careers might this knowledge be necessary?

Cornstarch: The cornstarch can be used to demonstrate how dust explosions occur in coal mines or grain elevators. Cornstarch can also be used to explain how bread becomes toast.

Baking soda: The reaction of baking soda and vinegar results in the release of carbon dioxide gas. This gas can be used as a fire extinguisher. Most dry-powder extinguishers utilize baking soda; it can also be used to smother fires.

Plaster of Paris: This is nothing more than hydrated calcium sulfate. When mixed into a paste with water, it sets quickly and expands. It is because of this property that it is used as a fine casting material.

Salt: Salt can be used to lower the freezing point of water; examples are road salts and salt used in ice cream makers.

Sugar: Its numerous uses in foods are obvious, but also our knowledge of the chemical composition of sugar and the food calories it provides have led people to discover sweeteners that work like sugar but with fewer calories.

4. EVALUATION: How will the students show what they have learned?

Upon completing the activities the students will be able to:

- when given five unknown powders, demonstrate the steps necessary to identify them by using physical properties;
- demonstrate how water, iodine, vinegar, and heat can be used to identify an unknown powder;
- explain the advantages of an indicator test over reliance on merely physical properties to identify an unknown.

Using the Scientific Method to Solve Problems

Concepts to be invented

Main idea—Problems should be thought out before action is taken to solve them. The *scientific method* is a useful tool in problem solving.

Concepts that are important to expansion

Matter can be combined in many ways. It can become a mixture, a solution, a suspension, or a colloid.

Materials needed

1-liter 7-Up soft drink	2 pounds cornstarch
1 liter water	Efferdent tablets or Alka-Seltzer
400 ml alcohol (90 percent	tablets
or higher concentration)	plastic bins or buckets
1 gallon vinegar	paper towels for clean-up
1 pound flour	balloons

The teacher may also want to obtain any other clear liquids or unknown white powders the students decide to use in the experiments they design.

➡ **Safety precautions:** Goggles should be worn by teacher and students during all activities.

Teacher preparation

For clear liquid: Pour about 400 ml of alcohol as close to 100 percent pure as possible into a container. Typical rubbing alcohol is 70 percent; the water content will cause the Efferdent to dissolve slowly. Therefore, 98 percent rubbing alcohol, also available over the counter, will be more effective.

For white powder: Add 1 cup of cornstarch to a large container or plastic bin (old dishwashing containers work well). Slowly add water until a gooey consistency is reached. This material will pour or drip slowly but will not splatter when struck with a quick blow. This is a non-Newtonian fluid. Rather than a solution or mixture, it is called a *colloid:* The starch is suspended in the water.

1. EXPLORATION: Which process skills will be used?

Problem solving, communicating, inferring, designing an experiment, recording data, measuring, observing, defining operationally, synthesizing and analyzing information

What will the students do?

Exploring with Efferdent Tablets

Ask the students to imagine traveling through space. All of a sudden the spaceship crash-lands. Tell them, "You have no idea where you landed. You do find several objects on the planet. Your hope is that manipulating these objects will give you some clues about the place where you have landed." Show them a container with a clear liquid in it. This is one of the things found at the landing site. Other items found were several packages of Efferdent tablets, used on earth to clean dentures. Ask them what they think will happen if you drop two tablets into the clear liquid. Encourage a variety of predictions. Now drop the tablets into the liquid. Did you predict accurately? What do you think this liquid could be? In a few moments you will be given a chance to experiment to determine what it is and if there is a way to get the Efferdent to dissolve in it.

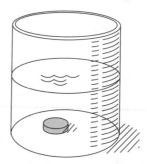

Explain to the students that in addition to the clear liquid and Efferdent tablets, they found some white powder and mixed it with water from their spaceship. Show them the mixture you created. Tell them, "You were trying to figure out what the powder was, especially because it didn't get all gooey like the paste you use at school. Some of you will need to design an experiment to determine what this white powder is."

Now assign the students on one side of the room to solve for one of the unknowns (what the clear liquid is—7-Up or vinegar, for example) and the students on the other side to solve for the other unknown (what the white powder is—flour or baking soda, for example). Encourage use of the scientific method to solve for the unknowns. Use the following guide questions to help plan student experiments: What do you think the problem is? How will you go about solving the problem? What materials do you think you will need? What will you do with those materials to help solve your problem? Do you think it will be important to keep accurate records of the information you collect while doing the experiment you designed?

2. EXPLANATION/CONCEPT INVENTION: What is the main idea? How will the main idea be constructed?

Concept: Problems should be thought out before action is taken to solve them. The *scientific method* is a useful tool in problem solving.

Ask the students to share with you the methods they used to go about solving their problem. Key questions to get them to share are: Do you think it is important to plan before you act? Why? What steps did you use in designing your experiment?

This methodical way of problem solving is called the *scientific method*. The steps to be followed are:

1. State the problem.
2. Generate predictions or hypotheses to help solve the problem.
3. Design an experiment to help solve the problem.
4. Create a list of materials needed to solve the problem.
5. Gather the materials and act on the experimental design.
6. Collect and record the data.
7. Draw conclusions and share them with peers.

3. EXPANSION OF THE IDEA: Which process skills will be used?

Problem solving, communicating, inferring, designing an experiment, recording data, measuring, observing, defining operationally, synthesizing and analyzing information

How will the idea be expanded?

Exploring with Cornstarch

Ask the students from the different sides of the room to communicate the results of their experiment to one another. The students on each side will need to communicate clearly to the students on the other side exactly what they did so that the students on the other side can replicate their experiment. Allow the students time to replicate experiments. Now ask them where they think they landed. The students should reason that since they found objects on earth that behaved in ways they weren't familiar with, perhaps they could still be on earth.

Once the students from each side of the room have discovered what the unknowns were, the students may want to play with the ooze formed with the cornstarch and water. Demonstrate to the students the balloon method for car-

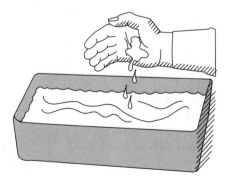

rying their ooze in space. Obtain a plastic 1- or 2-liter soda bottle. Remove the cap and cut off the top of the bottle about 2 to 3 inches from the neck. Invert this, place a balloon over the bottle opening, pour the ooze into the funnel, and milk it into the attached balloon. Knot the balloon. Stretch the balloon into various shapes. What happens? Why can you do this?

Science in Personal and Social Perspectives

- Do you think you can use the scientific method to help you solve personal problems you have?
- How would you go about explaining an important event that happened in your life to a friend? Will the story have the same impact if you leave out important details?
- Do you think it is as important to be able to communicate accurately your feelings about some issue as it is important to be able to give directions for performing a particular task?

Science and Technology

- How important do you think it is to have motor oil that is the right weight in your car's engine? Can these differences in the oil's weight be affected if dirt particles were dissolved in the oil? Will dirt particles dissolve in the oil, or will they create a colloid?
- Can solutions be created when the materials involved are at temperatures close to freezing? Do you think this knowledge will be important as we try to create space stations hundreds of miles from earth?

Science as Inquiry

- What are the differences among solutions, mixtures, suspensions, and colloids?
- What steps are involved in the scientific method?

History and Nature of Science

- If you were an auto mechanic, would knowledge of solutions be beneficial? What kinds of solutions does an auto mechanic work with?
- What other careers rely on knowledge of the differences among solutions, suspensions, colloids, and mixtures? Name three and state why.

4. EVALUATION: How will the students show what they have learned?

Upon completing the activities the students will be able to:

- take a given problem and design an experiment to solve it, using the steps in the scientific method;
- demonstrate examples of mixtures, solutions, suspensions, and colloids;
- upon looking at a diagram of a mixture, solution, suspension, or colloid, identify each combination of matter.

Heat Energy

Concept to be invented
Main idea—Adding heat energy to solids causes them to liquefy.

Concepts that are important to expansion
Removing heat energy from liquids causes them to solidify.

Materials needed

hot plate   aluminum foil
ten birthday candles   tablespoon
saucepan (double boiler)

➡ **Safety precautions:** Do not move too close to the hot plate. Do not touch the hot melted wax. Be sure to use a hot plate that has adjustable settings. Melt wax slowly. To avoid fires, melt in a double boiler.

1. **EXPLORATION:** Which process skills will be used?

    Classifying, observing, inferring, generalizing, communicating

    What will the students do?

Liquid Birthday   Allow the students to handle the birthday candles. Ask them to determine whether they are a liquid or a solid. Collect their responses. Once there is consensus as to their solid state, ask for suggestions on how the solid candle could

be turned into a liquid. During this discussion, if no student suggests it, suggest using the hot plate to melt the candles. Place the candles in the double boiler over the hot plate, set at a low setting, and melt them. Ask the students to make observations as heat energy is added to the candles.

2. EXPLANATION/CONCEPT INVENTION: What is the main idea? How will the main idea be constructed?

Concept: Adding energy to solids causes them to liquefy.

To help the students create this concept, ask the following questions: If you place your hand close to the pan (do not touch it!), does it sense that the pan is hot? What happens to the candles as the heat energy moves from the hot plate to the pan? Can you explain why this is happening? What is a common way in which birthday candles are melted? What other types of things in your home release heat energy? As the hot plate releases heat energy to the saucepan, it is transferred to the candles, causing them to melt. What can you do to change the candles back into solids?

3. EXPANSION OF THE IDEA: Which process skills will be used?

Inferring, questioning, observing, communicating

How will the idea be expanded?

Liquids to Solids   Ask the students to make predictions about what will happen to the candles once the double boiler is taken off the hot plate. Give each child a piece of aluminum foil and a drop of the liquid wax. Ask the students to make observations of their wax. Divide the class in half. Ask half to determine ways in which they can turn the liquid wax back to a solid in the shortest time possible, the other half to determine ways to keep their drops in the liquid state. In which case do you need to add heat energy? Where is heat energy removed?

Science in Personal and Social Perspectives

- Imagine you are riding in a car on a long trip through Florida in July. During the long ride you spend time coloring and drawing pictures. You leave your crayons on the car seat when you stop to eat lunch. What do you think you will find when you return to the car after lunch? Why?
- Where in your home would be a good place to store candles? Why?

Science and Technology

- Why do you think it is important to understand why heat energy can melt a solid? Describe how this concept is applied in manufacturing glass objects, such as vases and mirrors.
- The oil used in a car engine is in a liquid state, yet when cool, it is very thick. What do you think will happen to it as the car engine continues to run? Will this affect the design of an engine?

PHYSICAL SCIENCE

Science as Inquiry

- What does it take to change a solid object into a liquid state?
- Can objects change their state of matter without gaining or losing heat energy?

History and Nature of Science

- Aside from automobile engineers, are there other careers in which people must understand that the addition or subtraction of heat energy will change an object's state of matter?
- How do you think a hairdresser utilizes the concept identified in these activities? If you were having your hair done by a hairdresser, would you feel more comfortable if this person understood something about heat energy?

4. EVALUATION: How will the students show what they have learned?

Upon completing the activities the students will be able to:

- demonstrate how heat energy can be added to a rubber band without using fire or a hot plate,
- demonstrate how heat energy can be removed from an ice cube, draw a picture of it, and write three sentences describing how this is done.

Structure Strength

GRADE
5–8
DISCIPLINE
Physical
Science

Concept to be invented
Main idea—The strength of a structure depends on the arrangement of the materials used in construction.

Concepts that are important to expansion
A variety of materials can be used to create a structure. A triangular arrangement of materials provides a more stable structure than a square.

Materials needed

straws	toothpicks	toilet paper tubes
clay	popsicle sticks	paper towel tubes
glue	string	rolled sheets of newspaper
pins		

➡ **Safety precautions:** Use care in handling the pins to attach straws together. Do not stand on chairs when building tall structures; ask the teacher for help. Do not throw any of the building materials.

1. EXPLORATION: Which process skills will be used?

Observing, predicting, manipulating materials, hypothesizing, inferring

What will the students do?

*Simple
Construction*

Divide the class into five working groups. Provide one group with straws, another with toothpicks, another with popsicle sticks, the fourth with toilet paper or paper towel tubes, and the fifth with sheets of newspaper rolled slightly longer than the paper towel tubes but just about the same diameter. Allow each group access to clay, pins, glue, or string to attach the building materials together.

Ask the students to make observations about the materials provided. Ask them to make predictions about how the materials could be used. Encourage the students to think beyond the usual uses for the materials. Allow them to manipulate the materials and to put them together in as many ways as possible. Ask the students to draw pictures of the different creations. Ask them to identify which of their creations remained standing the longest.

2. EXPLANATION/CONCEPT INVENTION: What is the main idea? How will the main idea be constructed?

Concept: The strength of a structure depends on the arrangement of the materials used in construction. A variety of materials can be used to create a structure.

Key questions to ask to help identify these concepts are:

- What kinds of things did you create with these materials?
- Did anyone create a structure that remained standing?
- What did that structure look like?
- What kinds of materials did you use?
- How long did your structure remain standing?
- Why do you think one structure stood longer than another?
- Do you think you could use the same materials yet make your structure stronger? How do you think you could do that?

3. EXPANSION OF THE IDEA: Which process skills will be used?

Observing, predicting, manipulating materials, hypothesizing, inferring

How will the idea be expanded?

*Triangle
Construction*

Allow those students who originally created some sort of building to work on making it stronger using the same materials. Encourage students who did not originally create a building to do so, trying to create as strong a structure as possible. Encourage all of the students to share with one another the structures they created. Take the time to point out which structures were sturdier than others and why. Assist the students in realizing that structures in which materials like

PHYSICAL SCIENCE

the straws, toothpicks, popsicle sticks, or paper tubes are arranged in a triangular shape are stronger than those left as squares.

Science in Personal and Social Perspectives

- Take a field trip with an adult family member to the attic or basement of your house or that of a friend. What kinds of support systems are found in the house? What materials were used? In what arrangements are those support systems placed?
- Think of some common objects found around your house that you typically use once and throw away. Do you think you could use them to create a structure? How long do you think a structure would last if it was built out of the material you have in mind?

Science and Technology

- Can you name three famous buildings that are known for the uniqueness of their structure?
- Why do you think that certain areas in the United States have strict laws about the types of structures that can be built there?

Science as Inquiry

- Can you make a house out of a deck of cards? How is it possible? Why is it possible?

PHYSICAL SCIENCE

- Do you think you can support a 2-pound weight in a structure made out of old newspapers? How will you manipulate the newspapers to make this possible? Try it.

History and Nature of Science

- Choose one of the following occupations and explain how important knowledge of structural arrangement and strength is to that occupation: mechanical engineer, civil engineer, architect, contractor.
- Do you think a paper carrier or someone working in a fast-food restaurant would use the ideas you discovered through these activities in his or her work? How?

4. EVALUATION: How will the students show what they have learned?

Upon completing the activities the students will be able to:

- work in cooperative groups of four and use drinking straws and clay to build a bridge that spans across the classroom. The strength of the structure built will be tested using metal washers.
- view two toothpick structures and determine which of the two has the greater strength and be able to explain why (create them according to the accompanying picture).
- draw a picture of a structure that could survive in an area where strong winds occur often. Write a narrative explaining what the structure is and why it was so designed.

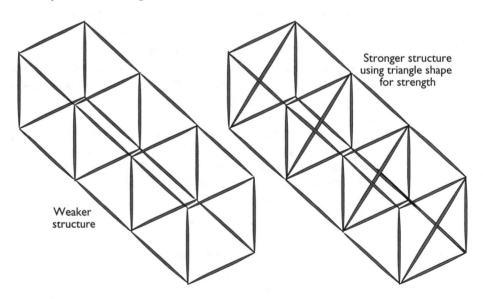

Stronger structure
using triangle shape
for strength

Weaker
structure

Mirrors and Reflection

GRADE
2–4
DISCIPLINE
Physical
Science

Concepts to be invented

Main idea—An object must be shiny, smooth, and reflect light to be called a *mirror*. Light bouncing off a shiny surface is called *reflection*.

Concepts that are important to expansion

Mirrors with a bowl-shaped surface are called *concave;* those that are rounded outward are called *convex*.

Materials needed

For each student group:

at least one 2-inch square mirror	black paper
one metal spoon	scrap paper
aluminum foil	pencils
clear plastic	Mylar paper

➡ **Safety precautions:** Be sure that rough edges on mirrors are filed or taped. Demonstrate to the students the proper handling of mirrors and Mylar paper: hold them by the edges to avoid fingerprints. Stress the importance of sharing.

PHYSICAL SCIENCE

1. EXPLORATION: Which process skills will be used?

Observing, predicting, making assumptions, brainstorming, recording data

What will the students do?

Mirrors and Reflectors

Allow the students to observe various materials and predict if they will be able to see themselves. Ask the students to brainstorm ideas of when and where they have seen mirrorlike materials such as the ones they are working with. Manipulate the materials to see if they can see images of objects in them. Ask the students to describe their observations. Encourage the students to think about the position of that object in the mirrorlike materials versus what it looks like when they look at it directly. Ask the students to predict what their name will look like after they write it on the paper, and look at it in each of the materials. Instruct the students to write their name and view it in the mirror and each of the other materials. Can you see it in all of the objects? Does it look the same as it is written? Why or why not? Can you write it so that you can read it correctly when you look in the mirror?

2. EXPLANATION/CONCEPT INVENTION: What is the main idea? How will the main idea be constructed?

Concept: An object must be shiny, smooth, and reflect light to be called a *mirror.* Light bouncing off a shiny surface is called *reflection.*

Assist the students in creating these concepts by doing the following: Refer back to the list brainstormed during the exploration phase. If terms like *smooth, reflect, light,* and *shiny* are not listed, add them to the list. Ask the students to help explain the meaning of those terms. Can an object be considered a mirror without light? Does the surface of the object need to be shiny? Can surfaces that are rough or bumpy give images as clear as shiny, smooth surfaces?

3. EXPANSION OF THE IDEA: Which process skills will be used?

Observing, predicting, manipulating materials, classifying, inferring

How will the idea be expanded?

What's a Mirror? Using the same materials from the exploration activity, ask the students to classify them into groups of things that are shiny, things that are smooth, and things that reflect light. Were you able to classify all of the materials? Could some of the materials fall into more than one group? Which materials were shiny and smooth and reflected light? Can you call these objects mirrors?

Can the spoon be considered a mirror? Describe the images seen inside the spoon. Where have you seen mirrors like these before? Have you ever been to a grocery store and seen these kinds of mirrors? What purpose do these mirrors serve? Mirrors with a bowl-shaped surface are called *concave;* those that are rounded outward are called *convex.*

Science in Personal and Social Perspectives

- Mirrors are used quite a bit in our everyday lives. When and where have you seen mirrors? What is their purpose?
- How often do you use a mirror? Describe the mirrors that you use.

Science and Technology

- How do different people use mirrors? What can be learned by looking in a mirror?
- How do scientists use mirrors? Have you ever used a microscope that uses mirrors? Did you ever see a telescope that makes use of mirrors?
- Can you list at least three machines that make use of mirrors? Draw a working diagram of one of them.

Science as Inquiry

- Why is a light source needed in order for an object to be considered a mirror?
- Which type of mirror would you use if you wanted objects to appear larger than they actually are: concave or convex?
- Why do words appear to be written backward when viewed in a mirror?

PHYSICAL SCIENCE

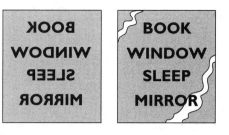

History and Nature of Science

- What careers are linked to the use of mirrors? Do your parents use mirrors in their work?
- Would some careers be more difficult without mirrors? Think of your school bus driver.
- The German chemist Justus von Liebig was instrumental in creating the mirror that we currently use. Trace the history of the mirror, describing the role von Liebig played.

4. EVALUATION: How will the students show what they have learned?

Upon completing the activities the students will be able to:

- write their names upside down and backward on a piece of paper to illustrate their knowledge of what a mirror can do,
- describe the three properties of a mirror or mirrorlike object and use them in sentences,
- classify materials into *shiny, smooth,* and *reflects light* categories.

Paper Chromatography

**GRADE
5–8
DISCIPLINE
Physical
Science**

Concept to be invented
Main idea—Paper chromatography is the separation of a mixture into its different parts through preferential absorption by a strip of filter paper.

Concepts that are important to expansion
Black ink is made up of many colors.

Materials needed
Per student group:
One rectangular basin at least the size of a shoebox, enough water to fill the container to about ½ inch, paper towels for spills, several sheets of filter paper (inexpensive coffee filters or white paper towels work just as well), three rubber

bands, paper clips, one set of colored felt-tip pens, five or more different brands of black water-soluble felt-tip pens (each labeled with the name of a different person), scissors to make multicolored coffee filter snow flakes during expansion phase.

➡ **Safety precautions:** Encourage the students to use caution when carrying the water-filled basins. Clean up all spills immediately. Do not poke one another with markers. Keep markers away from eyes.

1. EXPLORATION: Which process skills will be used?

Observing, predicting, questioning, making assumptions, brainstorming, recording data

What will the students do?

Moving Black Ink Dots

Set the stage for this lesson by explaining that for different holidays you like to decorate the outside of your house. You had a decoration in front of your house, and one Monday morning you woke to find it had been taken. Taped to your front door was this message: "I have your decorations. If you want them back you must bake me some cookies by Friday or else!" Ask the students to help you find out which friend took your decorations. Tell them that you don't have time to make cookies for all of your friends. You want to narrow it down so you have to make cookies for only that one friend.

Pick a number based on the number of different felt-tip black pens you were able to collect. Explain that you went to that number of friends' homes and innocently asked them if you could borrow their pen with the promise of returning it by Friday. Show the students the ransom letter and the pens. Ask them to help brainstorm ideas on how they could figure out who wrote the let-

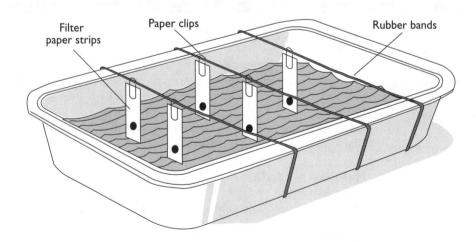

Filter paper strips

Paper clips

Rubber bands

ter, using their pens and the ransom letter. Record these suggestions. After as many suggestions as possible are offered, review the suggestions. Help the students decide which suggestions will really work. Show them the basin with water and the filter paper. Ask them if they think they can use these to help solve your problem. If they can't figure it out, demonstrate to them by cutting a word off the ransom letter and placing it in the water. Ask the students to observe what happens to the ink as the paper becomes wet. Allow the paper to dry. Let the students examine the various colors that bled from the letters. While that word is drying, encourage the students to think about how they could use the black pens to see the colors in the ink.

Show the students one efficient set-up to separate the ink: Stretch three rubber bands across the rectangular basin. Use the filter paper to make strips about 1 to 2 inches wide. Place a dot about the size of a dime about ¼ inch from one end of the strip. Hang the strips over the rubber bands so that about ⅛ inch of the paper end closest to the dot is sitting in the water. Use the paper clips to clip the top of the strip to the rubber band. Let these strips sit until the dot slowly moves up the strip. An illustration may help in set-up.

2. EXPLANATION/CONCEPT INVENTION: What is the main idea? How will the main idea be constructed?

Concept: Paper chromatography is the separation of a mixture into its different parts through preferential absorption by a strip of filter paper. Black ink is made up of many colors.

Ask the students to share their observations about the word from the ransom note when it was placed in the water. What happened to the black ink? When you placed the paper strips with the dots from each of the pens in the water, what happened to the dots? Did they appear to crawl up the paper? Did they all remain the same color? What colors did you observe? Why do you think that happened?

Assist the students in understanding that as the water moves up the filter paper, it takes some of the ink with it. Black ink is made up of many colors. The different colors separate out of the spot of ink. The heavy colors stay near the dot; the light ones move up the strip. Different pen manufacturers use different formulas for their black inks. This will cause a difference in the chromatogram (the colored strip of separated black ink) that is formed. When we compare the different colors in the strips to the different colors from the ransom word, we can determine whose pen wrote the note. According to your data, which friend took your decoration?

3. EXPANSION OF THE IDEA: Which process skills will be used?

Observing, predicting, manipulating materials, recording data, inferring

PHYSICAL SCIENCE

Moving Colored Ink Dots and Snowflakes

How will the idea be expanded?

Start this phase by reminding the students about their discoveries from the exploration phase. Ask them if they think colored markers will behave the same way as black felt-tip pens. Allow the students to make and record their predictions. Provide the students with one piece of filter paper. Ask them to make several strips and place a dot from a different colored pen on each. Hang these in the basin. Do the colors separate out? Do all of the colored pens create a chromatogram? Why or why not?

As an extra activity, give each child another piece or two of filter paper. Ask the students to use the colored and black pens to create a design in the middle of the circular filter paper (inexpensive coffee filters are great for this activity). Fold the filter paper so that the center is at the pointed end of a triangle. Ask them to make predictions about what will happen to that design after you dip the pointed tip into the basin of water. Record those predictions; then dip. Open the paper and allow it to dry. After it has dried and the various colors have bled throughout, encourage the students to refold the paper and cut out various designs. When they open it up, they will have created a snowflake.

Science in Personal and Social Perspectives

- Do you think you could trick your friends using paper chromatography? How?
- In what ways have you ever mixed different colors together to get a different one? When you did that, did you ever wish you could separate them again? Do you think you could separate them in all cases? Why or why not?

Science and Technology

- In industry, paper chromatography is not used as much as solid chromatography, in which solids are used to separate mixtures into their parts. In what industries do you think this type of chromatography is used?
- Do you think the paint industry has benefited from knowledge of chromatography? Why or why not?

Science as Inquiry

- Can all black inks be separated into their component parts?
- What do you call separating a mixture into its parts by using a solid or paper to pull out those parts?
- How would you design an experiment to determine who wrote you an anonymous letter?

History and Nature of Science

- Do you think the FBI makes use of paper chromatography? How do you think FBI agents might use it?
- Would a cake decorator need to understand chromatography? Why or why not?
- How do you think paint stores know how many drops of each color paint to put into a can of white to get it to match the color on the paint sample strip?

4. EVALUATION: How will the students show what they have learned?

Upon completing the activities the students will be able to:

- design an experiment to determine who wrote an anonymous letter,
- explain the concept of paper chromatography to a peer,
- explain why some ink colors merely bleed while others bleed and separate.

GRADE
5–8
DISCIPLINE
Physical
Science

Toys in Space

Concept to be invented
Main idea—Things that behave one way on earth will behave differently in space due to zero gravity conditions.

Concepts that are important to expansion
An astronaut will experience weightlessness while traveling through space. Toys can be used to explain a variety of scientific principles.

Materials needed
Toys in Space video (available from NASA, Lewis Research Center, Cleveland, OH) and toys used in video: wheel-o, yo-yo, paddle ball, ball and jacks, self-propelling car, magnetic marbles, spinning top, Play-Skool Flip Mouse, gyroscope.

➡ **Safety precautions:** Teacher and students should wear goggles to be sure that no eye injuries occur.

PHYSICAL SCIENCE

1. EXPLORATION: Which process skills will be used?

Observing, predicting, manipulating materials, hypothesizing, inferring

What will the students do?

Toy Behavior in Zero Gravity   Provide the students with the toys from the materials list. Ask them to play with the toys and make observations about how they function. After adequate time has been spent playing with the toys, ask the students to make predictions as to how they think the toys would function in zero gravity. Encourage the students to make as many predictions as possible.

2. EXPLANATION/CONCEPT INVENTION: What is the main idea? How will the main idea be constructed?

Concept: Things that behave one way on earth will behave differently in space due to zero gravity conditions.

To assist the students in developing this concept, ask them the following questions: How do the toys work in the classroom? Can you demonstrate them for me? How does gravity behave on earth? What does it do to objects on earth? If there were no gravity on earth, how do you think these toys would behave? Have you ever seen movies of astronauts as they travel in space? How do they look?

3. EXPANSION OF THE IDEA: Which process skills will be used?

Observing, predicting, manipulating materials, hypothesizing, inferring

How will the idea be expanded?

Toys and Newton   After much student discussion about their predictions, show the NASA videotape *Toys in Space.* Discuss afterward the discrepancies between the students' predictions and what really happened. An astronaut will experience weightlessness while traveling through space.

Toys can be used to explain a variety of scientific principles. If the students really show an interest in the behavior of the toys under zero gravity conditions, you may want to introduce the students to some of Newton's laws, which govern the behavior of these toys on earth. If you want the students to really understand them, then take care to plan additional activities that engage the students in science processes to enhance their understanding of these laws. The laws are as follows:

1. *Law of inertia*: Every body continues in its state of rest or of uniform motion in a straight line, except insofar as it is compelled by forces to change that state.
2. Force equals mass times acceleration.
3. The force exerted by an object A on another object B is equal in magnitude and opposite in direction to the force exerted by object B on object A.

PHYSICAL SCIENCE

Science in Personal and Social Perspectives

- How do you decide what kinds of toys to play with? Did you ever think that you could use them to help explain science concepts?
- Why do you think you or your friends choose particular toys to play with? Is it important that you play with the same things as your friends? Why or why not?
- Can you choose one of your toys and explain how or why it works? Ask your friends to help you decide which science concept is applied to explain why your toy works.

Science and Technology

- Toys are actually like models of particular systems. Why do you think it would be easier to make a toy model of some invention first? What advantage would that give to certain industries?

Science as Inquiry

- Is it possible for toys on earth to behave the same way when under zero gravity conditions? Is it possible for toys in space to behave the same way when on earth?
- Describe two different scientific concepts that can be explained using a bicycle.

History and Nature of Science

- Do you think a wheel-o could have been invented if the creator did not understand something about magnetism?
- If you were to become a toy designer, would knowledge of science concepts be useful in your career?

4. EVALUATION: How will the students show what they have learned?

Upon completing the activities the students will be able to:

- describe one scientific concept that can be explained with the use of a roller skate,
- create a toy using materials of their choice that can be fun and explain a scientific concept,
- design a toy that can still function in the absence of gravity and write a few sentences to describe it.

Simple Machines: The Lever

GRADE
5–8
DISCIPLINE
Physical
Science

Concept to be invented

Main idea—A lever is a rigid bar that pivots around a point that is used to move an object at a second point by a force applied at a third point. The pivot point is the *fulcrum*, the object moved is the *load*, and the place where the force is applied is the *effort*.

PHYSICAL SCIENCE

Concepts that are important to expansion

There are three kinds of levers. A *first-class lever* is a fulcrum between effort and load; the effort moves in the opposite direction of the load, as in a seesaw or a balance. A *second-class lever* is a load between the fulcrum and the effort; effort is applied in the same direction as the load should be moved, as in a wheelbarrow or a bottle opener. A *third-class lever* is an effort between the fulcrum and the load, which magnifies the distance moved by the load but reduces its force, as in a hammer, a catapult, or a fishing rod. Additional terms that may be introduced in this lesson are *resistance, friction, work,* and *machine.*

Materials needed

Per student group, for the discrepant event:

sandpaper	cooking oil
water	hand lotion
marbles or beads	paper towels or wipes

For exploration:

Goggles, one long piece of board (18" × ¼" works well), one fulcrum (proportional in size to the long board—for the 18-inch board, triangular pieces cut out of a 2 × 4 work well), any proportionally sized objects to be used as load, such as blocks of wood, small books, metal chunks, or cylinders.

For expansion:

goggles	one rubber band
two plastic spoons	peanuts

➡ **Safety precautions:** Remind students that safety goggles must be worn at all times. Discourage students from sending the load material flying across the room. Warn them of the potential danger to themselves and other students.

Discrepant event

Which process skills will be used?

Observing, hypothesizing, inferring, drawing conclusions

What will the teacher and students do?

Do not show the students what you are giving them. Ask them to put out their hands and place a small amount of one of the following in their hands: sandpaper, nothing, water, hand lotion, cooking oil, two or three marbles or beads. Tell them to be sure not to let anyone else see what they have. Once everyone has received one of the items, then ask the class to rub their hands together (all at the same time) with the objects still in their hands. After the students have had time to do this and to comment on what just happened, then ask questions such as: What did your hands feel like? Who had the hardest time rubbing his or her hands together? the easiest? Why? Did your hands change temperature? What do you think caused your hands to get hot/cold/no change? Why was it easy for some and not for others? What do you think is prohibiting you from sliding or rolling the objects in your hands? (Resistance.) What is this resistance to movement called? (Friction.) What did you need to do to overcome friction? (Exert some energy—effort.) By using effort to move your hands over a distance, you have done work. What do we call an object that will do the work for us? (A machine.)

1. EXPLORATION: Which process skills will be used?

Manipulating materials, collecting and recording data, communicating, observing, hypothesizing, predicting, inferring

What will the students do?

Lever Creations   *Instructions:* Use a long board and a triangular-shaped block in as many combinations as you think possible to move the weighted object (blocks, books, metal pieces). Draw the methods you tried. Discuss possible solutions with your peers. Try to record the results of those as well.

2. EXPLANATION/CONCEPT INVENTION: What is the main idea? How will the main idea be constructed?

Concept: A lever is a rigid bar that pivots around a point, which is used to move an object at a second point by a force applied at a third point.

Have the students draw the results of their manipulations on the board. With help from the class, identify on their drawings the pivot point, the object being moved, and the place where they had to apply a force to get the object to move. Solicit class ideas as to names for these points. Identify the pivot point as the *fulcrum,* the object moved as the *load,* and the place where force was applied as the *effort.*

Key questions to ask: Did these inventions make it easier for you to do work? What do we call objects that make our work easier? What has the machine we invented allowed us to do? What do you think we call it? Why? Once the concept *lever* has been invented, ask the students if they can see any differences in the placement of the three points on any of their diagrams. If necessary, supply diagrams that show different placements of the points. Key questions: Is there any advantage to changing the position of the three points? What happens to the direction of the effort and load in each of the diagrams? Can you see some practical uses for the different positions of the points? As you go through the different arrangements of the points, identify the three classes of levers: A *first-class lever* is a fulcrum between effort and load; the effort moves in the opposite direction of the load, as in a seesaw or a balance. A *second-class lever* is a load between the fulcrum and the effort; effort is applied in the same direction as the load should be moved, as in a wheelbarrow or a bottle opener. A *third-class lever* is an effort between the fulcrum and the load, which magnifies the distance moved by the load but reduces its force, as in a hammer, a catapult, or a fishing rod.

PHYSICAL SCIENCE

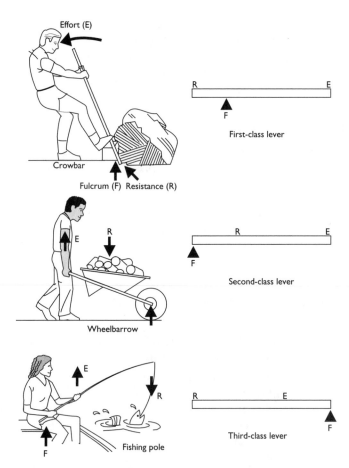

3. EXPANSION OF THE IDEA: Which process skills will be used?

Hypothesizing, inferring, manipulating materials, observing, communicating, collecting and recording data, making assumptions, predicting, formulating models

How will the idea be expanded?

Spoons and Nuts   *Instructions:* Given two plastic spoons, a rubber band, and some peanuts, design and demonstrate a first-, second-, and third-class lever. Share your inventions with the class.

Home extension: Which process skills will be used?

Inferring, manipulating materials, making assumptions, formulating models, observing, analyzing, classifying

What will the students do?

Lever Scavenger Hunt

Have the students ask an adult to go with them on a lever scavenger hunt. Make a list of all of the places where levers are being used in some form or another. How many of these are combination levers? How many are compound levers of the first, second, or third class? Bring these lists back to school to share with the class.

Science in Personal and Social Perspectives

- Where in your home did you find a lever being used? Did any of these places surprise you? Were any of these uses a case where two of the lever types were used in combination? (Nail clippers, manual typewriter, piano.) Did you find any compound levers? (Scissors, pliers, nutcracker, tweezers.)
- When you need to cut a piece of paper, why is it easier to use scissors instead of a knife? What advantage does using a pair of scissors have over using a knife for cutting?
- Which simple machine makes it possible for people to play a piano?

Science and Technology

- Why would it be difficult for you to wear your ice skates in the house but not your roller skates? How have industries used this information to overcome friction?
- How do you think the invention of the parking meter has affected your city? How about cities like Chicago or New York?

Science as Inquiry

- Students will be able to explain the function of the fulcrum, load, and effort; various combinations of these points can create a first-, second-, or third-class lever. They will be able to explain how machines help us to do work and to overcome friction.
- This activity lays the foundation for new concepts to be identified in new lessons, such as the relationship between effort and work, mechanical advantage, other types of simple machines, and so on.

History and Nature of Science

- Archimedes of Syracuse was perhaps the greatest of the Greek mathematicians and scientists. He lived from 287 to 212 B.C. He is credited with inventing the catapult, which the Greeks used during the Second Punic War against the Roman army. It is said that Archimedes was slain during this war while he was studying mathematical figures, which he habitually drew in the dust. What do you think he meant when he said, "Give me a fulcrum on which to rest, and I will move the earth"?
- Who needs to know about levers? Which careers rely on the use and/or knowledge of levers? (Manufacturers of playground equipment, laborers, dock workers, piano makers, typewriter manufacturers, parking meter repair persons.)

4. EVALUATION: How will the students show what they have learned?

Upon completing the activities the students will be able to:

- classify the following items as a first-, second-, or third-class lever: hammer, nutcracker, seesaw, wheelbarrow, balance, bottle opener, fishing rod;
- identify the fulcrum, the effort, and the load on each item, when given a hammer, wheelbarrow, and nail extractor;
- predict the direction of the load when effort is applied with each of the following: fishing rod, balance, bottle opener.

Earth and Space Science Lessons

Lesson Name	Content Standards	Grade Level	Activities
Astronomy			
The Solar System and the Universe	Objects in the Sky	K–3	Rhythm Activity • Postcard Writing
The Expanding Universe	Earth in the Solar System	5–8	Expanding Balloon/Universe • Build a Solar System Salad
Constellations	Earth in the Solar System	5–8	Connect the Stars • Evening Field Trip • Create a Constellation
Geology			
Earth Layers	Properties of Earth Materials	K–4	Clay Earth Layers • Clay Continents
Fossils	Properties of Earth Materials	2–4	Fossil Observations • Plaster Molds and Casts
Soil Formation	Structure of the Earth System	5–8	Soil Separation and Rock Crushing • Soil Components
Rock Types	Structure of the Earth System	5–8	Rock Categorization • Rock Collection Field Trip
Cooling Crystals	Structure of the Earth System	5–8	PDB Crystal Formation • Rock Type versus Crystal Formation
Weathering	Structure of the Earth System	5–8	Freezing Bottle • Weathering Field Trip • Rock Identification • Chemical Weathering • Mechanical Weathering
Crustal Plate Movement	Earth's History	5–8	Moving Plates • Mapping Volcanoes and Earthquakes • Oatmeal and Cracker Plate Tectonics
Meteorology			
Rain Formation	Objects in the Sky	K–4	Rain in a Jar • Water Drop Attraction
Dew Formation	Objects in the Sky	K–4	Soda Bottle Condensation • Thermometer Reading and Dew Point
Radiant Energy	Objects in the Sky	2–4	Temperature and Colored Surfaces • Temperature: Sun versus Shade • Magnifiers: Capture the Sun • Sun Tea
Weather Forecasting	Structure of the Earth System	5–8	Weather Log Creation • Weather Map Symbols • Weather Data Collection
Weather Predictions	Structure of the Earth System	5–8	Weather Map Information • Recording Weather Data and Predicting Weather
Air Mass Movement	Structure of the Earth System	5–8	Coriolis Effect: Globe • Coriolis Effect: Top • Air Movement: Dry Ice • Oil and Water Fronts • Create a Rain Gauge • Air Masses and Parachutes
Air Pressure	Structure of the Earth System	5–8	Balloon Balance • Paper Blowing • Newspaper Strength
Solar Heating	Earth in the Solar System	5–8	Temperature versus Surface Color • Optimum Thermometer Placement
Air Movement and Surface Temperature	Structure of the Earth System	5–8	Convection Current and Surface Temperature in an Observation Box • Paper Bag Balance
Uneven Heating of the Earth	Structure of the Earth System	5–8	Tower of Water • Aneroid Barometer • Uneven Heating and Air Pressure • Air Pressure versus Water Temperature • Air Temperature versus Movement of Air • Heat Transfer on a Wire • Heat Movement Through Air • Heat Transfer Through Metal • Movement of Smoke over Hot and Cold Surfaces: Clouds • Movement of Smoke over Hot and Cold Surfaces: Wind Patterns

EARTH SCIENCE

The Solar System and the Universe

**GRADE
K–3
DISCIPLINE
Earth
Science**

Concept to be invented
Main idea—The earth is part of the solar system.

Concepts that are important to expansion
Planets differ from one another.

Materials needed
For exploration:
Books on planets, such as Jeff Davidson, *Voyage to the Planets* (Worthington, OH: Willowisp Press, 1990) and Joanna Cole, *The Magic School Bus Lost in Space* (New York: Scholastic, 1988).
For expansion:
Postcard outline, poster paper, paints, and markers.

➧ **Safety precautions:** The students should be reminded to sit and listen without poking or hitting one another. During the expansion activity, they should be sure to clean up any paint spills immediately, and they should not put markers or paint brushes in their mouths.

1. **EXPLORATION:** Which process skills will be used?

   Observing, questioning

   What will the students do?

Rhythm Activity
   • You should read such books as *Voyage to the Planets* or *The Magic School Bus Lost in Space* to the students. Ask them recall questions as you are sharing the book with them.
   • Teach the students the following chant, clapping the beat. Allow them to fill in the planet of their choice once they get the rhythm down:

   A–B–CDE, How many planets can there be?
   F–G–HIJ, There are nine we know of today.
   K–L–MNO, To which one would you like to go?
   P–Q–RST, I'd like to visit Mercury.
   U–V–WXY, I've been watching it in the sky.
   Z–Z–ZZZ, Know anyone who'll come with me?

2. **EXPLANATION/CONCEPT INVENTION:** What is the main idea? How will the main idea be constructed?

   Concept: The earth is part of the solar system.

It has been found through observations of the nighttime sky and satellite observations that the earth is just one of nine planets that move around the sun. Each of the planets has unique characteristics because of its distance from the sun. Questions students ask during the reading of the book will also assist in developing the concepts.

3. EXPANSION OF THE IDEA: Which process skills will be used?

Inferring, observing, questioning

How will the idea be expanded?

Postcard Writing   Once the students know the chant and sing it with all nine planet names, ask them to choose one of the nine as a place they'd like to go on vacation. Break the students into nine planet vacation groups. Ask them to plan a drawing of their planet as close to reality as possible, and then work as a cooperative group to create one drawing of that planet. Draw a sun on your mural paper. Ask the different groups to come up to the mural and place their planet in its appropriate order from the sun.

Give each student a copy of the postcard outline. Ask them to write postcards to family members, describing their trips to the planets they drew. Teach them how to address a postcard. Ask them to design an appropriate stamp for

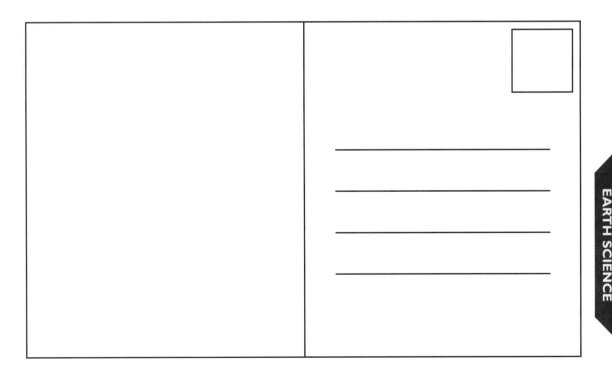

the planet they visited. When all of these are completed, tape the postcards near the planet of origin.

Questions that help invent additional concepts

- Is the earth all alone in space? (No, there are eight other planets.)
- What else is found in the earth's neighborhood? (Planets, moons, dust, meteorites.)
- How do we know there are other planets in our neighborhood? Has anyone ever seen them? (We can see them in the sky; they look like stars. We have satellites that have gone close to them and sent back pictures to earth.)
- What is unique about your planet? (Answers will vary.)
- How close to the sun is your planet? (Answers will vary.)
- Are all the planets the same size? (No. Go into detail about their planets.)
- Do you think you could live on your vacation planet as easily as you can on earth? Why or why not?

Students will apply knowledge they learned about their planets to answer these questions.

Science in Personal and Social Perspectives

- Do you think if the earth were as close to the sun as Mercury you could still live on it? Why or why not?
- If someone told you he or she could take you on a plane ride to the planet Mars, would you believe it? Why or why not?

Science and Technology

- Do you think a person can invent a way so that it will be possible to live on any of the other planets? How do you think we can do this?

Science as Inquiry

- Students will be able to name the nine planets, list their order from the sun, and discuss one characteristic of each after completing and participating in the above activities.

History and Nature of Science

- Do you think that a person responsible for monitoring the air quality of the planet Earth can learn anything from understanding what the atmosphere is like on the planet Jupiter?
- How important is it that space scientists know the positions of the planets before launching satellites or rockets into space? What kinds of skills do space scientists need in order to do their jobs?

4. EVALUATION: How will the students show what they have learned?

Upon completing the activities the students will be able to:

- answer the questions included in the expansion phase of this lesson, as well as the new outcomes questions.

- draw lines from the picture of a planet to a group of words that briefly describe the planet. The picture question on the next page is an example of the kind of question that could be made for this assessment:

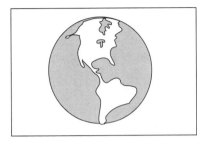

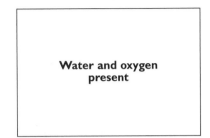

Water and oxygen present

- create a planet mobile (this can be done as a home extension) out of the following materials: wire coat hanger, paint, tape and/or glue, papier maché or balls of different sizes, string, and cardboard, paper, or newspaper.

The Expanding Universe

**GRADE
5–8
DISCIPLINE
Earth
Science**

Concepts to be invented
Main idea—Our universe appears to be expanding. Distances between parts of the universe are vast.

Concepts that are important to expansion
Planets orbit about the sun. The planets are very small and very far away from the sun.

Materials needed
For exploration:
Round balloons (one for each student), wide-tip felt markers (black and red).

For expansion:

one fresh pea	one dried pea	one small walnut
one larger walnut	one bean	one smaller bean
one 8-inch head of cabbage	one 9-inch head of cabbage	one grapefruit
one big orange		a bicycle
the school track		

➥ **Safety precautions:** Use extreme caution while blowing up the balloon. Do not allow children to chew on the balloon.

1. **EXPLORATION:** Which process skills will be used?

Observing, predicting, hypothesizing, inferring

EARTH SCIENCE

*Expanding
Balloon/Universe*

What will the students do?

Instruct each student to

1. inflate a round balloon partially, pinching the neck closed with thumb and forefinger,
2. make specks with a wide-tip felt marker all over the surface of the balloon, noting their positions and letting them dry,
3. blow more air into the balloon and look at it, again noting the position of the specks.

2. EXPLANATION/CONCEPT INVENTION: What is the main idea? How will the main idea be constructed?

Concept: Our universe appears to be expanding. Distances between parts of the universe are vast.

Help the students invent the concept by asking them such questions as:

- What has happened to the distance between the specks? (It has increased, expanded.)
- What do you think will happen to the specks if you continue to add air to the balloon? (They will continue to move away from one another.)
- Imagine that the balloon is space and one of the specks is the neighborhood the earth is found in. Put a red mark on one of the specks to represent the earth's neighborhood. Blow up the balloon some more while watching the red speck. What do you think you could say about space if you were on this red speck? (The earth is very far from other parts of the universe.)

3. EXPANSION OF THE IDEA: Which process skills will be used?

Observing, communicating, formulating models, recording data

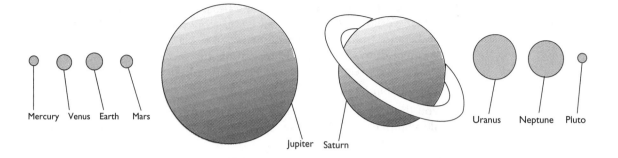

Mercury Venus Earth Mars

Jupiter Saturn

Uranus Neptune Pluto

How will the idea be expanded?

Build a Solar System Salad

Have students observe the fixings for a solar system salad (see materials needed). They should decide which of the items correspond to the nine planets and the earth's moon. The students should check with one another to come to some consensus. Then they will discuss decisions with the teacher.

After a discussion on relative sizes, take the salad items out to the school track. While bicycling around the track, drop off the planets to show their relative distance from each other. Allow all the students to participate. Some may be lap counters; others should do the riding. To make it really effective, each student should ride the bicycle. As the children grow tired, the vast distances between the planets will be apparent to them. Each lap represents 211,265 miles in space.

Mercury: 2/5 lap

Venus: 3/4 lap

Earth: 1 lap

Mars: 1½ laps

Jupiter: 5½ laps

Saturn: 9½ laps

Uranus: 19½ laps

Neptune: 30 laps

Pluto: 39–2/5 laps

Questions that help invent additional concepts:

- Which of the salad fixings did you have a hard time assigning a planet to?
- Did you find it necessary to look in some reference books to help you decide which item represents which planet?

Mercury: Fresh pea

Venus: Walnut

Earth: Larger walnut

Moon: Dried pea

Mars: Bean

Jupiter: 9-inch cabbage

Saturn: 8-inch cabbage

Uranus: Grapefruit

Neptune: Big orange

Pluto: Small bean

- How did your legs feel after you dropped off the solar system salad fixings?

- Imagine you are out in space dropping those items off at the different planets. What would be the total distance you would have traveled? (*Hint:* What is the distance from the sun to Pluto?)
- If the center of the football field represents the sun, what can you say about the planets with respect to the sun? What do the planets do?

Science in Personal and Social Perspectives

- Do you think it will ever be possible for you to travel to the other planets? Would you like to do this? Why or why not? What do you think you would need to pack for your trip?
- Would you purchase a ticket today to spend some time in a space station? Do you think you will live long enough to use the ticket?

Science and Technology

- Do you think space stations will solve the problems of pollution and over-population on earth?
- Do you think the vastness of space will allow us to ship our garbage out into space and never be affected by it on earth? How do you think this will be possible?

Science as Inquiry

- The students will be able to explain the concept of the expanding universe and discuss the implications that has for life as we presently know it on earth.
- Why is it possible to view planets in the nighttime sky? Do all of the planets always maintain the same orbital paths?

History and Nature of Science

- If it was your job to create a satellite that would move through outer space, sending back to earth information about other planets, what kinds of knowledge do you think you would need to have? What would be the qualifications for your job? Pretend you need to employ someone to fill such a job. Write a job description and give it a title. Do the race or sex of the person applying matter?

4. EVALUATION: How will the students show what they have learned?

Upon completing the activities the students will be able to:

- complete the activities above.
- write a few sentences after they participate in the bicycle activity about how they felt when they finished and what they think about the distances between the planets. Ask the students to share their feelings with one another. How tired they became and how much they want to share with others what they did will provide an effective measure of success.
- when provided with ten different kinds of vegetables for a solar salad, use these new items to arrange the members of the solar system. Also ask them

to decide how far they would have to be from one another if 1 inch equals 1 million miles.

Constellations

Concept to be invented
Main idea—Constellations are groups of stars.

Concepts that are important to expansion
Big Dipper, Little Dipper, Polaris or North Star, Cassiopeia, Perseus, and Pleiades found in Taurus.

Materials needed
For exploration:
construction paper   overhead projector
one pen or pencil per student   four or five flashlights

➡ **Safety precautions:** Remind students to be careful not to poke themselves or others with the pen or pencil.

1. EXPLORATION: Which process skills will be used?

Observing, predicting, hypothesizing, inferring

What will the students do?

Connect the Stars The students will view a dot-to-dot pattern presented to them and predict what the pattern will look like once the dots are connected. This pattern is made on the chalkboard by using an overhead projector and black construction paper with holes punched in it for dots as the transparency. Place several different patterns on the overhead. Have the students take turns connecting the dots on the chalkboard.

2. EXPLANATION/CONCEPT INVENTION: What is the main idea? How will the main idea be constructed?

Concept: Constellations are groups of stars found in the sky. Ask the students questions such as the following to help invent this concept: What do you think these patterns represent? Do you recall seeing these same patterns anywhere? Review each of the patterns again and ask once again if anyone recalls seeing these patterns anywhere.

Patterns represent star constellations. Star constellations are made up of a group of stars and are given a name traditionally based on the pattern they

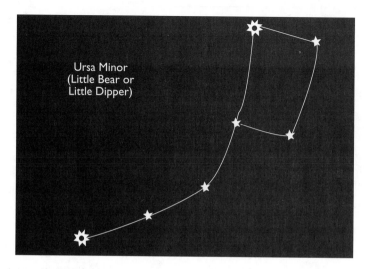

Ursa Minor
(Little Bear or
Little Dipper)

make in the sky. These constellations were named by people in the past and usually have a story or legend attached to them.

Once again, project the patterns up on the board, again connecting the dots. This time go through the names of the constellations presented, and give a brief history of how they got their names. Some easy constellations to showcase are the Big Dipper, the Little Dipper, Cassiopeia, Perseus, and Pleiades found in Taurus.

Identify the North Star—Polaris—for the students. Explain how all the other constellations in the Northern Hemisphere appear to revolve around this star. Thus, at different times of the year only certain constellations are visible in the nighttime sky in the Northern Hemisphere.

3. EXPANSION OF THE IDEA: Which process skills will be used?

Observing, communicating, formulating models, recording data

How will the idea be expanded?

Evening Field Trip
- Take the students on an evening field trip to an area where electric lights are minimal. Be sure you pick a clear night. Ask everyone to bring a blanket and lie on the grass. Try to identify as many constellations as possible.

Create a Constellation
- Ask the students to create a constellation of their own and name it, much as the ancient Greeks and Indians did as they observed stars in the nighttime sky. Have them write reports about how their constellations got their names. Share the reports orally with the class.

Science in Personal and Social Perspectives

- How can star constellations help you if you get lost at night?
- How can you develop watching stars into a hobby?

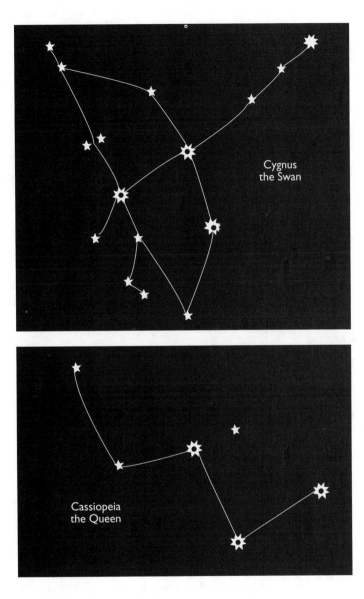

Cygnus
the Swan

Cassiopeia
the Queen

Science and Technology

- What kind of equipment can you use to improve your view of the stars?
- How has astronomy equipment been perfected since the time of Galileo's first telescope?

Science as Inquiry

- How can we use our knowledge of constellations to find a particular star in the sky?

- Why do all stars in the Northern Hemisphere appear to revolve around Polaris? Is this our closest star?

History and Nature of Science

- How are constellations used by astronomers who study other phenomena in the sky?
- Is there any difference between an astronomer and an astrologer? Do they both use their knowledge of constellations in some form? How?

4. EVALUATION: How will the students show what they have learned?

Upon completing the activities the students will be able to:

- identify Polaris, the North Star,
- identify the Big and Little Dippers in the northern sky,
- explain how at least two different constellations got their names,
- identify the star closest to earth.

Earth Layers

GRADE
K–4
DISCIPLINE
Earth
Science

Concept to be invented
Main idea—The planet earth is made up of three layers: the *core, mantle,* and *crust.*

Concepts that are important to expansion
Large land masses found on the crust of the earth are called *continents.* Large bodies of water on the crust are called *oceans.*

Materials needed
For exploration (one per student):
2-inch diameter ball of red, yellow, and gray clay; plastic knife; white construction paper; three crayons of red, yellow, and gray.

For exploration (for entire class):
Green and blue clay, green crayon, globe of the earth, tennis ball, soccer ball. Maps of ocean floors are useful but optional.

➡ **Safety precautions:** Remind students to be careful not to poke themselves or others with the plastic knife. Be sure to wash hands after using the clay. Remind them not to eat the clay.

1. EXPLORATION: Which process skills will be used?

Observing, manipulating materials, predicting

What will the students do?

Clay Earth Layers   Guide the students through this portion of the lesson by first asking them to pick up the red clay and work it into a ball. Ask them to then flatten out the yellow clay and wrap it around the red ball of clay. Finally ask them to flatten out the gray clay and then wrap it around the yellow-covered ball of clay. Ask the students to use their plastic knives carefully to cut the clay ball in half. Ask them to draw on their construction paper what the sliced-open clay ball looks like.

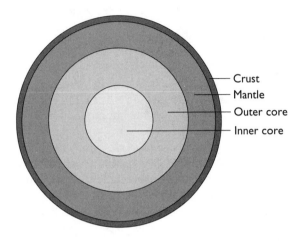

2. EXPLANATION/CONCEPT INVENTION: What is the main idea? How will the main idea be constructed?

Concept: The planet earth is made up of three layers: the *core, mantle,* and *crust.*

Help the students invent the concept by asking them such questions as: What do you think this ball of clay with the different colored layers represents? Accept as many suggestions as possible and provide appropriate responses, all the while steering the students toward thinking about the earth. If this suggestion is never given, then tell the students you'd like them to think of the clay ball as a representation of the earth and its layers. Since the students are most familiar with things found on the surface of the earth, ask them to give you suggestions of things they find there. If possible, draw pictures of their suggestions or write the names on the board. Ask if anyone has an idea for another name to call the earth's surface. You may make an analogy to a pie that has a different material on the inside than outside. What do you call the outer covering of the pie? *Crust*—this same name is given to the outer surface of the earth. Ask the students to label the gray layer on their diagram the *crust.*

Ask the students what they think the yellow layer may be like on the earth and if they have any ideas as to its name. The yellow clay represents the mantle. This layer of the earth is in a slightly liquid form. It is under enough pressure to heat the rock and melt it. Ask the students to label the yellow layer on their diagram the *mantle*.

Continue with questions to get the children to think about what the very middle of something is usually referred to. Get the students to think about what they call the center of an apple. The *core* is represented by the red ball. Because the core is under such great pressure it is very hot, but also in a solid state. Ask the students to label the red layer on their diagram the *core*.

3. EXPANSION OF THE IDEA: Which process skills will be used?

Manipulating materials, observing, hypothesizing, inferring

How will the idea be expanded?

Clay Continents   Hold up the tennis ball. Ask the students how they think the tennis ball is like the earth. Encourage them to use the terms *crust, mantle,* and *core.* Hold up a soccer ball. Ask the students how the soccer ball is like the earth. Hold up the globe. Tell them that this represents what the earth would look like if they were up in the sky looking down. Ask the students to observe the globe carefully. After they look at the globe, ask the students if they think the soccer ball or the tennis ball is more like the earth's surface. Engage the students in a conversation about how the soccer ball is not one solid piece but many pieces sewn together. The crust of the earth does not look like one solid piece but like many pieces separated by water. The pieces appear to fit together. Ask the students for suggested names for the land masses and the bodies of water. If none are given, tell the students that the land masses are called *continents* and the bodies of water are called *oceans.* If maps of the ocean floor are available, share them with the students. Be sure to point out that the crust still exists below the ocean water.

Provide the students with some green and blue clay. Ask them to put their two halves of clay back together again, gently sealing the gray clay so that they have one ball of clay again. Ask the students to use the green clay to place some land masses or continents on their earth. Ask them to add blue clay between the continents to represent the oceans. Then ask them to use their green and blue crayons to draw the continents and oceans on their drawings and to label them.

Science in Personal and Social Perspectives

- It has been found that the movement of the semiliquid material in the mantle of the earth causes the crust to move. When the crust moves, earthquakes occur. Have earthquakes ever occurred where you live? What should be done to protect people during earthquakes?
- What continent do you live on?

Science and Technology

- How has knowledge about continent movement changed the way we construct buildings?
- Can earthquakes be detected? How?

EARTH SCIENCE

- Do you think if technology could come up with a way to drain the oceans that would be better for life on earth? Why or why not?

Science as Inquiry

- Which layer of the earth is very hot yet still in a solid state?
- The land masses on the surface of the earth appear to fit together, yet many are far apart. Do you think they were once together? If so, why?
- Is there crust under the oceans? How do we know this?

History and Nature of Science

- A seismologist would need to understand that the earth is in layers. Why do you think this is true? What do you think a seismologist does?
- Should oceanographers be concerned about the earth's layers?
- Many oil companies get their oil out of the North Sea. Do you think these companies used their knowledge of the earth's layers to find their drilling sites? Why or why not?

4. EVALUATION: How will the students show what they have learned?

Upon completing the activities the students will be able to:

- draw a diagram of a cross-section of the earth and label the continents, oceans, crust, mantle, and core;
- identify from a diagram the different layers of the earth;
- explain how the earth can be compared to a soccer ball;
- point out continents and oceans on a globe.

Fossils

GRADE
2–4
DISCIPLINE
Earth
Science

Concept to be invented
Main idea—A record of an ancient animal or plant found in sedimentary rocks is called a *fossil*.

Concepts that are important to expansion
Fossils provide clues to ancient environments. Evidence that humans were present during primitive times is called an *artifact*. A hollow space left in sedimentary rock when a plant or animal body decays is called a *mold*. When sediments fill the hollow space and harden, the hardened sediments formed in the shape of the plant or animal are called *casts*.

Materials needed
For exploration:
A variety of fossil samples for class observations, construction paper, and crayons or markers.

For expansion:

Seashells (one or two per student)	plaster of Paris
leaves or plants	water
one aluminum pie tin per student	one plastic spoon per student
petroleum jelly	paper towels
two paper cups per student	old newspapers

Note: The plastic samples of seashells, readily available through science equipment suppliers, may be preferred over the actual seashells. Young children will find these easier to work with.

➡ **Safety precautions:** Students should be reminded not to eat the plaster. Take care to avoid water spills. Should they occur, wipe them up immediately.

1. EXPLORATION: Which process skills will be used?

Observing, brainstorming, predicting, hypothesizing, communicating

What will the students do?

Fossil Observations

Pass the fossil samples around to the students without telling them what they are looking at. Ask the students to make careful observations about these unknown objects and to share their observations with the class. Encourage the students to think about what these things could possibly be. Is it a plant or an animal? Is it an image of a plant or an animal, or a piece of the real thing? Do you think it is still on the earth? How do you think this could have been formed? Allow the students sufficient time to brainstorm with one another ideas on their possible origins. Ask the students to draw the unknown object and to color it the way they think it would look if the actual object (plant or animal) were right in front of them. If the students are capable of writing sentences, ask them to write three or four sentences below their pictures describing how they think the image in the rock was formed.

2. EXPLANATION/CONCEPT INVENTION: What is the main idea? How will the main idea be constructed?

Concept: A record of an ancient animal or plant found in sedimentary rock is called a *fossil.*

Help the students invent the concept by asking them to share with the class the drawings they created. Some questions to ask the students to help invent the concept are:

- Why did you choose those colors for your drawing?
- Depending on the unknown you observed, was it easy or difficult for you to decide what this would look like if it were right in front of you? Why?
- How do you think this was formed?
- Will you please share with us your ideas?

Through this line of questioning the process of fossilization can be brought out. When an animal or plant dies, it is covered with mud, rocks, sand, and so on. Pressure is applied over many years, so the layers turn to stone, leaving an imprint of the plant or animal. The records of ancient animals and plants found in sedimentary rocks are called *fossils.* Additional source books or films on fossils may be shared with the class at this time. Also share examples of local fossils.

3. EXPANSION OF THE IDEA: Which process skills will be used?

Observing, manipulating materials, predicting

How will the idea be expanded?

Plaster Molds and Casts

Ask the students to bring in seashells or leaves to use in making an image, or provide these or plastic models for them. Ask the students to use the old newspapers to cover their desk tops. Give each student a pie tin. Provide enough petroleum jelly so that the students can spread a thin to medium film over the bottom and sides of the pie tin. Remind them to be sure that the entire inside of the tin is covered with jelly. Once they have chosen the item they want to make an image of, instruct the students to cover the shell or plant with a thin layer of petroleum jelly. Place the shell or plant in the bottom of the pie tin so that the flattest side rests on the bottom of the pan.

In one of the cups for each student, place enough dry plaster of Paris so that when mixed it will be enough to cover the bottom of the pie tin with about 15 mm (½ inch) of plaster. In the second cup place enough water so that each student will have created the proper consistency of plaster once he or she mixes (using the plastic spoon) the dry powder with the water. Once the students have mixed their plaster, instruct them to pour it carefully over the shell or plant into the pie tin. They should allow about 1 hour for the plaster to harden. Remember: As the plaster dries it will become quite warm and then cool. Wait until it has cooled before removing it from the tin.

Once the plaster has hardened, turn the pie tin upside down over the paper-covered desk and tap the tin lightly to remove the plaster cast. The plaster will still be quite wet at this time, so the students need to be reminded to use care as they remove their shells or plants from the plaster. Once the shells or plants are removed, set the plaster casts in a safe place to cure fully (dry out and harden). This should take at least a day. Once the casts are cured, the students will have what is known as a *negative imprint* or *mold* of a plant or animal. If desired, a *positive imprint* or *cast* can now be created by spreading additional petroleum jelly over the surface of the negative imprint and placing it back into a deeper petroleum-jelly-lined pie tin. On top of the first cast pour additional plaster. After it has hardened (about 1 hour) carefully turn the tin upside down and remove the old and new plaster casts. Since the surface of the old cast was thoroughly covered with petroleum jelly, the two casts should readily come apart with a knife blade. The new cast formed from the negative imprint is called a *positive imprint.* After this has had a chance to harden thoroughly (about

EARTH SCIENCE

Step 1. Pour plaster into pie dish.

Step 2. Push shell into plaster; after drying an hour, pop out cast and allow to dry overnight.

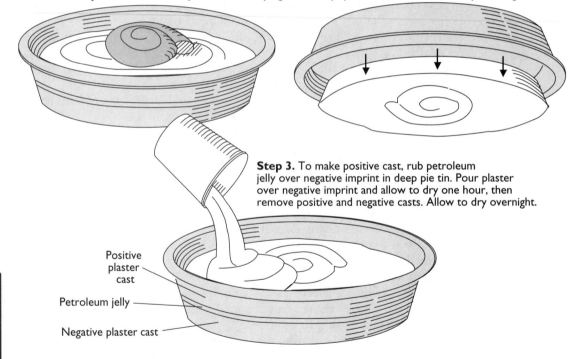

Step 3. To make positive cast, rub petroleum jelly over negative imprint in deep pie tin. Pour plaster over negative imprint and allow to dry one hour, then remove positive and negative casts. Allow to dry overnight.

Positive plaster cast

Petroleum jelly

Negative plaster cast

one day), the students may want to paint or color with markers their newly formed fossils.

Science in Personal and Social Perspectives

- Why do you want to know about fossils? Has our study of fossils given you any ideas about what life was like in the past?

- Do you think you could have lived during the time when dinosaurs roamed the land? Why or why not?

Science and Technology

- How can fossils tell us what ancient environments were like?
- Evidence left by early people is called an *artifact*. Some examples are arrowheads, ancient beads, and animal skins used as clothing. Why do you think we don't call them fossils?

Science as Inquiry

- Why can fossils be found only in sedimentary rocks?
- Can you find fossils where you live? Where do you think you would go to look for fossils?

History and Nature of Science

- Paleontologists (fossil experts) study and learn from fossils. If you were a paleontologist, what kind of information would you share with others on the imprints you just made?
- How is an archeologist's job different from a paleontologist's? An excellent book for this topic is Gloria and Esther Goldreich, *What Can She Be? A Geologist* (New York: Lothrop, Lee and Shepard, 1976).
- Describe how the Leakeys (Louis, Mary, and son Richard) used fossil evidence to determine the changes in human body form throughout history.

4. EVALUATION: How will the students show what they have learned?

Upon completing the activities the students will be able to:

- demonstrate how a fossil can be formed by using sand, water, and a seashell;
- pick out the fossils when given several items to choose from, such as a seashell, a leaf, a sedimentary rock with a shell imprint or leaf imprint on it, a geode, or an igneous rock such as obsidian;
- tell or write in their own words what a fossil is and what information it can provide humans.

Soil Formation

**GRADE
5–8
DISCIPLINE
Earth
Science**

Concept to be invented
Main idea—Soil is made from finely ground rock and organic material.

Concepts that are important to expansion
The rocks and plants found in the local area will determine the kind of soil that is formed. Large amounts of weathered sandstone will create a sandy soil. Slightly smaller particles create a silty soil. Very fine particles will make a clay soil.

Materials needed

For exploration:

soil samples from local area

one piece of white construction paper per student

local sedimentary rock samples (these are easily broken)

hammer

old newspapers

one magnifying glass per student

one pair of goggles per student

For expansion:

sand

organic matter such as leaves or grass clippings

soil samples from local area

two small baby food jars with lids for each cooperative group

water

➡ **Safety precautions:** Make sure that all students are wearing goggles while smashing rocks with hammers. Wrap the rocks in newspaper and then strike them with a hammer. This will prevent rock pieces from flying everywhere.

If you choose to take the students outside to collect soil samples, be sure proper safety procedures are followed. Pair up the students and make sure they know the boundaries for soil sample collection.

1. EXPLORATION: Which process skills will be used?

Observing, recording data, classifying

What will the students do?

Soil Separation and Rock Crushing   Provide the class with soil samples collected from the local area, or if possible, take the students around the school grounds to collect soil samples. Ask the students to cover their desktops with old newspapers and then place the white construction paper on top of the newspaper. Arrange the students in cooperative groups of three to four to make observations of the soil samples. Use the magnifying glasses to make detailed observations of the individual particles. Encourage students to draw or write a description of their observations.

After the students have made as many observations as possible, ask them to try to separate their soil samples into different parts. How many different ways can you separate the soil samples?

Give each cooperative group a hammer and several pieces of local sedimentary rocks like sandstone or limestone. Remind students to *put on and keep on* their goggles at all times during this section of the activity. Over the newspaper-covered desks, ask the students to wrap the rock samples in newspaper and then pound the rocks with hammers. Do the materials formed look similar to the materials you separated out from the local soil sample?

2. EXPLANATION/CONCEPT INVENTION: What is the main idea? How will the main idea be constructed?

Concept: Soil is made from finely ground rocks and organic material.

Ask the students to share the results of their observations. What kinds of things did you observe? Were all parts of the soil the same size? How many different ways did you separate your soil samples? Suggestions may include size or color; rocklike or plantlike. What did your rock look like before you crushed it with the hammer? What about afterward? Is there any similarity between the crushed rock and your soil sample? Continue questioning students until they come to the conclusion that soil is made up of small pieces of rock and plant matter.

3. EXPANSION OF THE IDEA: Which process skills will be used?

Manipulating materials, observing, inferring, classifying, estimating, predicting

How will the idea be expanded?

Soil Components   Provide each cooperative group with two small baby food jars with lids. Ask the students to label one jar *local soil* and the second *homemade soil*. Ask the students to fill the first jar up halfway with one of the local soil samples. Ask the students to place in the second jars some of the crushed rock they just smashed, some sand, and some grass clippings or leaves, so that half of the jar is filled. Into both jars pour enough water to cover all of the solid materials. Place the lids on the jars and shake vigorously. Solicit predictions about what will happen in each jar after it has sat for 1 hour, for 3 hours, and overnight. Ask the students to record their predictions and then place the jars where they will not be disturbed for the times indicated. Ask the students the following questions to help them conclude that the rocks and plants found in the local area will determine the kind of soil formed. Weathered sandstone will create a sandy soil, more finely ground particles will create a silty soil, and very fine particles will create a clay soil. What did the two samples look like after 1 hour? after 3 hours? the next day? If you did not look at jar labels and just at samples, could you tell the difference between the soil in the two jars? How were they similar? different? Look at the settled materials. Can you estimate how much of the sample is sand? silt? clay? How would you classify the soil? What do you think will happen to the grass or leaves if you let the jar sit for one week, one month, or three months? Solicit predictions and then set the jar in a safe place so that students can observe it over a three-month period.

Science in Personal and Social Perspectives

- What kind of soil is found around your home? Would it be a good soil if you wanted to grow potatoes in your garden?
- Should people be concerned about farmers using excessive amounts of fertilizers in soils? What can be done to prevent excessive use of fertilizers?
- Do you think it is better to have a sandy or a silty soil in your garden? Do you put fertilizers on your soil? If so, why?

Science and Technology

- As you have discovered, not all soils are alike. Do you think it was important to keep this fact in mind as tractor tires were developed?
- What do you think *no-till* means, and why would farmers be urged to use this method of farming?

Science as Inquiry

- List at least three components of soil.
- What influence does local bedrock have on the type of soil found in an area?
- Does the rate of weathering and erosion in an area affect the formation of soil?
- Where do you think the minerals found in soils come from?

History and Nature of Science

- What are the responsibilities of a soil agronomist?
- How important is it for a land developer to understand soil formation?
- What is organic farming? How do these methods of farming differ from other methods?

4. EVALUATION: How will the students show what they have learned?

Upon completing the activities the students will be able to:

- take a given soil sample and demonstrate the steps necessary to estimate the amount of sand, silt, and clay in the sample;

- explain how the type of soil found in a local area is dependent on the local bedrock and ground cover;
- write a persuasive argument on why grass is necessary to cover soil or on how soil is different from dirt.

Rock Types

Concept to be invented

Main idea—Rocks may be classified into three groups: *igneous, sedimentary,* and *metamorphic.*

Concepts that are important to expansion

Igneous means "fire formed." Cooled magma and lava create igneous rocks such as granite and obsidian. *Sedimentary* rocks are formed in water due to layers of sediments building up from weathered igneous, metamorphic, and other sedimentary rocks, or decaying organic matter; examples are limestone and sandstone. *Metamorphic* rocks are very hard rocks that may be formed from igneous or sedimentary rocks under extreme heat and pressure; marble and gneiss are examples.

Materials needed

For exploration (for each cooperative group of students):
several samples of igneous rocks, sedimentary rocks, metamorphic rocks, one jar, two sheets of construction paper, sand, mud, and pebbles.

For expansion (for each student):
Goggles, hammer and chisel, collection bag, three empty egg cartons, old newspapers, and a marker.

➡ **Safety precautions:** Remind students to handle rock samples carefully. No throwing rocks! If you choose to take the students outside to collect rock samples, be sure proper safety procedures are followed. Pair up the students and make sure they know the boundaries for rock sample collection.

1. EXPLORATION: Which process skills will be used?

Observing, classifying, inferring

What will the students do?

Rock Categorization

Divide the class into cooperative learning groups of three or four students. Provide each group with sand, numerous rock types, and pebbles. Ask the students to categorize the rocks. What's different about them? How are they alike? After the students have shared the results of their categorizing, ask them to set those samples aside in the categories they identified.

Give each cooperative group a jar and ask them to put rocks, sand, mud, and water into it. Put a lid on the jar and shake it for a few moments. Ask the students to draw a picture of what the jar looks like after the materials have settled.

2. EXPLANATION/CONCEPT INVENTION: What is the main idea? How will the main idea be constructed?

Concept: Rocks may be classified into three groups: igneous, sedimentary, and metamorphic.

Ask the students to fold a sheet of construction paper into three parts. Now go back to the different piles of rocks the students first categorized. Ask them what kinds of differences they noted. Explain that rocks come in all shapes, colors, and sizes. However, they weren't all made the same way. Use the example of lava from a volcano. What happens to the lava when it dries? It becomes a hard rock called *igneous,* meaning "fire formed." Cooled magma and lava create igneous rocks like granite and obsidian. In the first part of the construction paper, draw or describe how igneous rock is formed. Provide the students with various samples of igneous rocks to observe.

Refer back to the shaken jar. What does it currently look like? Steer the students toward looking at the layers of materials. Did your group classify any of the rock samples based on whether you could see layers? What do you think rocks formed from the buildup of materials in layers are called? *Sedimentary* rocks are formed in water due to layers of sediments building up from weathered igneous, metamorphic, and other sedimentary rocks, or decaying organic matter. Limestone and sandstone are sedimentary. In the second part of the construction paper, draw or describe how sedimentary rocks are formed. Provide the students with various samples of sedimentary rocks to observe.

Ask the students if they think they classified any rocks that have not yet been described. Have the students share those rocks with the rest of the class. Make sure they do not fit under igneous or sedimentary categories. Explain to the students that the igneous or sedimentary rocks can be put under extreme heat and pressure inside the earth, which changes the look of the rock. These are called *metamorphic* rocks; examples are marble and gneiss. Metamorphic rocks are very hard. In the third part of the construction paper, draw or describe how metamorphic rocks are formed. Provide the students with various samples of metamorphic rocks to observe.

3. EXPANSION OF THE IDEA: Which process skills will be used?

Observing, classifying, collecting, comparing, communicating

How will the idea be expanded?

Rock Collection Field Trip

This expansion activity may be done as a home extension activity or as a class field trip. Identify a site where students will be permitted to collect rock samples. Either take them as a class or provide instructions to parents to take the students to the collection site. Be sure the students are given instruction on how to use the hammer and chisel to extract rock samples from the bedrock. Encourage the students to break their samples into pieces small enough to fit into the egg carton depressions. Remind the students to think about the different colors and textures that different kinds of rocks have. Classify the collection into igneous, sedimentary, and metamorphic, and designate one egg carton for each rock type. After a sufficient amount of time has passed (one or two months), ask the students to bring their collections to school to share with the class.

Science in Personal and Social Perspectives

- If you were going to build a home along the ocean, would you want the underlying rock to be igneous, sedimentary, or metamorphic? Why?
- Have you ever washed your hands with a pumice-based soap? Have you ever used a pumice stone to smooth away rough skin? Where do you think this comes from?

Science and Technology

- Which type of rock is best used for building purposes?
- Would you trust a bridge made of sedimentary rocks? Do you think it would last as long as a bridge made with igneous rocks? What about a bridge made of metamorphic rock?
- Which type of rock would be a wise choice to build a dam with?

Science as Inquiry

- Where in the world would I easily find an igneous rock? a sedimentary rock? a metamorphic rock?
- Can an igneous rock be formed from a sedimentary one? Can a sedimentary rock be formed from a metamorphic or igneous rock?
- What kind of rock is the local bedrock?

History and Nature of Science

- Would a civil engineer responsible for placing a bridge across the Mississippi River between Illinois and Missouri need to understand the type of bedrock found in the area before plans for the bridge could be made? Why or why not?
- As a construction worker you decide to build your own home. You want to make it out of stone. Which kind of rock type would you use, and why? Is it important that a construction worker or even a home owner know the differences among igneous, sedimentary, and metamorphic rocks?

4. EVALUATION: How will the students show what they have learned?

Upon completing the activities the students will be able to:

- look at six different rocks and identify whether they are igneous, sedimentary, or metamorphic;

- identify different areas of the world where the three different rock types can be found;
- reflect, and then write a description of an igneous rock formed when lava cooled outside the earth.

Cooling Crystals

Concept to be invented
Main idea—The rate at which a crystal cools affects the size of the crystal.

Concepts that are important to expansion
Crystals can be seen in many rocks.

Materials needed
For exploration (for each group):

three glass caster cups

three small test tubes (10 ml)

test tube holder

paradichlorobenzine (PDB) flakes
    (found in supermarkets,
    hardware stores, pharmacies)

one hand lens per student

grease pencil

crushed ice

two 500-ml beakers

one 150-ml beaker

tongs

For exploration (for entire class):
hot plates, paper towels

For expansion:
Samples of the igneous rocks rhyolite, granite, and obsidian; one hand lens per student.

➥ **Safety precautions:** Extreme care should be used near the hot plate and in handling the hot water and PDB. Goggles should be worn at all times. Be sure the room is well ventilated when melting the PDB.

1. EXPLORATION: Which process skills will be used?

Observing, predicting, manipulating materials, recording data, drawing conclusions

What will the students do?

*PDB Crystal
Formation*

Ask the students to fill one of the 500-ml beakers with 300 ml of water. Place a caster cup in the beaker. Boil the water on the hot plate. Fill the other 500-ml beaker with crushed ice. Place the second caster cup in the beaker. Leave the third caster cup at room temperature.

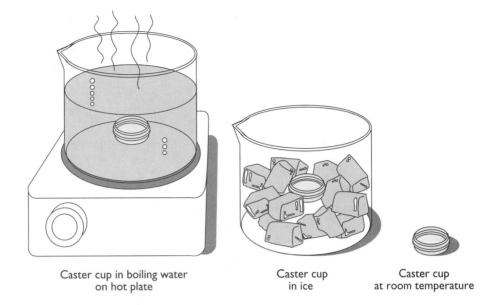

Caster cup in boiling water
on hot plate

Caster cup
in ice

Caster cup
at room temperature

Carefully observe some PDB flakes. Record those observations. Fill each of the three small test tubes with PDB flakes. Half-fill the 150-ml beaker with water. Place the three test tubes in the beaker. Place the beaker with the test tubes on the hot plate. Heat the beaker gently until the PDB melts.

Using the tongs, carefully remove the caster cup from the boiling water. Dry the cup and label it *A*. Using the test tube holder, remove one test tube and pour the PDB into this caster cup. Time how long it takes for the PDB to completely become a solid. Record the time. Record your observations of the PDB flakes for cup A.

Remove the second caster cup from the beaker with ice. Dry the cup quickly and completely. Label it *B*. Pour the second test tube of PDB into this cup. Time how long it takes for the PDB to turn completely solid. Record the time. Record your observations of the PDB flakes for cup B.

Pour the third test tube of PDB into the cup at room temperature. Label it *C*. Again, time how long it takes for this PDB to solidify completely. Record the time. Record your observations of the PDB flakes for cup C.

2. EXPLANATION/CONCEPT INVENTION: *What is the main idea? How will the main idea be constructed?*

Concept: The rate at which a crystal cools affects the size of the crystal.

How does the rate of cooling affect the size of crystals? Record the cooling times for samples A, B, and C on the board. Look at the contents of each caster cup with the magnifying glass. Draw the contents of each caster cup on your paper.

EARTH SCIENCE

When the PDB was placed into the test tubes, there was no difference between tubes. Once it was placed into cups A, B, and C, a change occurred. How are they different? What caused this difference? What conclusions can you draw? The students should conclude that the rate at which a crystal cools affects the size of the crystal formed.

3. EXPANSION OF THE IDEA: Which process skills will be used?

Observing, recording data, generalizing, formulating models

How will the idea be expanded?

Rock Type versus Crystal Formation   Ask the students to observe the crystals in the samples of granite, rhyolite, and obsidian with a magnifying glass. Draw the crystals in each sample on your paper. Compare the crystals in the caster cups to the samples of granite, rhyolite, and obsidian. Which PDB crystals are most similar to the crystals in the rock samples? (Cup A, granite; cup B, obsidian; cup C, rhyolite.)

Granite, rhyolite, and obsidian are igneous rocks essentially made of the same material. Explain why they look different. Where would igneous rocks have a chance to cool slowly? Where would igneous rock cool rapidly? If you saw a rock that contained large interlocking crystals, what would you say about the way it formed? The more slowly a crystal cools, the larger the crystals are. Granite cooled slowly and crystals were able to form. Rhyolite cooled more rapidly than granite, but more slowly than obsidian. Igneous rocks cool slowly deep in the earth. They cool rapidly on the surface. Large interlocking crystals form slowly inside the earth.

Science in Personal and Social Perspectives

- What kinds of crystals do you eat regularly? (Salt and sugar)
- How does the size of a crystal determine its quality? Do you think your knowledge of how crystals form will assist you in determining the quality of precious rocks and gems?

Science and Technology

- The strength and quality of rocks are important for construction. What is the best type of rock for long-lasting buildings?
- How has the scarcity of quality gems on the market affected your life, your community, or the world?

Science as Inquiry

- What kinds of rocks are found in the area where you live? Can you classify them according to their crystal structure?
- Can crystals be found in sedimentary rocks? Why or why not?

History and Nature of Science

- What kinds of careers would use information on crystal formation? Some possibilities include geologist, geophysicist, volcanologist, jeweler, sculptor, and geographer.

- Choose one of the career suggestions from the question above and research the skills necessary to enter that career. Provide an oral report to the class.

4. EVALUATION: How will the students show what they have learned?

Upon completing the activities the students will be able to:

- identify where a crystal cooled (on the earth's surface or inside the earth) and at what rate when given drawings of crystals of different shapes and sizes;
- examine samples of igneous rocks and explain why they have different-sized crystals;
- explain how the prices of precious jewels are affected by crystal formation.

Weathering

Concept to be invented
Main idea—*Weathering* is the name given to the various mechanical and chemical processes that break down rock.

Concepts that are important to expansion
Erosion, soil formation, rock formation—igneous, sedimentary, metamorphic.

Materials needed
For discrepant event:
Soda bottle and cap, water, freezer.

For exploration:
Field site to collect data, stereomicroscope, hammer.

For expansion:
Dilute hydrochloric acid (HCl); igneous, sedimentary, and metamorphic rock samples.

➡ **Safety precautions:** Review with the students ahead of time the rules that should be followed for everyone's safety during the field trip. Visit the field site before the students do to guard against any possible hazards at the site.

Freezing Bottle   The day before you begin this lesson, take a glass soda bottle and ask a student to fill it with water all the way to the top. Cap the bottle so that no water can escape. Now ask the students what they think will happen to this bottle if you place it in the freezer for a day. Record their predictions on the board, where they will remain untouched until the next day. Twenty-four hours later remove the bottle from the freezer. If the bottle was totally filled before freezing, it should now be cracked, as the ice expanded upon freezing. Ask the students what they observe. Did it behave according to their predictions? Why did this happen? What happens to water when it freezes? Based on your observations, do you think water could do this to other items besides glass? Think about this as we engage in today's activity.

1. EXPLORATION: Which process skills will be used?

Observing, hypothesizing, predicting, measuring, using spatial relationships, recording data

What will the students do?

Weathering Field Trip

The students will go on a field trip around the school grounds. An old road or empty prairie or field will be an ideal site. Before beginning the trip, the students will be reminded about appropriate care of a collection site. Remind them to take care as they travel through the site and to try not to destroy any animal homes or wildflowers or plant growth. Ask the students to look for rocks that appear to be broken apart. They are to record a description of the area in which they find them, taking care to note the soil conditions (wet, dry, sandy, clayey), an estimate of the original size of the rock, a physical description of the rock (color, shininess, hardness, porosity), and a prediction based on their findings as to what they think caused the rock to break apart. A small sample of the rock should be collected for further study in the classroom. Upon returning to the classroom, the students will make a composite chart of their field observations. Headings for this chart could include *collection site, soil conditions, rock size, physical properties* (color, luster, hardness, pore size), *possible cause for breakage.*

2. EXPLANATION/CONCEPT INVENTION: What is the main idea? How will the main idea be constructed?

Concept: Weathering is the name given to the various mechanical and chemical processes that break down rock.

Draw the students' attention to the composite chart in the front of the room. In order to guide the students in inventing the concept of *weathering*, ask such questions as: In looking at this chart, are there any we can group together? Do any of them sound as if the different groups of investigators were looking at the same rocks?

Ask the students to bring up the sample rocks whose descriptions sound similar. Do you think these are the same rocks?

Once double sightings have been eliminated, begin to focus on the chart again, this time asking, "Is there any one area where broken rocks were found more often than any other? Or is there any one soil condition where broken rocks are found more often than any other?"

If this is the case, then ask the students if they think this soil condition contributed to the presence of broken rocks. If it is a very wet area, then you can relate this back to the discrepant event—how the freezing and thawing of water will contribute to the cracking of the rocks. If this is a dry area, ask the students

EARTH SCIENCE

if they made note of any vegetation growing in the area. They may have found the broken rocks due to roots growing through the surface of the rock. It may be a very dry area where wind blows through rather rapidly, causing the rocks to break up.

Ask the students if they know of a term to describe the breaking up of rock due to running water, wind, rain, or roots. Introduce the term *weathering* at this point.

What happens to the rock pieces as they are carried by the rain, wind, or running water? What term can we use to describe the carrying away of this weathered material? (Erosion.) Ask the students if they observed the soil where they found the rock. Was it similar in composition to the rock itself? Engage the students in a discussion of how the weathering of rocks assists in soil formation.

3. EXPANSION OF THE IDEA: Which process skills will be used?

Observing, classifying, experimenting, predicting, inferring, interpreting data, recording data, communicating

How will the idea be expanded?

Rock Identification

If your students collected rock samples that fell into one type (all igneous, or all sedimentary, or all metamorphic), then in addition to their samples, provide them with rock samples from the missing rock groups. Ask the students to try to group the rock samples according to the characteristics from the composite chart from the first activity. Suggest to them that based on hardness, porosity, and composition, they should be able to group their rock samples into three different groups.

Once they have their samples in three groups, the students can perform the following experiments to determine possible sources of weathering.

Chemical Weathering

Acid Test. Take one sample from each rock group. Predict what will happen to the rock when you drop three drops of dilute HCl on it. Do you think each rock will react the same way? Which one do you think will weather the most? In nature, what type of weathering could we consider this to be? (This is known as *chemical weathering.*)

Rust/Oxidation. Do you notice any color changes in your rock? Are there what appear to be rust spots on the rock? What do you think causes this?

Mechanical Weathering

Water. Cover the three different rock samples with water and place them in a freezer for a day. Do the rocks crumble easily in your hands? If you strike them with a hammer lightly, do they fall apart? Are the insides still wet? Which rock type was most susceptible to the freezing water? Since the water simply froze and broke the rock apart, this is known as *mechanical weathering.*

Roots. In what area did you find this rock? Are there still traces of plant matter on the rock? Did you see any roots pushing up right through the surface of the rock? Do the roots cause chemical or mechanical weathering? Overall, which rocks are most easily weathered and which are most difficult to weather?

Can you guess how each of these rock groups was originally formed based on your weathering observations? Lead to a discussion on rock formations: igneous, sedimentary, and metamorphic. Detailed discussions will be provided in a separate lesson for each rock type.

Science in Personal and Social Perspectives

- Why does one need to use special fishing lures if a river or lake is muddy or murky due to erosion?
- What would you suspect was happening if the water in your favorite fishing stream looked clean, yet the number of fish began to dwindle? You have noticed that some of the rocks along the bank are beginning to crumble and wash downstream. What could you do to verify your suspicions? Whom would you talk to about this problem?

Science and Technology

- What role does strip-mining of coal or clear-cutting of timber play in allowing the forces of weather to affect erosion?

- How has an increased understanding of the forces of weathering and erosion caused us to change our farming practices since the Dust Bowl days of the 1930s?

Science as Inquiry

- How does weathering differ from erosion? What factors contribute to soil formation? What processes have occurred to create the different rock types? Can you name the three different rock types?
- In which rock formation would you most likely place a building like the Sears Tower? Why? Which rock type would you be least likely to choose to build a house of? Why?

History and Nature of Science

- Why would a civil engineer need to understand the processes of weathering and erosion?
- Do you think a contractor or cement finisher would find knowledge of weathering, erosion, soil and rock types useful in his or her work?
- Research the great pyramids of Egypt. How were they built? What are they made of? When were they built? Would they still exist if they were first built in Chicago?

4. EVALUATION: How will the students show what they have learned?

Upon completing the activities the students will be able to:

- draw a diagram showing the relationships among rock types, soil types, weathering, and erosion;
- when given a weathered rock sample and a description of where the sample was found, suggest the most probable source for its weathering;
- list at least four agents of erosion;
- discriminate between constructive and destructive geologic forces.

Crustal Plate Movement

GRADE 5–8
DISCIPLINE Earth Science

Concept to be invented
Main idea—The theory of plate tectonics states that the crust of the earth is not one solid piece but rather several separate plates that are in motion on top of molten material.

Concepts that are important to expansion
Continental drift, earthquakes, volcanoes.

Materials needed
For exploration (for each group of four to six students):
four wood blocks
1 liter of water

plastic shoebox (heavy plastic type, which will not melt under light bulb)

a heat lamp or 150–200-watt   food coloring
   bulb and socket   stacks of books to raise box above lamp

For expansion:
Maps of the world showing the crustal plate boundaries, a list of places famous
for volcanic eruptions, a list of sites of recent earthquakes.

➥ **Safety precautions:** The students should be reminded to use care with the heat
source. Don't place the heat source too close to the plastic box or books. Use care
around water and electricity. Wipe up any water spills immediately. Do not
touch heat source with wet hands.

1. EXPLORATION: Which process skills will be used?

Experimenting, observing, predicting, inferring

What will the students do?

Moving Plates   Each student group should place its plastic box on two stacks of books. The box
should be high enough so that a heat source (lamp) will fit beneath. Pour water
into the box. Place the four small wood blocks in the box. All the blocks should
touch, forming a square. Place the heat source beneath the box directly under
the center of the blocks. Turn the light on and place a drop of food coloring in
the water where the four blocks meet. Observe the blocks for about 5 to 10 minutes. What happens to each of the four wood blocks? What happens to the food
coloring?

2. EXPLANATION/CONCEPT INVENTION: What is the main idea? How will the main idea be constructed?

Concept: The theory of plate tectonics states that the crust of the earth is not one
solid piece, but rather several separate plates that are in motion on top of
molten material.

Ask the students to share their observations on the movement of the four wood
blocks and the food coloring. Why do you think this happened? If you were to
relate this activity to the earth's crust, what do you think the blocks represent?
(Early land masses that separated millions of years ago.) What would the water
represent? (The molten layer of the earth called the *mantle.*) What happened to
the temperature of the water over time? (It warmed up.) What happened to the
food coloring? (It slowly moved along the surface as the water continued to
warm.) Through questioning along this line, help the students to conclude that
the theory of plate tectonics states that the crust of the earth is not one solid piece
but rather several separate plates that are in motion on top of molten material.

3. EXPANSION OF THE IDEA: Which process skills will be used?

Observing, predicting, making conclusions

EARTH SCIENCE

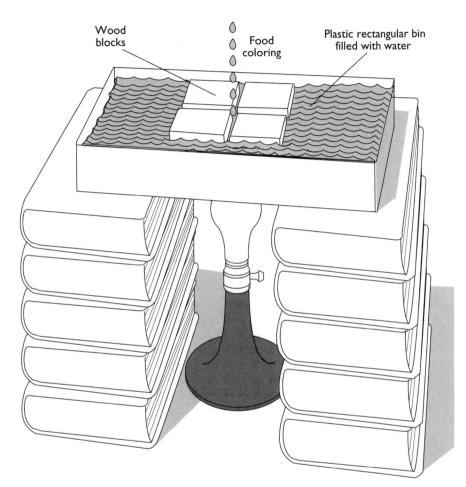

Wood blocks

Food coloring

Plastic rectangular bin filled with water

How will the idea be expanded?

Mapping Volcanoes and Earthquakes

Pair up the students. Provide each pair with a world map indicating the boundaries for the crustal plates. The students should be free to mark on the maps you provide. Provide the students with a recent list of volcanic and earthquake activity. Ask them to plot on the map the places where the most recent earthquakes and volcanoes have occurred. You may give them a list of volcanic and earthquake activity for the past fifty years to plot. Ask the students to share some observations they have made about the relationship between earthquakes and volcanoes from this exercise. The students should conclude that most earthquake and volcanic activity occurs where two or more crustal plates come together.

Science in Personal and Social Perspectives

- Would you choose to live along a crustal plate boundary? If you did, how might it affect your life?

EARTH SCIENCE

- Do you think the government should help pay to repair homes for people who chose to build their homes on a known crustal boundary?

Science and Technology

- Are you aware of any other theories about formation or movement of the earth's crust? What part do you think technology has played in theory change and advanced knowledge about different phenomena?
- How do we use our knowledge about movement of the earth's crust when we construct buildings in areas where crustal plates are known to move?

Science as Inquiry

- Is there still movement of the earth's crust? How do we know?
- A lot of volcanic activity occurs in the Hawaiian Islands. Are they on the edge of a crustal plate? If not, what is causing the volcanic activity? Research the formation of these volcanic islands.
- Explain how a solid crust can move. What does the mantle layer of the earth have to do with this movement?

History and Nature of Science

- Who is Charles Lyell? What career changes led him to many geological discoveries?
- Would a seismologist be concerned with crustal plate movement? Why?
- Why would a civil engineer be concerned with the location of crustal plate boundaries? What does a civil engineer do?

4. EVALUATION: How will the students show what they have learned?

Oatmeal and Cracker Plate Tectonics

On completing the activities the students will be able to:

- demonstrate the theory of plate tectonics by using a bowl of oatmeal and some soda crackers;
- identify the area known as the Ring of Fire on a world map and explain what it is;
- briefly explain the theory of plate tectonics.

EARTH SCIENCE

GRADE
K–4
DISCIPLINE
Earth
Science

Rain Formation

Concept to be invented
Main idea—Raindrops form as water vapor condenses and falls from the sky.

Concepts that are important to expansion
Water cycle, condensation, evaporation, precipitation.

Materials needed

For exploration (for each group of four to six children):
1-quart glass jar with lid, hot-to-boiling water, ice cubes.

For expansion:
Clear plastic lid (coffee can lid), pencil, water, plastic cup, eye dropper, paper towels.

➡ **Safety precautions:** The students should be reminded to avoid bumping the tables once the exploration activity is set up. If the hot water spills out, it could hurt the children. If the glass jar breaks, it could cut someone.

1. **EXPLORATION:** Which process skills will be used?

Observing, predicting, recording data

What will the students do?

Rain in a Jar
Set groups of four to six students around a table. In the middle of the table place a 1-quart jar with enough hot-to-nearly-boiling water to cover the bottom of the jar. The teacher should ask the students to make predictions about what will happen when they cover the jar with the lid turned upside down, holding three or four ice cubes. After the students have recorded their predictions and shared them with the class, instruct someone from each group to place the lid carefully over the jar and place the ice cubes on top of the inverted lid. Ask the students to watch the jar for 4 or 5 minutes. What did you observe? Was it as you predicted? Record those observations.

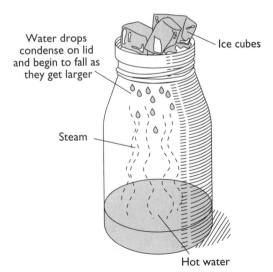

Water drops condense on lid and begin to fall as they get larger

Ice cubes

Steam

Hot water

2. EXPLANATION/CONCEPT INVENTION: What is the main idea? How will the main idea be constructed?

Concept: Raindrops form as water vapor condenses and falls from the sky.

The students should have observed that water drops collected on the inside of the lid. As time progressed more water drops formed. As the drops became bigger, it got to the point that the lid could no longer hold the drops, and the drops began to fall back into the jar. Ask the students the following questions to help them conclude that raindrops form as water vapor condenses and falls from the sky. What observations did you record? Where do you think the drops of water on the lid came from? (From the *condensation* of water vapor inside the jar. The hot water in the jar *evaporated* and changed into a *gas*—water vapor. When the water vapor hit the cool lid, it *condensed* and changed back to a *liquid*.) What happened to the drops of water as they collected on the lid? (They got bigger as more water vapor *condensed* and collected on the jar lid.) At what point did the water drops start to fall from the jar lid? (As they collected on the lid, they grew bigger and soon pulled together with other drops. Their weight pulled them down.) What do you call water drops that fall from the sky? (Rain.)

3. EXPANSION OF THE IDEA: Which process skills will be used?

Observing, inferring, measuring

How will the idea be expanded?

Water Drop Attraction

Pair up the students. Provide each pair with a plastic coffee can lid or the like, an eye dropper, a cup of water, and some paper towels. Ask the student pairs to do the following: One student should hold the plastic lid bottom side up. The other student should fill the eye dropper with water and squeeze as many separate drops of water on the lid as possible. The child holding the lid should then quickly turn the lid over. Hold the lid at least 8 to 10 inches over the table top, directly over some paper towels. Ask the student not holding the lid to use the point of a pencil to move the tiny drops together. What happens when you do this? Ask the students to switch roles, allowing one to hold the lid and flip it and the other to use the eye dropper and pencil. Did the same thing occur?

The water molecules appear to attract one another. As you pull them together it seems as if they readily jump to one another. As they grow bigger, they eventually are overcome by gravity and fall from the lid. Water may fall like this from the sky, not just in the form of rain. The teacher may solicit ideas from the students on other forms in which water falls from the sky (snow, sleet, hail). Explain to the students that all of these are called *precipitation*.

Science in Personal and Social Perspectives

- Why do you think it rains more in certain places than in others?
- Read the poem "Little Raindrops," by Aunt Effie (Jane Euphemia Browne), to the class. After it is read ask the students if they think they are affected by emotional changes with changes in the weather.

EARTH SCIENCE

Science and Technology

- Why do you think meteorologists study rain patterns? Do these patterns affect where people will build cities?
- Why do scientists *seed* rain clouds in dry areas? Do you think farmers in these areas want to be able to make it rain when water is scarce? Why?

Science as Inquiry

- What do you call it when water turns into water vapor? (Evaporation.)
- When water vapor collects on an object to form water droplets, what is it called? (Condensation.)
- What do you call water that falls from the sky? (Precipitation.)
- What do we call the process by which water evaporates, condenses, and falls from the sky? (The water cycle.)

History and Nature of Science

- How important do you think it is for a farmer to understand the water cycle?
- If you were a botanist working in the desert, why would you be curious about how a cactus grows?
- When you watch a local weather forecast, does the meteorologist help explain where the next rainfall will come from?

4. EVALUATION: How will the students show what they have learned?

Upon completing the activities the students will be able to:

- show how they can make rain when given a jar of hot water, a pie tin, and some ice cubes;
- explain where evaporation, condensation, and precipitation are occurring in the jar demonstration they set up;
- draw a picture of something they think they would not have in their life if it did not rain. Ask them to explain the reasoning behind choosing that object.

Dew Formation

GRADE
K–4
DISCIPLINE
Earth
Science

Concept to be invented
Main idea—Cold surfaces collect more water drops than warm surfaces do.

Concepts that are important to expansion
Dew, frost, temperature measurement with a thermometer, dew point.

Materials needed
For exploration (for each group of four to six children):
Minute timer or clock with minutes marked off, glass soda bottle, clear container large enough for the bottle to fit in, ice cubes, water, paper towels.

EARTH SCIENCE

For expansion:
Drinking glass, thermometer, ice cubes, water, paper towels

➡ **Safety precautions:** The students should be reminded to use care when handling the bottles. Wipe up any water spills so that students do not slip on wet surfaces.

1. EXPLORATION: Which process skills will be used?

Observing, predicting, measuring, inferring, recording data

What will the students do?

Soda Bottle Condensation

Set groups of four to six children around a table. In the middle of the table place a container large enough to hold a soda bottle. In this jar place four or five ice cubes and enough water so that once the bottle is placed in the jar, it will be covered with cold water up to its neck. Give one child in the group a glass soda bottle. Remind the other students that they each will get a turn. If enough bottles are available, each child may be given one at this time. Ask the children to wrap their hands around the bottle for 2 minutes to try to get it very warm. When the 2 minutes are up, ask the students to exhale inside the bottle. What did you observe? Record those observations.

Then ask the students to make predictions about what will happen after they put the bottle into the container of ice water for 2 minutes, take it out, quickly wipe it off, and again exhale into the bottle. After they have recorded their predictions and shared them with the class, the students should take turns putting their bottles into the ice water container, taking them out, wiping off the excess water, and then exhaling inside them. What did you observe? Was it as you predicted? Record those observations.

2. EXPLANATION/CONCEPT INVENTION: What is the main idea? How will the main idea be constructed?

Concept: Cold surfaces collect more water drops than warm surfaces.

When the students exhaled into their warmed bottles, they may have observed some condensation, but very little. Their warm breath and the warmed bottle did not differ greatly in temperature. Therefore, water vapor did not condense readily. When the students exhaled into the cooled bottles, the difference in temperature between their breath and the bottles was enough to make water drops collect on the cold bottles. The students will be able to conclude that cold surfaces collect more water drops than warm surfaces when you ask them the following questions about what they did. What observations did you record when you exhaled on the warmed bottle? What observations did you record when you exhaled on the cooled bottle? Was there a difference between the two? Why do you think this happened? Do you ever walk through grass on a spring or summer morning? What happens to your shoes on those mornings? (If the students said yes, they may begin to think about getting wet shoes as they walk through the grass. If the students start to respond along these lines, then ask the next set of questions.) Why do you think your shoes got wet? Do you think the grass or the air was warmer? Which was cooler? (The cool grass allowed water vapor to come out of the warm air and condense on the grass.) Do you know what we call the water you find on grass in the morning? (Dew.) When it's a cold morning this dew appears to be frozen. What name do we give it then? (Frost.)

3. EXPANSION OF THE IDEA: Which process skills will be used?

Observing, measuring, comparing, recording data

How will the idea be expanded?

Thermometer Reading and Dew Point

Pair up the students. Give each pair a thermometer. Practice reading the thermometer. Be sure each student knows how this is done. As the students work in pairs, ask them to fill a glass with ice and add enough water to cover the ice. Record the temperature their thermometer is reading. Place the thermometer in the glass. Watch the outside of the glass and record the temperature at which water begins to form on the outside of the glass. Explain to the students that for this particular day, with this particular amount of moisture in the air, the temperature they just recorded would be called the *dew point* for the day. When the air reaches that temperature, then *dew* will begin to form on the grass outside.

Science in Personal and Social Perspectives

- Other than the noise involved, why do you think it is not a good idea to mow grass very early on a summer morning?

EARTH SCIENCE

- Explain how your feet could get wet when you run through the grass in the spring.
- Why does frost form on car windows in the winter?

Science and Technology

- Do you think auto manufacturers are concerned with dew formation when they build new cars? Do you think the auto manufacturers think carefully about the kind of paint they put on new cars because they know dew may form on them? What would happen to a car if dew formed on it day after day and there was no protective paint on it? Would the same thing happen to your bicycle?
- How does a rear window defogger/deicer eliminate frost on the car window?

Science as Inquiry

- What do you call it when water turns into water vapor? (Evaporation.)
- When water vapor collects on an object to form water droplets, what is it called? (Condensation.)
- When water collects on a cold surface what may form? (Dew or frost.)
- What is a *dew point?*

History and Nature of Science

- Why would a landscaper be concerned about dew/frost formation? Have you ever seen plants wrapped in cloth or covered in plastic bags? Why do you think landscapers or homeowners do this?
- Do you think a person in the lawn-care business should pay attention to weather forecasts that give the dew point? Do you think it could be used to help the person decide when to start work in the morning?

4. EVALUATION: How will the students show what they have learned?

Upon completing the activities the students will be able to:

- use a bottle and a bowl of ice water to demonstrate how dew can form,
- demonstrate how to determine dew point using a glass, ice cubes, and a thermometer,
- explain why their shoes get wet when they run through grass on a sunny summer morning.

Radiant Energy

Concept to be invented
Main idea—The sun produces energy in the form of heat, referred to as *radiant energy.*

Concepts that are important to expansion
The sun's heat can be used to perform work.

Materials needed
For Activity 1:
Two pie pans, sand, two coins, two black plastic bags.
For Activity 2:
Large glass jar with lid, water, thermometer, graph paper.
For Activity 3:
Magnifying glasses, sheets of paper.
For expansion activity:
6 tea bags, large jar.

➡ **Safety precautions:** Before starting the activities go over the following safety rules:

- The students should call the teacher if the thermometer is dropped and broken. Avoid touching broken glass or the liquid inside the thermometer.
- Activity 3 should be done only by a teacher or other adult.
- Avoid playing with the magnifying glass or placing a hand between the paper and magnifying glass.
- Do not let children stare at or touch the point of light during Activity 3.

1. EXPLORATION: Which process skills will be used?

Predicting, observing, hypothesizing, measuring, recording and analyzing data, graphing

What will the students do?

Temperature and Colored Surfaces

Activity 1. Ask the children to fill the pie pans with sand. Put one pan of sand, one coin, and one garbage bag in direct sunlight. Put the other pan, coin, and bag in shade. Predict what the differences will be between the objects in the sun and those in the shade. After a while have the children feel and compare the objects. How did the objects that were in the sun feel? What about the ones that were in the shade? Why do the things that were in the sun feel warm? Why do they feel cool if they were in the shade?

Temperature: Sun versus Shade

Activity 2. On the second day, have the students fill two jars with water. Record their starting temperatures. Place one of the jars in the sun and one in the shade. Predict how much temperature change will take place in both as time progresses. Have students record the temperatures of the two jars every half hour for a total of 3 hours. Take a final temperature reading. Graph the results with a bar graph using different colors for the sunny and shady sites.

Magnifiers: Capture the Sun

Activity 3. (Do this on day 2 while waiting for the results of Activity 2). On a sunny day, hold the magnifying glass over a piece of paper until the light comes

EARTH SCIENCE

to a point. Hold it there for a few seconds. What happens to the paper? What made the hole in the paper? What does this tell you about what the sun does for us? What can the sun do to your skin and eyes?

2. EXPLANATION/CONCEPT INVENTION: What is the main idea? How will the main idea be constructed?

Concept: The sun produces energy in the form of heat, referred to as *radiant energy.*

What does your graph tell you about a sunny environment versus a shady one? Why do you think there were such temperature differences at the two sites? What does the sun do for the earth? What do you think might happen if the earth were closer to the sun? What if the earth were farther from the sun? What would life be like in either case?

3. EXPANSION OF THE IDEA: Which process skills will be used?

Predicting, observing, inferring, hypothesizing

How will the idea be expanded?

Sun Tea

Fill a large jar with water and six tea bags. Record its temperature. Predict what will happen to the water after a few hours. (Suggest to the students that they might want to think about more than just a temperature change.) Decide where you would place the jar if you wanted to make tea. Place the jar in that spot. Throughout the day check the jar and record the changes. Ask: "What do you think is happening inside the jar? How did the water change into tea? What part did the sun play in this process? What other ways can the sun's heat be harnessed to help things to work?"

Science in Personal and Social Perspectives

- Why is the sun important to us?
- What are some of the things we need to be aware of when we are in the sun?

Science and Technology

- What are some ways in which people use solar energy? (Solar batteries, skylights, heating water to warm rooms, and so on.)
- Are these beneficial? In what ways?
- Why might we need to explore ways to use solar energy in the future?
- Why do clothing manufacturers create lighter-colored clothing for the summer months? Would a manufacturer make more money selling black or white t-shirts in the summer?

Science as Inquiry

- Why are people more careful about being exposed to the sun during the summer than during the winter?

- New concepts to be identified for invention in new lessons: global warming, the ozone layer, the greenhouse effect.

History and Nature of Science

- What are some careers in which people can work with solar energy?
- Why would it be important for a botanist, a florist, or a gardener to understand how the sun heats the earth?

4. EVALUATION: How will the students show what they have learned?

Upon completing the activities the students will be able to:

- while blindfolded, tell which objects were in the sun and which were in shade, and give reasons for the answers;
- create a collage showing the many uses of solar energy;
- draw pictures showing ways they can protect themselves from the damaging effects of the sun.

Weather Forecasting

**GRADE
5–8
DISCIPLINE
Earth
Science**

Concept to be invented
Main idea—Weather data can be collected and reported.

Concepts that are important to expansion
Controlling variables, use of symbols, cloud types.

Materials needed
For exploration:

barometer	wind vane	anemometer
thermometer	rain gauge	clinometer
sling psychrometer	cloud charts	nephoscope

The students should have had prior experience with this equipment as they were learning about individual weather phenomena such as air pressure, humidity, temperature, air masses, fronts.

For expansion and evaluation:
Weather instruments listed above, collection of weather maps from newspapers.

➡ **Safety precautions:** Use care with weather instruments when collecting data. Outdoors, obey school rules. Avoid talking to strangers, and exercise caution if inclement weather prohibits data collection.

EARTH SCIENCE

1. **EXPLORATION:** Which process skills will be used?

Brainstorming, observing, formulating models, predicting, measuring, questioning

Teacher introduction: How many of you have nicknames? When you write letters or your name in school, do you write your full name or your nickname? Which is easier for you to write?

Try to picture in your mind a McDonald's or a Kentucky Fried Chicken restaurant. Imagine you are in the parking lot, or you are riding down the road and you spot one of these places. What image comes to mind first? How many of you remembered a shape or a symbol for the restaurant first?

Can you think of any other things in your life, like toys, games, or bicycles, where you might remember the symbol for the manufacturer rather than the actual name of the company?

For which stores, restaurants, toys, or games do you find the symbol easiest to remember? How often do you use the item or frequent the store? Do you find that the more you use the item or frequent the store, the easier it is to remember the symbol?

Now imagine you're a meteorologist and you collect weather data every day for years. Just like you and your nickname or McDonald's and their golden arches, would it help the meteorologist to have symbols to record data with instead of words? Why or why not?

What will the students do?

Weather Log Creation

Challenge the students to prepare a weather log or a data chart that they will use to collect weather information. Encourage them to keep in mind the previous discussion. Allow the students to break into their own groups. This will help when the students eventually collect weather information on weekends.

Try to give as little input as possible. Give the students time to brainstorm all the factors that may be important to forecast weather. Have the instruments available for them to look over as they try to think of what they need to create a good weather forecast.

Encourage the students to use their designed chart for 1 week. At the start of the next week, ask the student groups to share the information they obtained. As a class, determine the group that was the most accurate in predicting daily weather.

2. **EXPLANATION/CONCEPT INVENTION:** What is the main idea? How will the main idea be constructed?

Concept: Weather data can be collected and reported.

Controlling variables is important to making reliable weather observations. Each separate weather measurement is a variable that cannot be controlled. Ask the students the following questions to help them invent the concept:

EARTH SCIENCE

- Did the weather factors you chose to observe give you enough information to forecast the weather?
- Could you have been more accurate had you collected other types of data?
- Which factors could increase error in your data?
- Did you try to control any human factors that might have made your readings faulty?
- Can you simplify the way in which you recorded your data?

3. EXPANSION OF THE IDEA: Which process skills will be used?

Observing, interpreting data, inferring, creating models, making conclusions

How will the idea be expanded?

Weather Map Symbols

Symbols can be used to designate some weather observations. Collect a supply of weather maps from as many different newspapers as possible. Once you have a number of maps that vary in sophistication, distribute them to your students and ask if they can interpret them. Create a list on the board of all of the different symbols they observe on the maps. Encourage the students to speculate about what each symbol represents. After exploring the various symbols

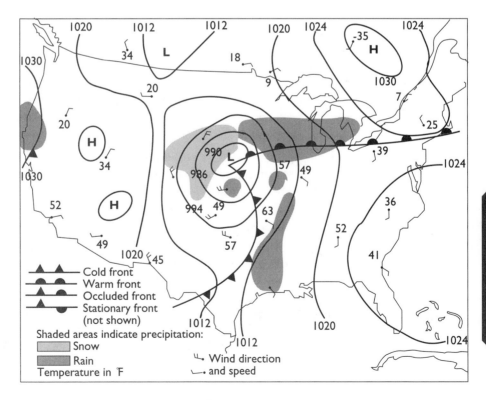

EARTH SCIENCE

found on the map, break the class up into six groups. Assign each group one of the following tasks:

1. Draw a station model diagram that shows wind direction and speed, type of high cloud, type of middle cloud, sea-level pressure, pressure change, type of low cloud, dew point, sky cover, present state of weather, air temperature.
2. Create a chart that shows the weather map symbols for highs, lows, fronts, isobars, and air masses.
3. Create a chart titled "Present State of the Weather" that shows and briefly describes the symbols for precipitation.
4. Create a chart titled "Sky Cover" that shows the symbols for the different fractions of cloud coverage.
5. Create a chart titled "Major Cloud Types" that shows the symbols for and names of the major cloud types.
6. Create a chart titled "Wind Scale" that lists the speed and shows the symbols for the wind.

Weather Data Collection

As the student groups report on the symbols they discovered to represent the various weather phenomena, ask them to decide how they could use some of this information to make recording weather information easier. How can you use this information to predict weather?

Science in Personal and Social Perspectives

- What changes have you experienced in the amount of attention you pay to weather forecasts now that you have had a chance to collect weather information yourself?
- Do you think you can create a family weather station at your house without spending a large amount of money on expensive weather equipment? What types of weather instruments could you create?

Science and Technology

- In the summer of 1990 a sudden flood wiped out the town of Shadyside, Ohio. Could an improved weather radar system have helped to save lives? Could it have prevented the sudden flood?

Science as Inquiry

- Create graphs for each of the weather factors collected over the one-week time period. Study your graphs. Do you see any great fluctuations in any of the readings over time? If so, with which weather factor?
- Was there ever a dramatic rise or decrease in the barometric pressure?
- Did you examine your graphs to see if any other factor changed dramatically when the barometer did? If you did find some changes, with what other factors?
- What kind of pressure system was over the area when the barometer changed dramatically?

- What conclusions can you draw about the relationships among different weather factors?

History and Nature of Science

- Survey local radio and television stations. Where do they get their weather forecast information from? Is there a resident meteorologist who prepares the forecast? If so, see if you can interview that person. Prepare some key questions you would like to have answered in the light of the experiences you have just had collecting your own weather data.

4. EVALUATION: How will the students show what they have learned?

Upon completing these activities the students will be able to demonstrate the use of symbols for collecting and reporting weather data by completing the following tasks:

- Ask the students to look at the data they collected from the exploration phase of this lesson and consider the following questions: Is there a weather factor you did not consider collecting that you would add now? Would it be important to be consistent in your data collection? In other words, did you consider things like making sure you collect your information at the same time every day, or that at least two people in the group are responsible for reading the instruments to check for accuracy?
- Revise your weather log to include all the factors necessary to make a sound weather forecast. You may ask the teacher for sample weather logs or suggestions on what data to collect. Be sure the variables that can be controlled are controlled!
- Once you have revised your log, show it to the teacher. If it is judged complete, then collect weather data for a month.

Some teachers may have their students so proficient on the various weather instruments that it becomes second nature to them. Collect weather data every day for the entire school year. Your class may want to give a daily weather report to the school on the intercom each day.

Weather Predictions

GRADE
5–8
DISCIPLINE
Earth
Science

Concept to be invented
Main idea—Many aspects of weather need to be considered before one can make an accurate prediction of the weather.

Concepts that are important to expansion
Types of storms, seasonal weather change, and climate zones.

EARTH SCIENCE

Materials needed

For exploration:

Numerous copies (at least two for each student) of weather maps from newspapers and/or those available from National Oceanic and Atmospheric Association, weather map symbol key.

For expansion:

rain gauge	sling psychrometer
wind vane and anemometer or an aerovane that combines the two	mercury barometer or the more convenient aneroid barometer
thermometer	cloud charts

➡ **Safety precautions:** Handle weather instruments with care. Avoid dropping them. Be sure you understand how they are used to prevent damage.

1. **EXPLORATION:** Which process skills will be used?

Hypothesizing, recording data, classifying, predicting, formulating models, analyzing, making conclusions, evaluating, communicating

What will the students do?

Weather Map Information

Ask the students to generate a list of variables that need to be taken into account in order to predict the weather in their area accurately. Place this list on the board, numbering each item. (This part of the activity requires them to reflect on results of previous activities in which they studied phenomena like air pressure, cloud types, temperature, relative humidity, air masses, wind speed, and so on.) After the class has had ample opportunity to add to this list, ask the students to take two or more of the weather maps and go on a scavenger hunt. They are to use the weather map key to help them in their hunt. Circle the items from the list on the board that are found on the map. Place the number from the list on the board next to the circle on the map. Do your maps contain enough data to predict accurately what the weather will be in your area? If so, predict the weather. If not, what do you think is missing? Why?

2. **EXPLANATION/CONCEPT INVENTION:** What is the main idea? How will the main idea be constructed?

Concept: Elements of the weather can be recorded and used to forecast weather change.

- What role do air pressure, relative humidity, wind speed and direction, and cloud cover play in predicting weather?
- Without being aware of any other weather component, if your city was trapped under a low-pressure system, what kind of weather would you predict you would have?

EARTH SCIENCE

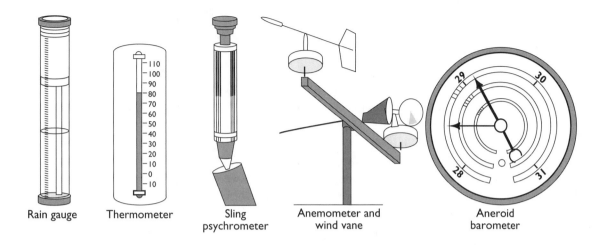

Rain gauge   Thermometer   Sling psychrometer   Anemometer and wind vane   Aneroid barometer

- What types of storms can form in a low-pressure system?
- What types of information are better than others for making accurate forecasts? Time should also be set aside for problems students had in making predictions.

3. EXPANSION OF THE IDEA: Which process skills will be used?

Observing, questioning, measuring, predicting, using numbers, mapping, recording data, making assumptions, formulating models, inferring, analyzing, interpreting data.

How will the idea be expanded?

Recording Weather Data and Predicting Weather The students will generate a list of materials needed to create an amateur weather station on the school grounds. The students will work with the teacher to obtain these materials. They will work together to learn how to use these instruments. Divide the class into groups, assigning each group a week in which they will be responsible for reading and recording the weather instruments each day. From their observations, the use of weather maps, and how they chart the air movements on their own weather maps, the group is to predict the weather each day for one week. Offer a prize to the group that gives the most accurate weather forecast. After each group has had a week to predict the weather, determine the winning group and award the prize!

Science in Personal and Social Perspectives

- Why is it is important to know proper safety procedures during severe storms?
- Do you think you are affected by emotional changes with changes in the weather?

- Why is it important for those who work outdoors to pay attention to daily weather reports on TV, radio, or newspapers?

Science and Technology

- How has the number of commuters into cities like Los Angeles or New York altered the weather conditions of these cities? How has the formation of smog in and around metropolitan areas altered the climate of the surrounding region?

Science as Inquiry

- Charts can be useful in organizing various kinds of data. Past experience can assist one in making accurate predictions of future events.
- What factors do you need to be aware of in order to make an accurate weather prediction?

History and Nature of Science

- How were many historic events shaped by changes in weather and climate? Examples are the potato famine in Ireland, the Dust Bowl days of the 1930s in the United States, the Shadyside floods in Ohio during the spring of 1990, and various Revolutionary War battles.
- In addition to meteorology, in what other careers is the accurate prediction of weather essential? Why?
- Why do those who install or make insulation, heat pumps, and air conditioners want to neutralize weather extremes?

4. EVALUATION: How will the students show what they have learned?

Upon completing the activities the students will be able to:

- make short-term forecasts or predictions of weather conditions using an available weather record with 75 percent accuracy,
- describe typical weather conditions for various climate zones,
- identify a weather trend on a weather map and use it to predict changes over twenty-four hours.

EARTH SCIENCE

Air Mass Movement

GRADE
5–8
DISCIPLINE
Earth
Science

Concept to be invented
Main idea—When moving air masses of different temperature and different moisture content come in contact, it results in precipitation and other identifiable weather phenomena.

Concepts that are important to expansion
Fronts, cold and warm.

Materials needed

For exploration:

globe of the earth	paper	thermometer
medicine dropper	marking pen	hammer
colored water	dry ice	matches
flat-sided top	container of water	string

For expansion:

clear bottle with screw cap   cold water
   (small juice bottles work well)   red and blue food coloring
cooking oil

➡ **Safety precautions:** Use extreme caution when handling the dry ice. If the students are immature, the teacher or another adult may need to handle the dry ice for that part of the experiment. Heavy-duty safety gloves should be made available for anyone handling the dry ice. Goggles should be worn. Care should be taken when handling any of the instruments. Exercise care with glass containers.

1. EXPLORATION: Which process skills will be used?

Observing, measuring, recording data, formulating models

What will the students do?

Coriolis Effect: Globe

Station A. Spin the globe quickly so that it moves in a west-to-east direction. Pretending that you are on the globe at the North Pole, use the medicine dropper to start some colored water rolling in a stream south toward the equator. Carefully record your observations, being sure to include the movement of the water both north and south of the equator.

Coriolis Effect: Top

Station B. Obtain a small flat-sided top. On a piece of paper draw a circle the size of the top. Push this down over the handle of the top and center it on the top. As you spin the top in a counterclockwise direction (from west to east) with one hand, hold a marker in your other hand and try to draw a straight line on the paper attached to the top. Record what happens when you do this.

Air Movement: Dry Ice

Station C. Break a piece of dry ice with a hammer and place a few small pieces into a container of water. Be sure to use caution when working with the dry ice (gloves and goggles). Observe the air around the container over a period of time. Measure the temperature of the air mass (1) just above the container, (2) about 1 meter above the container, and (3) near the base of the container. Record these readings.

   Light one end of a piece of string and then blow out the flame. The end should begin to smoke. Give the smoking string to the students and have them wave it around the container. Ask them to record their observations of the movement of the smoke.

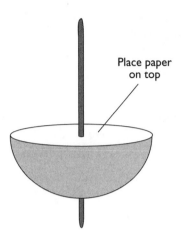

Place paper
on top

2. **EXPLANATION/CONCEPT INVENTION:** What is the main idea? How will the main idea be constructed?

Concept at Stations A and B: Air masses, low-pressure areas, and fronts move generally from west to east.

- At Station A, in what direction did the stream turn in the Northern Hemisphere? in the Southern Hemisphere?
- What effect do you think the land masses with their mountain ranges will have on the moving air?
- At Station B, what happened when you tried to draw a straight line on the paper from the center to the edge of the top?
- Because of the earth's rotation, the motion of a body as seen from earth appears to deflect to the right in the Northern Hemisphere. This fictitious deflecting force is also called the *Coriolis effect.* How do you think the *Coriolis effect* can help explain the results you obtained when trying to draw a straight line on the paper on the spinning top?

Concept at Station C: When moving air masses of different temperature and different moisture content come in contact, it results in precipitation and other identifiable weather phenomena.

- Where was the air mass the highest?
- What happened to the air as it cooled?
- What were your temperature readings around the container? If there were differences, why do you think they occurred?
- What happened when you waved some smoking string in the air around the container? In what direction did the air flow around the container?
- What kind of precipitation do you think could occur if warm air were blown over the cold air flowing from the container?

3. EXPANSION OF THE IDEA: Which process skills will be used?

Manipulating materials, formulating models, hypothesizing, inferring

How will the idea be expanded?

*Oil and
Water Fronts*
Half-fill a bottle with cooking oil. Add some red food coloring, cap the bottle, and shake well. This will represent a warm air mass. In a separate container, add blue food coloring to cold water. What do you think will happen as you pour the cold water into the bottle of oil? Slowly pour the water into the bottle.

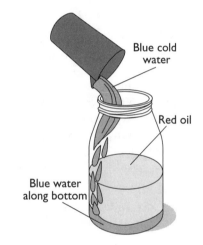

Blue cold
water

Red oil

Blue water
along bottom

The following concepts can be demonstrated with this arrangement of materials:

- Lines of temperature differences between two air masses are called *fronts*.
- A *warm front* is caused by a relatively warm mass of air advancing over a mass of relatively cold air.
- A *cold front* is caused by a mass of relatively cold air displacing relatively warm air.
- Advancing cold fronts lift warm air. Advancing warm fronts result in the warm air being lifted.
- Fronts do not all move at the same speed or in the same direction.
- The amount of moisture in the air controls the kind of weather along the front.

Questions that help students invent expansion concepts:

- What happened when you poured the cold water into the oil? Did it behave as you predicted? Which liquid is denser? How do you know?
- Place the screw cap on the bottle. Slowly turn the bottle on its side. How does the heavier liquid move, and what is its final position?
- If a cold air mass moves toward a warm air mass, would the leading edge of the cold air mass be at the ground level or above the ground? Why?

(Remember that the blue water represents the cold air mass, and the red oil is the warm air mass.)

- If a warm air mass moves toward a cold air mass, would the leading edge of the warm air mass be at the ground or above the ground? Why?
- How would you describe a stationary front? What factors affect its formation?

Science in Personal and Social Perspectives

- If you were planning a picnic for Saturday and you heard on a Thursday weather forecast that a warm front would be moving into the region on Friday evening, would you switch the day of your picnic to Sunday? Why or why not?

Science and Technology

- What effect do extremes in precipitation have upon area populations (not just human)?
- How do you think knowledge of such weather phenomena as air masses, fronts, and precipitation have assisted in the invention of the material Gore-tex, which is now used in running clothes, tents, tarpaulins, and so on? How has this invention allowed us to enjoy our environment more, no matter what the weather conditions?

Science as Inquiry

- What kind of pressure system do you think would bring your area a large amount of precipitation? a small amount? Create your own rain gauge to measure precipitation by following the steps below.

Create a Rain Gauge

Use the following materials to create your own rain gauge: large straight-sided jar, long narrow jar or large test tube, meter stick, metric ruler, and masking tape. Place a ruler vertically in the large jar and pour in water until it reaches the 10-mm mark on the ruler. Pour this water into the narrow jar, to which you have attached a strip of masking tape. Mark the masking tape at the exact level of the water. This represents 10 mm in the jar. Repeat this procedure for levels of 20 mm, 30 mm, and so on.

Place the large jar outside, away from any obstruction, to collect rain. Why is that important? The top of the jar should be about 30.5 cm above the ground. To read the amount of rain, empty it into the measuring jar at the same time each day. Keep a daily record in a chart form.

Do you think you can determine how much snow you would have had if you had 50 mm of rain collected in your gauge? What about if you have 50 mm of snow? How much rain would that be? The student can do two things here: (1) Obtain a tall, straight-sided container, such as an empty juice can. Carefully fill it with loose snow, but do not pack the snow in the can. Heat the snow until it is completely melted. Use the rain gauge to measure the amount of water. If you know the length of the can, you can compare amount of snow to rain. (2) The student could guesstimate the amount of rain the snow is equal to by knowing that the ratio of snow to rain is usually 10 to 1. A wet, heavy snow may have a ratio as low as 6 to 1, while in dry, fluffy, new-fallen snow, the ratio may be as high as 30 to 1.

History and Nature of Science

- How is it possible for airplanes to fly in the eye of the storm during a hurricane? What kind of information do pilots need to understand about air masses in order to do this?
- Create a list of all of the types of jobs that can be affected when air masses of different temperatures and moisture contents come in contact. Are any of those jobs in areas in which you would like to work?

4. EVALUATION: How will the students show what they have learned?

Air Masses and Parachutes

The following parachute activity, as well as the questions covering personal development, science-technology-society, academic growth, and career awareness could be used to assess the students' knowledge of the relationships among air masses, fronts, and precipitation.

Parachute materials

12-inch square sheet of tissue paper   washer for weight
eight glue-backed hole reinforcers   paper person (for decorative
four strings 10 inches in length each   purposes only)

Punch a hole in each corner of the tissue with a pencil point. Place a hole reinforcer on each side of the hole. Tie the four strings to each hole. Tie the loose ends of the strings together around the washer. Be sure the strings end up being of equal length. Decorate with a paper person attached to the washer. You may

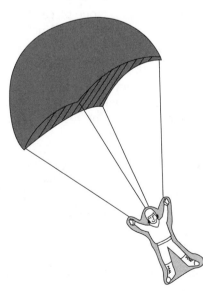

find that a small hole in the very center of the tissue will help the parachute open more quickly.

Fold up your chute and throw it into the air. Have a partner time from the moment you release it until the moment it begins to descend. Time its descent.

- How does the parachute depend on air pressure?
- What if your parachute came from several hundred meters above the earth's surface? Would it fall any differently?
- Would the parachute fall differently if a cold front were in the area? What about a warm front?
- What if a warm front were just moving into the area, replacing a cold front. Would it be safe to parachute during that time? Why or why not?

Air Pressure

**GRADE
5–8
DISCIPLINE
Earth
Science**

Concept to be invented
Main idea—Air has weight.

Concepts that are important to expansion
Air can exert pressure. Temperature and air movement are factors that influence air pressure.

Materials needed
For each student group:

modeling clay	three balloons	straw
pencil	two books	one index card
yardstick	one piece of 8½-inch	one glass of water
string	by 11-inch paper	one sandwich bag

For teacher demonstration:
one beach ball

For Science as Inquiry and evaluation:

two paper lunch bags	one lamp or candle
two balloons and string for	one straw and one Ping-Pong ball
each student group	per student

➡ **Safety precautions:** The students should take care that when blowing during the activities they don't hyperventilate and get dizzy. Have a paper bag available for any hyperventilating student to breathe into slowly. This will balance the oxygen-carbon dioxide ratio and return the student to normal.

1. **EXPLORATION:** Which process skills will be used?

Observing, predicting, comparing, questioning, describing, manipulating materials, recording data

What will the students do?

Balloon Balance   Provide the students with modeling clay, pencil, yardstick, three balloons, and a string. Ask them to manipulate these materials so that they can create a balance such as in the diagram.

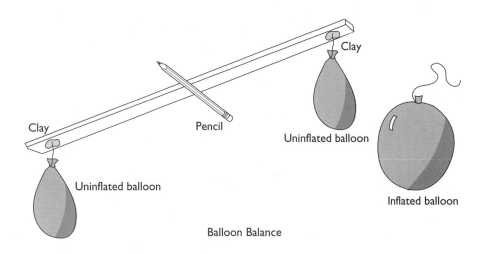

Balloon Balance

Suspend and balance two uninflated balloons. Ask the students to record their observations. Then ask them to predict what would happen to this balanced system if they were to replace one of the uninflated balloons with an inflated balloon. Record their predictions. Now replace one of the uninflated balloons with an inflated balloon. Record students' observations. Do they match their predictions?

2. EXPLANATION/CONCEPT INVENTION: What is the main idea? How will the main idea be constructed?

Concept: Air has weight.

What kind of data did you collect? Did you obtain results as you predicted? Hold up an uninflated beach ball. Ask the students to help you weigh it. Now ask one of the students to blow it up. Ask for their predictions as to whether it now weighs the same. How is this demonstration similar to the balance you just created? What happened with your balance when you replaced the uninflated balloon with an inflated balloon? Weigh it. Does it weigh the same? Why? (Air has weight.)

3. EXPANSION OF THE IDEA: Which process skills will be used?

Observing, predicting, comparing, manipulating materials, recording data, hypothesizing

How will the idea be expanded?

Paper Blowing

Ask the students to place two books (at least a quarter- to a half-inch thick) 3 inches apart on a desk top. Place a sheet of 8½-inch by 11-inch paper across the book lengthwise. Have the students predict if they can blow the paper off the books by blowing into the space between the books. Record your predictions, then try it! Repeat the experiment, this time using a straw placed just under the edge of the paper to blow between the books.

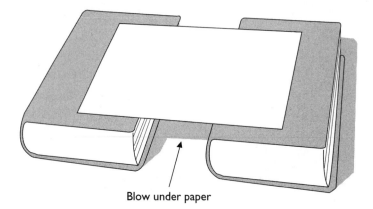

Blow under paper

What happened to the paper when you blew without the straw? with the straw? Were you able to blow the paper off the books either time? Did the paper move at all? If so, how? This activity demonstrates that air has pressure. Air moving fast, such as the air you blew out between the books and underneath the paper, creates a lower pressure than the pressure above the books. Thus you see a slight dip in the paper. When you use a straw to blow through, the straw creates a narrow high-speed path of low pressure between the books. Now the pressure underneath the paper bridge is much lower than the pressure above the paper; thus you observe a big dip in the paper bridge. This dip is caused by the higher air pressure on top of the paper. Thus, air exerts pressure.

Newspaper Strength

A good teacher demonstration is to take a yardstick or some other relatively long, thin piece of wood and place it on a table top. Smooth out a large piece of newspaper over the wood. Leave about 6 to 8 inches of wood sticking out one side. Make sure there are no air spaces between the newspaper and the table top. Ask the students if they think you can hit this stick and make the paper go flying. Once you take several predictions, hit the stick. What happened? The stick broke and the paper remained on the table top. Why? Because on every square inch of that paper, air is exerting a pressure of 14.7 pounds per square inch. A full sheet of newspaper is typically 27 inches by 23 inches, or 621 square inches. If there are 14.7 pounds of pressure exerted on every square inch of the newspaper, that means that there is 621 square inches times 14.7 pounds per

square inch, or 9128.7 pounds of pressure being exerted by the air on that paper. You would have to hit the stick with a force equal to that amount to get the paper to move!

Science in Personal and Social Perspectives

- What does air pressure have to do with a smooth ride on your bike or in a car?
- What happens when your bike gets a flat tire? What does this do to the air pressure in the tire?

Science and Technology

- In the second activity you found that faster-moving air causes lower air pressure. How do you think this fact has influenced the design of airplanes?
- Ask a student to demonstrate lift by taping a narrow strip of paper to a pencil. Hold the pencil by your mouth and blow over the strip of paper. What happens to it? How do you think this movement is similar to air blowing over the wing of an airplane?

Science as Inquiry

- Does all air have the same weight? Ask the students to replace their uninflated balloons in the balanced system with two paper lunch bags. Get the system to balance. Now place a lit lamp or candle several inches below one of the bags. What happened to that balanced system? Which weighs more: cold or hot air?
- What kind of air pressure do you think would be associated with a cold front? a warm front?

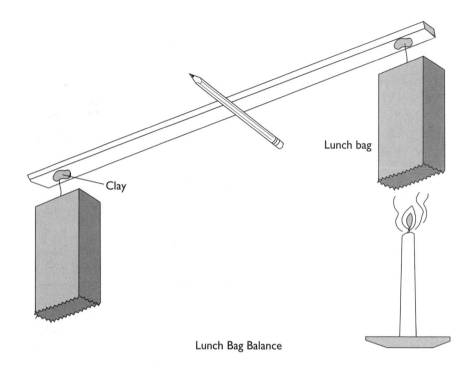

Lunch bag

Clay

Lunch Bag Balance

History and Nature of Science

- Ask the students to share information with one another on Daniel Bernoulli (1700–1782). He was a Swiss doctor, mathematician, biologist, physiologist, physicist, astronomer, and oceanographer. Can you think of any people today who are as well versed in as many areas as Daniel Bernoulli was? Do you think it is more difficult to be an expert in all of these areas today? Why?
- Invite a pilot to speak to your class. Ask him or her to explain how knowledge of air pressure helps him or her to control an airplane.

4. EVALUATION: How will the students show what they have learned?

Upon completing these activities the students will be able to:

- predict and then explain why two balloons suspended on equal-length strings about 3 inches apart come closer together when the students blow between them. They will be able to demonstrate this phenomenon.
- look at a picture of an unbalanced system, in which one balloon is inflated and the other is uninflated, and explain why this system is unbalanced.
- demonstrate that a Ping-Pong ball can hover over the end of a drinking straw. They will also be able to explain why this happens and be able to share and explain this phenomenon to children in a primary grade.

Solar Heating

Concept to be invented
Main idea—The earth's surfaces are heated unevenly.

Concepts that are important to expansion
Uneven heating creates wind and makes the water cycle occur. The sun is the source of energy that determines the weather on earth.

Materials needed
For exploration (per student group):

three paper cups   three thermometers
dark soil   one lamp
light sand   satellite photographs
water   of the earth's surface

For evaluation:
three metal cans   matte black paint
white enamel paint   Styrofoam cups

For expansion (per student group):
One thermometer

➡ **Safety precautions:** The students should be careful when using the lamp and around electricity.

1. EXPLORATION: Which process skills will be used?

Observing, predicting, comparing, questioning, describing, manipulating materials, recording data

What will the students do?

Temperature versus Surface Color Ask the students to cut the tops off the paper cups so that they are about 4 cm deep. Fill one with dark-colored soil, one with light-colored sand, and the third with water. Instruct the students to place a thermometer into each cup, covering the bulb with about 0.5 cm of soil, sand, or water. Record the temperature of each surface. Place a lit lamp so its bulb is about 15 cm from the tops of the cups. After 5 minutes, record the temperature of each cup. Identify which cup gained heat the fastest, and record this information. Remove the lamp from the cups. Predict which cup you think will lose heat the fastest. Record your prediction. Leave the cups untouched, and after 10 minutes, record the temperature of each cup. Which lost heat the fastest? Record these data. Did you predict correctly?

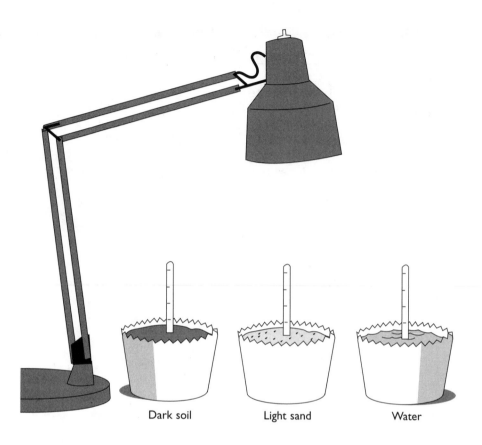

Dark soil   Light sand   Water

2. EXPLANATION/CONCEPT INVENTION: *What is the main idea? How will the main idea be constructed?*

> *Concept:* The earth's surfaces are heated unevenly.
>
> What kinds of data did you collect? Did you obtain results as you predicted? How do you think this activity helps explain the uneven heating of the earth's surfaces?
>
> Look at satellite pictures of the earth. Describe the different surfaces. Why do dark-colored surfaces absorb more heat energy from the sun? What do lighter-colored surfaces do that would prevent as much absorption of the sun's energy as dark surfaces? (The lighter surfaces reflect more of the sun's energy, whereas dark land absorbs it. Also, dark land loses its heat faster than water.)

3. EXPANSION OF THE IDEA: *Which process skills will be used?*

> Observing, predicting, comparing, manipulating materials, recording data, hypothesizing

How will the idea be expanded?

Optimum Thermometer Placement

Ask the students where they think they should place a thermometer to measure the air temperature every day. Ask the students to predict and then record air temperature taken on blacktop, grass, in the shade of a tree, a sandy area, and a gravel area. Take these readings at ground level and at 1 meter from the ground. Does this make a difference? Will the time of day make a difference? Have the students record the temperature at these various sites during different times of the school day. Which gives the most accurate reading for actual air temperature? Once the class decides this, then at that site and time, daily temperature readings can be taken for a weather log for the class. The students can also practice taking temperature readings in degrees Celsius and Fahrenheit.

Science in Personal and Social Perspectives

- What are ways of staying cool on a hot day or warm on a cold day?
- Why are swimming pools, ponds, lakes, or oceans good places to cool off?
- What kinds of clothes will help keep you cool in summer? What kinds will keep you warm in winter? How and why?

Science and Technology

- How do we attempt to control the temperature in our homes? What kinds of heating and cooling systems do we utilize?
- What alternative sources of energy, aside from fossil fuels, should we continue to develop? How efficient do you think these are or will be?

Science as Inquiry

- Aside from unequal heating of the different-colored surfaces of the earth, temperature is also determined by many other factors. Discuss how the following could affect air temperature: cloud cover, time of day, time of year, wind, latitude, altitude, and oceans or other large bodies of water.
- At what temperature in degrees Celsius does water freeze? boil? At what temperature will water freeze and boil in degrees Fahrenheit?

History and Nature of Science

- Who helps supply energy to keep our homes cool in summer and warm in winter? (Coal miner, lumberjack, oil-field worker, power plant operator, heating–ventilation–air conditioning personnel, and so on.) Choose one of these jobs and identify how they supply energy. What raw material do they make use of?

4. EVALUATION: How will the students show what they have learned?

Upon completing these activities the students will be able to:

- fill three identical-sized cans with tap water. Insert a thermometer through a cover made out of the bottom of a Styrofoam cup. One can should be painted

EARTH SCIENCE

dull black, one left shiny metal, and the last painted shiny white. Ask the students to predict what will happen to the temperature of the water when the cans are placed in direct sunlight or equally distanced from a 150- to 300-watt light bulb. The students should be able to record the temperature of the water in the cans at 1-minute intervals. They should be able to write a short report of their observations.

- record the temperature of the cans in Celsius and Fahrenheit.
- choose an optimal location outdoors to record daily temperature observations.

Air Movement and Surface Temperature

GRADE
5–8
DISCIPLINE
Earth
Science

Concept to be invented
Main idea—Air moves downward over cold surfaces and upward over warm surfaces.

Concepts that are important to expansion
A volume of warm air has less mass than an equal volume of cool air; particles of warm air are farther apart than particles of cool air. Cold air, being heavier than warm air, sinks, pushing warm air upward.

Materials needed
For exploration to make an observation box:

one cardboard box (about 30 cm × 30 cm × 50 cm)	plastic tape
clear plastic food wrap	one plastic straw

Remove the top of the box. Leave a 3-cm edge for strength. Turn the box over. Cut a window in the new top, leaving half of the top intact. Cut out one side, again leaving a 3-cm edge for strength. Tape clear plastic food wrap to the side and the half window on top. In one end of the box, cut a small hole just large enough to insert a plastic straw. See figure for assistance in construction.

Additional materials for exploration:

one 35-ml syringe	matches
one plastic straw (cut into three even pieces)	ice water
	hot water
heavy cotton string (three 4-cm pieces)	aluminum pan
	metric ruler
scissors	

For expansion:
one dowel rod (3 feet long × ¾-inch wide) with hole drilled exactly in center
one dowel rod (1 foot long × ¼-inch wide) to be placed through hole in larger rod

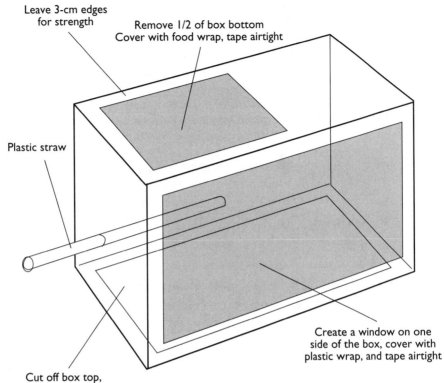

Leave 3-cm edges
for strength

Remove 1/2 of box bottom
Cover with food wrap, tape airtight

Plastic straw

Create a window on one
side of the box, cover with
plastic wrap, and tape airtight

Cut off box top,
leave 3-cm edge for strengh

one paper clip used as a sliding clip to balance the rod
two small paper bags of equal size
two thumbtacks of equal size and weight
one 150-watt bulb and socket
extension cord if necessary

➡ **Safety precautions:** Use caution around open flame.

1. EXPLORATION: Which process skills will be used?

Observing, experimenting, formulating models, questioning, communicating, inferring

What will the students do?

Convection Current and Surface Temperature in an Observation Box

Take a piece of string and fold it in half. Place the folded end into one of the pieces of straw, allowing about 0.5 cm to hang out the end. Be sure it fits snugly in the end. Do this for each piece of straw.

Slip the open end of the prepared straw onto the syringe. Light the string. Collect smoke in the cylinder by slowly pulling out the plunger. Remove the straw and lay it aside where it won't burn anything. You may need more smoke later.

Place a pan of ice water inside the observation box. Be sure the straw is in place through the end of the box, but not hanging over the pan. Let the pan sit for 3 or 4 minutes. After the wait, insert the smoke-filled syringe into the straw of the observation box. Gently force the smoke through the straw into the box. Carefully observe what happens to the smoke as it moves over the pan of ice water.

Complete the procedure using a pan of hot water instead. Once again, make careful observations of the smoke as it moves over the hot water.

2. EXPLANATION/CONCEPT INVENTION: What is the main idea? How will the main idea be constructed?

Concept: Air moves downward over colder surfaces and upward over warm surfaces.

- What path did the smoke take as it moved over the cold surface? (It spread out slowly over the pan, staying close to the pan's surface.)
- What path did the smoke take as it moved over the hot surface? (It slowly spread out and upward.)
- Do you think a force is acting on the smoke as it moves above the warm or cold surfaces? (A force is something that causes a change in shape or a change in motion of a body. It is easy to see the change in shape; this also shows the change in motion.)

3. EXPANSION OF THE IDEA: Which process skills will be used?

Experimenting, making conclusions, evaluating, generalizing

How will the idea be expanded?

Paper Bag Balance   Set up the dowel rod balance as in the figure. Fasten the two paper bags to the balance rod using the thumbtacks. Balance the rod using the sliding paper clip. Hold the rod stationary. Put the lighted bulb just below the open end of the bag on one side. Keep the bulb under the bag for 30 seconds. Then gently let go of the bar. Observe the bag for several minutes.

Questions that help invent additional concepts:

- What happened to the bag on the side near the bulb?
- How do you know this?
- Was the temperature of the bag away from the bulb colder or warmer than the bag near the bulb?
- What happened when you gently released the balance?

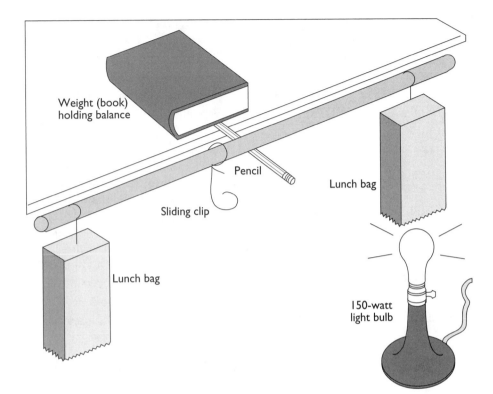

- From your observations, which has the greater mass? Is it the bag of warm air or the bag of cool air?
- The bags in this activity have the same volume. Which do you think has more gas particles? Why?
- What do you think this activity demonstrates about what happens to a substance when heated?

Warm air has less mass than an equal amount of cool air: particles of warm air are farther apart than particles of cool air. Cold air, being heavier than warm air, sinks, pushing warm air upward.

Science in Personal and Social Perspectives

- How would the absence of wind affect your life? Do you think life would be changed in any way if there never was a wind?
- How does the presence of wind affect you personally? How do you think strong winds would affect you if you lived in a coastal city?

Science and Technology

- How has wind power become a source of energy in some regions of the world? How has this harnessing of the wind changed the lives of people living there?

EARTH SCIENCE

- How has knowledge of air mass saved lives? In what circumstances?

Science as Inquiry

- The students will develop process skills needed to identify moving air as wind and to determine that air has mass.
- The students will be able to explain the movement of air over surfaces of varying temperatures and apply this knowledge to explain why wind occurs.

History and Nature of Science

- How will knowledge of wind behavior assist a pilot in flight? What kind of training must a pilot undergo in order to understand how wind behaves? Can just anyone become a pilot? What skills do you think are necessary to become a successful pilot?
- Read a book on Amelia Earhart. What do you think happened to her when she vanished in her plane over the Pacific Ocean?
- Can you list any other occupations in which knowledge of wind and its behavior is necessary?

4. EVALUATION: How will the students show what they have learned?

Upon completing the activities the students will be able to:

- answer all of the questions included in this lesson;
- demonstrate the movement of smoke over cold air and warm air to a group of younger students or parents and be able to explain the concept behind the movement;
- demonstrate that cold air sinks and warm air rises when given a thermometer, a pan of ice water, and a fan.

Uneven Heating of the Earth

GRADE
5–8
DISCIPLINE
Earth
Science

EARTH SCIENCE

Concept to be invented
Main idea—Uneven heating of the earth affects air pressure.

Concepts that are important to expansion
Uneven heating of the earth gives rise to wind patterns that move locally and around the globe.

Materials needed
For exploration:
long clear tube   six rubber bands
two rubber stoppers to fit   clear tape
   tube (clear caps)   one tongue depressor

tub of water
two baby food jars (one larger
    than the other)
balloon

one straw
scissors or knife
marking pen

For expansion:
two clear-glass drinking cups
    of the same size
water
food coloring
index card
wire
candle

two large can lids
clay
two tacks
small lamp with removable shade
oven mitt
glass beaker

➡ **Safety precautions:** The students should take care when using any glass containers. Exercise extreme caution when using the hot water to avoid burns. Also, when using the lamp, remember that the bulb can get hot. When using the candle, be watchful of the open flame. Be sure all sleeves are rolled up, all hair is pulled back, and no shirts are dangling into the flame.

1. **EXPLORATION:** Which process skills will be used?

Observing, measuring, questioning, recording data, predicting, formulating models

What will the students do?

The following two activities could be done ahead of time to introduce the concept of air pressure. Once the students understand this concept, then the third activity can be performed to teach the concept at hand.

Tower of Water   Close one end of a long, clear tube with a stopper or cap. Stand this in a tub of water. Fill the tube with water. Seal the top end of the tube with the stopper or cap. Remove the seal at the bottom, keeping the opening of the tube under water. What happens to the water in the tube? Why? What do you think will happen if you remove the stopper from the top of the tube? Try it! Was your prediction correct? Why does all of this happen?

Aneroid Barometer   Cut the open end off a balloon. Obtain a large-size baby food jar and extend the balloon over the mouth of the jar. Make sure the balloon is stretched taut. While you hold it, have your partner fasten it in place with a rubber band. Be sure to make a tight seal. Use the second rubber band to make sure the seal is tight. Why do you think a tight seal is important? Draw a sketch of your jar. Show what the balloon seal would look like if the pressure inside the jar were greater than the pressure outside of the jar. Cut one end of the straw at an angle to make it pointed. Gently place a 3-cm strip of tape on the uncut end. Place this on the center of the balloon-covered jar. Be sure it sits securely in the center. Attach a

EARTH SCIENCE

tongue depressor to the smaller jar at the top and the bottom of the jar, using two rubber bands at each location (a total of four). Place the two jars side by side on a level support so that the pointed straw is in front of the tongue depressor. Label the point where it hits 0 to show the starting position.

Questions for student activities:

- What do you think will happen to the pointer as the air pressure outside the jar increases?
- What about when the air pressure outside decreases?
- Try increasing the air pressure within the jar by placing your hands over the balloon jar for about 10 minutes. What happens to the pointer?
- Try decreasing the air pressure within the jar by placing the balloon jar in a pan of ice water. What happened to the pointer?

Uneven Heating and Air Pressure   Make use of the barometers created in the second activity or provide the students with commercially made aneroid barometers. After the students have had a chance to observe how their barometers work, divide the class into three groups. In the very beginning of the school day, instruct one third of the students to place their barometer in the same safe place in the playground in the sun on the blacktop or gravel; one third in the same safe place in the playground in the shade on the grass near a tree; one third in the same area of the classroom. Instruct each group to place a thermometer in their area also. Ask the students to take readings from their barometers and thermometers throughout the course of the school day. Instruct the students to note any changes that occur in the area where they placed the barometer, such as the amount of sunlight, changing shade conditions, or wind picking up or dying down. Remind them about the importance of keeping a careful record of their observations.

2. EXPLANATION/CONCEPT INVENTION: What is the main idea? How will the main idea be constructed?

Concept: Uneven heating of the earth affects air pressure.

If the students have made careful observations and recorded their data accurately, you should be able to create a class chart of data collected at the three sites. Ask the students from each of the groups to examine their data as a group first. If their data for the different time readings are not all the same, ask them to average the readings for that time period. These averages could be placed on the chart.

Through careful questioning and calling attention to the group data, the children may find that the barometric readings as well as thermometer readings were different at each of the sites. Ask them if they see some sort of relationship between the temperature at the site and what was happening with the barometer. What happened to the barometric reading as your temperature increased?

EARTH SCIENCE

as it decreased? Were the barometer readings any different in the shade than in the sun or the classroom? Why or why not?

The earth is heated unevenly due to varying types and colors of surfaces found on the earth. What was the color of the site where you placed your barometer and thermometer? Which color site had the warmest temperatures? the coolest? Were the barometer readings different for these sites? What conclusions can you draw about uneven heating of the earth and air pressure?

3. EXPANSION OF THE IDEA: Which process skills will be used?

Observing, hypothesizing, predicting, communicating

How will the idea be expanded?

Concept: Uneven heating of the earth gives rise to wind patterns that move locally and around the globe.

Set up stations around the classroom so that the children can practice the following:

Air Pressure versus Water Temperature   Fill two clear glasses with water. Place an index card on the top of one. Holding the card in place, invert the cup and place it on top of the other cup. Remove the card. Obtain some very hot water. Put food coloring into it. Use this to fill one of the clear glasses from your practice session above. Do the same with cold water and a different color of food coloring. Place a card over one of the cups. Be sure to wear an oven mitt to hold the hot glass. Try inverting the cold over hot and hot over cold. What happens in each set of cups? Why?

Air Temperature versus Movement of Air   Draw a spiraling line on an index card. Cut out this snake and tape a thread to the center of it. Blow on the snake from the bottom. What happens to the snake? What do you think will happen if you suspend it above a burning candle? Try it! Why is this snake moving?

Heat Transfer on a Wire   Light a candle and allow the melting wax to harden at different spots on a wire. Hold one end of the wire in a candle flame. What do you think will happen to the wax drops on the wire? Does something happen to all of the drops at the same time? How is heat transferred from one end of the wire to the next?

Heat Movement Through Air   Remove the shade from a lamp and plug it in. Place your hand carefully near the side of the bulb, keeping the light off. Turn on the lamp. Did you notice a change in the temperature of your hand? Place a cool beaker around the lit bulb. Can you feel the heat from the bulb?

Heat Transfer Through Metal   Cover one side of a large tin can lid with candle soot. Fix a tack to the opposite side with candle wax. Fix a tack to the side of a clean tin can lid. Support each lid in a clay mound so the tacks are directly opposite the candle flame, a small

EARTH SCIENCE

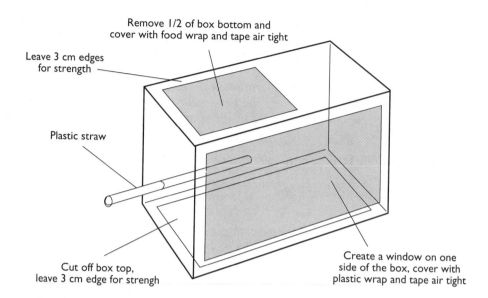

Remove 1/2 of box bottom and
cover with food wrap and tape air tight

Leave 3 cm edges
for strength

Plastic straw

Cut off box top,
leave 3 cm edge for strengh

Create a window on one
side of the box, cover with
plastic wrap and tape air tight

but equal distance away. Which tack do you think will fall first and why? Did it occur as you predicted?

As the students rotate through the five stations, set up a sixth demonstration area so that the small groups can observe the teacher perform the following activity.

Make an observation box before beginning the demonstration. The following materials will be needed: one cardboard box (about 30 cm × 30 cm × 50 cm), clear plastic food wrap, plastic tape, one plastic straw.

Remove the top of the box. Leave a 3-cm edge for strength. Turn the box over. Cut a window in the new top, leaving half of the top intact. Cut out one side, again leaving a 3-cm edge for strength. Tape clear plastic food wrap to the side and the half window on top. In one end of the box, cut a small hole just large enough to insert a plastic straw. See figure for assistance in construction.

Additional materials:

one 35-ml syringe   scissors
one plastic straw (cut into three   matches
   even pieces)   ice water
heavy cotton string (three 4-cm   aluminum pan
   pieces)   metric ruler

Movement of Smoke over Hot and Cold Surfaces: Clouds

Teacher demonstration:

1. Take a piece of string and fold it in half. Place the folded end into one of the pieces of straw, allowing about 0.5 cm to hang out the end. Be sure it fits snugly in the end. Do this for each piece of straw.

2. Slip the open end of the prepared straw onto the syringe. Light the string. Collect smoke in the cylinder by slowly drawing out the plunger. Remove the straw and lay it aside where it won't burn anything. You may need more smoke later.

3. Place a pan of ice water inside the observation box. Be sure the straw is in place through the end of the box but not hanging over the pan. Let the pan sit for 3 or 4 minutes. After the wait, insert the smoke-filled syringe into the straw of the observation box. Gently force the smoke through the straw into the box. Carefully observe what happens to the smoke as it moves over the pan of ice water.

4. Complete the procedure using a pan of hot water instead. Once again ask the students to make careful observations of the smoke as it moves over the hot water.

Additional activity/demonstration materials needed:

observation/convection box	paper clips	scissors
drinking straws	tape	empty soda bottle
straight pins	index cards	small fan
	clay	

Movement of Smoke over Hot and Cold Surfaces: Wind Patterns

Remove the pan of water used in the activity above and replace it with a candle. Cut a 10-cm hole in the observation box in the lid directly above the candle so that the observation box now looks like the figure below. Light the candle and place it inside the box directly under the hole. Once again inject air through the straw to keep the wick smoking. Observe the behavior of the smoke in the box. Which direction is the smoke in the straw coming from: horizontal or ver-

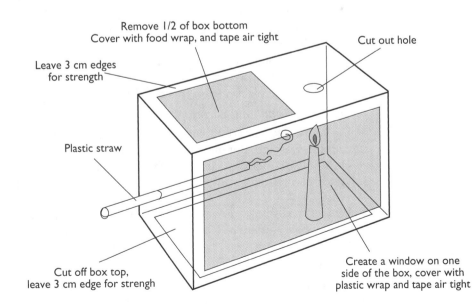

Remove 1/2 of box bottom
Cover with food wrap, and tape air tight

Cut out hole

Leave 3 cm edges for strength

Plastic straw

Cut off box top, leave 3 cm edge for strengh

Create a window on one side of the box, cover with plastic wrap and tape air tight

tical? Place a pan of ice cubes directly below the smoking wick and leave the burning candle in place. What happens to the smoke as it moves over the pan and on toward the candle?

Concept: Uneven heating of the earth gives rise to wind patterns that move locally and around the globe. *Convection* is hot air rising above cold. *Conduction* is heat transferred through surface of objects. *Radiation* is heat energy that travels in waves.

Questions for student activities:

- What three types of heating did you experience in the above activities?
- When warm air rises over cold air, what type of current does this represent?
- If you had a choice of the type of heating for your home, would you choose one that made use of conduction, convection currents, or radiation? Which do you think is the most efficient? the least efficient?
- How can a toaster be used to demonstrate the three different types of heating?

Questions for teacher demonstration:

- What path did the smoke take as it moved over the cold surface? (It spreads out slowly over the pan, staying close to the pan's surface.)
- What path did the smoke take as it moved over the hot surface? (It slowly spread out and upward.)
- What path did the smoke take as it moved over the ice and on toward the candle? (It stayed close to the pan's surface and then rose up over the candle.)
- Do you think a force is acting on the smoke as it moves above the warm or cold surfaces? (A force is something that causes a change in shape or a change in motion of a body. It is easy to see the change in shape; this also shows the change in motion.)
- What name could you give this change of motion? Why do you think it occurs? (Wind is caused by the uneven heating within the observation box. The teacher should elaborate on this concept of local and global winds.)

Science in Personal and Social Perspectives

- Do you think you could run a mile in Denver, Colorado, as easily as you could in Chicago, Illinois? Why or why not?
- On a hot summer day, can you feel a difference in your comfort level when you are wearing a dark-colored shirt compared to a light-colored shirt? Why?
- Why do you think you have to bake a boxed cake mix at a different temperature when you are in a place at a high altitude compared to a place closer to sea level?

Science and Technology

- What causes winds?
- Why is a desert climate different from a forest climate?

History and Nature of Science
- Who was Bernoulli and how did his work explain the concept of air pressure?

4. EVALUATION: How will the students show what they have learned?

Upon completing these activities the students will be able to:

- compare cloud patterns of different areas when given satellite photographs,
- look at an aerial map of a coastal state and be able to predict where most of the clouds will form,
- demonstrate the ability to read a barometer,
- explain the difference in barometric readings over land and sea,
- explain why you would expect the air to be warmer in the daytime over land than sea,
- engage in a reflective discussion on the cause of wind and its importance.

EARTH SCIENCE

National Science Education Standards: Content Standards for K–4 and 5–8

K–4 Physical Science Standards

Content Standard B—K–4:

All students should develop an understanding of:

- Properties of objects and materials
- Position and motion of objects
- Light, heat, electricity, and magnetism

Properties of objects and materials concepts

- Objects have many observable properties, including size, weight, shape, color, temperature, and the ability to react with other substances. These properties can be measured using tools such as rulers, balances, and thermometers.
- Objects are made of one or more materials, such as paper, wood, and metal. Objects can be described by the properties of the materials from which they are made, and these properties can be used to separate or sort a group of objects or materials.
- Materials have different states—solid, liquid, and gas. Some common materials such as water can be changed from one state to another by heating or cooling.

Position and motion of objects concepts

- The position of an object can be described by locating it relative to another object or the background.
- An object's motion can be described by indicating the change in its position over time.
- The position and motion of objects can be changed by pushing or pulling and the size of the change is related to the strength of the push or pull.
- Vibrating objects produce sound. The pitch of the sound can be varied by changing the rate of vibration.

Light, heat, electricity, and magnetism concepts

- Light travels in a straight line unless it strikes an object. Light can be reflected by a mirror, refracted by a lens, or absorbed by the object.

- Heat can be produced in many ways such as burning, rubbing, and mixing chemicals. The heat can move from one object to another by conduction.
- Electricity in circuits can produce light, heat, sound, and magnetic effects. Electrical circuits require a complete loop through which the electrical current can pass.
- Magnets attract and repel each other and certain kinds of metals.

K–4 Life Science Standards

Content Standard C—K–4:

All students should develop an understanding of:

- The characteristics of organisms
- Life cycles of organisms
- Organisms and environments

The characteristics of organisms concepts

- Organisms have basic needs, which for animals are air, water and food. Plants require air, water and light. Organisms can only survive in environments in which they can meet their needs. The world has many different environments, and distinct environments support the life of different types of organisms.
- Each plant or animal has different structures which serve different functions in growth, survival, and reproduction. For example, humans have distinct structures of the body for walking, holding, seeing, and talking.
- The behavior of individual organisms is influenced by internal cues such as hunger and by external cues such as an environmental change. Humans and other organisms have senses that help them detect internal and external cues.

Life cycles of organisms concepts

- Plants and animals have life cycles that include being born, developing into adults, reproducing, and eventu-

Source: National Research Council. (1996). Science content standards, *National Science Education Standards: Draft.* Washington, D.C.: National Academy Press, pp. 103–171.

ally dying. The details of this life cycle are different for different organisms.

- Plants and animals closely resemble their parents.
- Many characteristics of an organism are inherited from the parents of the organism, but other characteristics result from an individual's interactions with the environment. Inherited characteristics include the color of flowers and the number of limbs of an animal. Other features, such as the ability to play a musical instrument, are learned through interactions with the environment.

Organisms and their environments concepts

- All animals depend on plants. Some animals eat plants for food. Other animals eat animals that eat the plants.
- An organism's patterns of behavior are related to the nature of that organism's environment, including the kinds and numbers of other organisms present, the availability of food and resources, and the physical characteristics of the environment. When the environment changes, some plants and animals survive and reproduce, and others die or move to new locations.
- All organisms cause changes in the environment where they live. Some of these changes are detrimental to themselves or other organisms, whereas others are beneficial.
- Humans depend on both their natural and their constructed environment. Humans change environments in ways that can either be beneficial or detrimental for other organisms, including the humans themselves.

K–4 Earth and Space Science Standards

Content Standard D—K–4:

All students should develop an understanding of:
- Properties of Earth materials
- Objects in the sky

Properties of Earth materials concepts

- Earth materials are solid rocks and soils, liquid water, and the gases of the atmosphere. These varied materials have different physical and chemical properties. These properties make them useful, for example, as building materials, as sources of fuel, or for growing the plants we use as food. Earth materials provide many of the resources humans use.
- Soils have properties of color and texture, capacity to retain water and ability to support the growth of many kinds of plants, including those in our food supply. Other Earth materials are used to construct buildings, make plastics and provide fuel for generating electricity and operating cars and trucks.
- The surface of the Earth changes. Some changes are due to slow processes, such as erosion and weathering and

some changes are due to rapid processes such as land slides, volcanoes, and earthquakes.
- Fossils provide evidence about the plants and animals that lived long ago and nature of the environment at that time.

Objects in the sky concepts

- The sun, moon, stars, clouds, birds, and airplanes all have properties, locations, and movements that can be described and that may change.
- Objects in the sky have patterns of movement. The sun, for example, appears to move across the sky in the same way every day, but its path changes slowly over the seasons. The moon moves across the sky on a daily basis much like the sun. The shape of the moon seems to change from day to day in a cycle that lasts about a month.
- The sun provides the light and heat necessary to maintain the temperature of the Earth.
- Weather can change from day to day and over the season. Weather can be described by measurable quantities, such as temperature, wind direction and speed, precipitation, and humidity.

5–8 Physical Science Standards

Content Standard B—5–8:

All students should develop an understanding of:
- Properties and changes of properties in matter
- Motions and forces
- Transformations of energy

Properties and changes of properties in matter concepts

- Substances have characteristic properties such as density, boiling point, and solubility, which are independent of the amount of the sample. A mixture of substances can often be separated into the original substances by using one or more of these characteristic properties.
- Substances react chemically in characteristic ways with other substances to form new substances (compounds) with different characteristic properties. In chemical reactions the total mass is conserved. Substances are often placed in categories or groups if they react in similar ways, for example, metals.
- Chemical elements do not break down by normal laboratory reactions such as heating, electric current, or reaction with acids. There are more than 100 known elements which combine in a multitude of ways to produce compounds, which account for the living and nonliving substances that we encounter.

Motions and forces concepts

- The motion of an object can be described by its position, direction of motion, and speed.

- An object that is not being subjected to a force will continue to move at a constant speed and in a straight line.
- If more than one force acts on an object, then the forces can reinforce or cancel one another, depending on their direction and magnitude. Unbalanced forces will cause changes in the speed and/or direction of an object's motion.

Transformations of energy concepts

- Energy exists in many forms, including heat, light, chemical, nuclear, mechanical and electrical. Energy can be transformed from one form to another.
- Heat energy moves in predictable ways, flowing from warmer objects to cooler ones until both objects are at the same temperature.
- Light interacts with matter by transmission (including refraction), absorption, or scattering (including reflection).
- In most chemical reactions energy is released or added to the system in the form of heat, light, or electrical or mechanical energy.
- Electrical circuits provide a means of converting electrical energy into heat, light, sound, chemical or other forms of energy.
- The sun is a major source of energy for changes on the Earth's surface.

5–8 Life Science Standards

Content Standard C—5–8:

All students should develop an understanding of:

- Structure and function in living organisms
- Reproduction and heredity
- Regulation and behavior
- Populations and ecosystems
- Diversity and adaptions of organisms

Structure and function in living systems concepts

- Living systems at all levels of organization demonstrate complementary structure and function. Important levels of organization for structure and function include cells, organs, organ systems, whole organisms, and ecosystems.
- All organisms are composed of cells—the fundamental unit of life. Most organisms are single cells; other organisms, including humans, are multicellular.
- Cells carry on the many functions needed to sustain life. They grow and divide, producing more cells.
- Specialized cells perform specialized functions in multicellular organisms. Groups of specialized cells cooperate to form a tissue, such as a muscle. Different tissues are in turn grouped together to form larger functional units, called organs. Each type of cell, tissue, and organ has a distinct structure and set of functions that serve the or-

ganism as a whole. The human organism has systems for digestion, respiration, reproduction, circulation, excretion, movement, control and coordination, and for protection from disease.
- Disease represents a breakdown in structures or functions of an organism. Some diseases are the result of intrinsic failures of the system. Others are the result of infection by other organisms.

Reproduction and heredity concepts

- Reproduction is a characteristic of all living systems; since no individual organism lives forever, it is essential to the continuation of species. Some organisms reproduce asexually. Other organisms reproduce sexually.
- In many species, including humans, females produce eggs and males produce sperm. An egg and sperm unite beginning the development of a new individual. This new individual has an equal contribution of information from its mother (via the egg) and its father (via the sperm). Sexually produced offspring are never identical to either of their parents.
- Each organism requires a set of instructions for specifying its traits. Heredity is the passage of these instructions from one generation to another.
- Hereditary information is contained in genes, located in the chromosomes of each cell. Each gene carries a single unit of information, and an inherited trait of an individual can be determined by either one or many genes. A human cell contains many thousands of different genes.
- The characteristics of an organism can be described in terms of a combination of traits. Some traits are inherited and others result from interactions with the environment.

Regulation and behavior concepts

- All organisms must be able to obtain and use resources, grow, reproduce, and maintain a relatively stable internal environment while living in a constantly changing external environment.
- Regulation of an organism's internal environment involves sensing external changes in the environment and changing physiological activities to keep within the range required to survive.
- Behavior is one kind of response an organism may make to an internal or environmental stimulus. A behavioral response requires coordination and communication at many levels including cells, organ systems, and whole organisms. Behavioral response is a set of actions determined in part by heredity and in part from past experience.
- An organism's behavior has evolved through adaptation to its environment. How organisms move, obtain food,

reproduce, and respond to danger, all are based on the organism's evolutionary history.

Populations and ecosystems concepts

- Populations consist of all individuals of a species that occur together at a given place. All of the populations living together and the physical factors with which they interact compose an ecosystem.
- Populations of organisms can be categorized by the function they serve in an ecosystem. Plants and some microorganisms are producers—they make their own food. All animals, including humans, are consumers, which obtain food by eating other organisms. Decomposers, primarily bacteria and fungi, are consumers that use waste materials and dead organisms for food. Food webs identify the relationships among producers, consumers, and decomposers in an ecosystem.
- For ecosystems, the major source of energy is sunlight. Energy entering ecosystems as sunlight is converted by producers into stored chemical energy through photosynthesis. It then passes from organism to organism in food webs.
- The number of organisms an ecosystem can support depends on the resources available and abiotic factors such as quantity of light and water, range of temperatures, and the soil composition. Given adequate biotic and abiotic resources and no disease or predators, populations, including humans, increase at very rapid (exponential) rates. Limitations of resources and other factors such as predation and climate limit the growth of population in specific niches in the ecosystem.

Diversity and adaptations of organisms concepts

- There are millions of species of animals, plants, and microorganisms living today that differ from those that lived in the remote past. Each species lives in a specific and fairly uniform environment.
- Although different species look very different, the unity among organisms becomes apparent from an analysis of internal structures, the similarity of their chemical processes, and the evidence of common ancestry.
- Biological evolution accounts for a diversity of species developed through gradual processes over many generations. Species acquire many of their unique characteristics through biological adaptation which involves the selection of naturally occurring variations in populations. Biological adaptations include changes in structures, behaviors, or physiology that enhance reproductive success in a particular environment.
- Extinction of a species occurs when the environment changes and the adaptive characteristics of a species do not enable it to survive in competition with its neighbors. Fossils indicate that many organisms that lived long ago are now extinct. Extinction of species is common. Most of the species that have lived on the Earth no longer exist.

5–8 Earth and Space Science Standards

Content Standard D—5–8:

All students should develop an understanding of:
- Structure of the Earth's system
- Earth's history
- Earth in the solar system

Structure of the Earth system concepts

- The solid Earth is layered with a thin brittle crust, hot convecting mantle, and dense metallic core.
- Crustal plates on the scale of continents and oceans constantly move at rates of centimeters per year in response to movements in the mantle. Major geological events, such as earthquakes, volcanoes, and mountain building, result from these plate motions.
- Land forms are the result of a combination of constructive and destructive forces. Constructive forces include crustal deformation, volcanoes, and deposition of sediment, while destructive forces include weathering and erosion.
- Changes in the solid Earth can be described as the rock cycle. Old rocks weather at the Earth's surface, forming sediments that are buried, then compacted, heated, and often recrystallized into new rock. Eventually, these new rocks may be brought to the surface by the forces that drive plate motions, and the rock cycle continues.
- Soil consists of weathered rocks, decomposed organic material from dead plants, animals and bacteria. Soils are often found in layers, with each having a different chemical composition and texture.
- Water, which covers the majority of the Earth's surface, circulates through the crust, oceans, and atmosphere in what is known as the water cycle. Water evaporates from the Earth's surface, rises and cools as it moves to higher elevations, condenses as rain or snow, and falls to the surface where it collects in lakes, oceans, soil, and in rocks underground.
- Water is a solvent. As it passes through the water cycle it dissolves minerals and gases and carries them to the oceans.
- The atmosphere is a mixture of oxygen, nitrogen, and trace gases that include water vapor. The atmosphere has different properties at different elevations.
- Clouds, formed by the condensation of water vapor, affect weather and climate. Some do so by reflecting much of the sunlight that reaches Earth from the sun,

while others hold heat energy emitted from the Earth's surface.

- Global patterns of atmospheric movement influence local weather. Oceans have a major effect on climate, because water in the oceans holds a large amount of heat.
- Living organisms have played many roles in the Earth system, including affecting the composition of the atmosphere and contributing to the weathering of rocks.

Earth's history concepts

- The Earth processes we see today, including erosion, movement of crustal plates, and changes in atmospheric composition, are similar to those that occurred in the past. Earth history is also influenced by occasional catastrophes, such as the impact of an asteroid or comet.
- Fossils provide important evidence of how life and environmental conditions have changed.

Earth in the solar system concepts

- The Earth is the third planet from the sun in a system that includes the moon, the sun, eight other planets and their moons, and smaller objects such as asteroids and comets. The sun, an average star, is the central and largest body in the solar system.
- Most objects in the solar system are in regular and predictable motion. These motions explain such phenomena as the day, the year, phase of the moon, and eclipses.
- Gravity is the force that keeps planets in orbit around the sun and governs the rest of the motion in the solar system. Gravity alone holds us to the Earth's surface and explains the phenomena of the tides.
- The sun is the major source of energy for phenomena on the Earth's surface, such as growth of plants, winds, ocean currents, and the water cycle. Seasons result from variations in the amount of the sun's energy hitting the surface, due to the tilt of the Earth's rotation axis.

APPENDIX B   A NSTA Position Statement: Guidelines for Responsible Use of Animals in the Classroom*

These guidelines are recommended by the National Science Teachers Association for use by science educators and students. They apply, in particular, to the use of nonhuman animals in instructional activities planned and/or supervised by teachers who teach science at the precollege level.

Observation and experimentation with living organisms give students unique perspectives of life processes that are not provided by other modes of instruction. Studying animals in the classroom enables students to develop skills of observation and comparison, a sense of stewardship, and an appreciation for the unity, interrelationships, and complexity of life. This study, however, requires appropriate, humane care of the organism. Teachers are expected to be knowledgeable about the proper care of organisms under

*Adopted by the NSTA Board of Directors in July, 1991.

study and the safety of their students. These are the guidelines recommended by NSTA concerning the responsible use of animals in a school classroom laboratory:

- Acquisition and care of animals must be appropriate to the species.
- Student classwork and science projects involving animals must be under the supervision of a science teacher or other trained professional.
- Teachers sponsoring or supervising the use of animals in instructional activities—including acquisition, care, and disposition—will adhere to local, state, and national laws, policies, and regulations regarding the organisms.
- Teachers must instruct students on safety precautions for handling live animals or animal specimens.
- Plans for the future care or disposition of animals at the conclusion of the study must be developed and implemented.

- Laboratory and dissection activities must be conducted with consideration and appreciation for the organism.
- Laboratory and dissection activities must be conducted in a clean and organized work space with care and laboratory precision.
- Laboratory and dissection activities must be based on carefully planned objectives.
- Laboratory and dissection objectives must be appropriate to the maturity level of the student.
- Student views or beliefs sensitive to dissection must be considered; the teacher will respond appropriately.

For additional information concerning the responsible use of animals in the classroom, check the following Web sites:

http://www.nsta.org/handbook/animals.html
http://www.etsu_tn.edu/ospa/exosubf.html

A NSTA Position Statement: Liability of Teachers for Laboratory Safety and Field Trips*

The National Science Teachers Association (NSTA) issued the following position statement regarding liability and emphasizing the importance of safety in 1985:

Laboratory investigations and field trips are essential to effective science instruction. Teachers should be encouraged to use these instructional techniques, as physical on-site activity is important to the development of knowledge, concepts, processes, skills, and scientific attitudes. Inherent in such physical activities is the potential

for injury and possible resulting litigation. As such, liability must be shared by both school districts and teachers, utilizing clearly defined safety procedures and a prudent insurance plan. The NSTA recommends that school district and teachers adhere to the following guidelines:

I. School districts should develop and implement safety procedures for laboratory investigations and field trips.

*Adopted by the NSTA Board of Directors in July, 1985.

II. School districts should be responsible for the actions of their teachers and be supportive of the use of laboratory activities and field trips as teaching techniques.

III. School districts should look to NSTA for help in informing teachers about safety procedures and encouraging them to act responsibly in matters of safety and related liability.

IV. School districts should provide liability and tort insurance for their teachers.

V. Teachers, acting as agents of the school districts, should utilize laboratory investigations and field trips as instructional techniques.

VI. Teachers should learn safe procedures for laboratory activities and field trips and follow them as a matter of policy.

VII. Teachers should exercise reasonable judgment and supervision during laboratory investigations and field trips.

VIII. Teachers should expect to be held liable if they fail to follow district policy and litigation ensues.

IX. School districts and teachers should share the responsibilities of establishing standards and seeing that they are adhered to.

Index